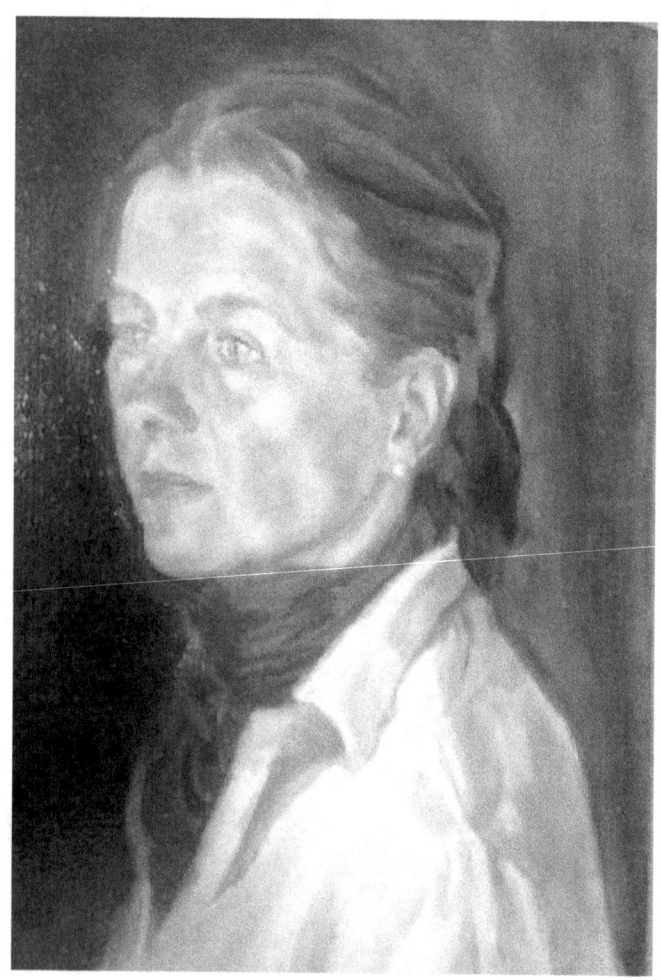

Portrait of Helen by Leszek Sobocki, 1987

Helen de Borchgrave is a fine art conservator and consultant, specializing in oil painting restoration. She trained at the Byam Shaw School of Art and with Professor Ruhemann of the National Gallery in London. She also has M.A. in Creative Non-Fiction from the University of East Anglia. She has contributed articles to various publications. Specifically she has published accounts of her experiences in Poland in: *Arts Review, Art and Artists, Jewish Chronicle* and *Country Life*. She is a member of the Association of International Art Critics and Society of Authors, and has led art tours to Poland, and throughout Europe.

Helen is the author of *A Journey into Christian Art* (Lion, 1999).

Praise for *A Journey into Christian Art*:

'Helen de Borchgrave has achieved a balance between text and picture which opens the doors of perception and feeds the imagination.'

Richard Chartres, Bishop of London.

'This book is an excellent text for either art or history enthusiasts. The work of each artist...is placed deftly into historical context...with a freshness that is very welcome...[the author's] deep knowledge and love for the subject is evident on every page...'

Daniel Turnbull, Catholic Times

RESTORATION

An Art Restorer's Journey through Communist Poland

Helen de Borchgrave

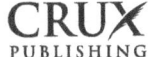

First published in the United Kingdom in 2021
by Crux Publishing Ltd.

ISBN: 978-1-913613-05-1

Acknowledgements

D URING THE LONG gestation of this book I have received help and encouragement from many sources, especially my friends and colleagues in Gdansk, Krakow and Warsaw, without whom this story could not have been written. Each one, in their own way, supported and enlightened me.

My thanks to William Fiennes and Helen Smith at UEA, Boguslaw Rostworowski and Agata Wolska who checked for Polish inaccuracies, Dr Tony Grey (who read an early draft of the manuscript) and Annie Power, who introduced me to the Oxford Centre of Life Writing. Above all, my heartfelt thanks go to Dr Kate Kennedy, Director of the OCLW at Wolfson College and her OCLW group, for their unstinting support and encouragement, especially during the period of Covid when we met weekly on zoom. And to Christopher Lascelles who patiently published the book with a sharp eye for detail.

For technical advice, I am indebted to William Sharpe, ever ready over the years to save my book from extinction.

This book is dedicated to my sons, Rupert and Simon,
with love and admiration

"...Whipped cream and icing sugar white as snow
Covered the centrepiece, which seemed to show
A winter landscape. In the midst you see
A darkling forest of confectionery,
And village houses round about it gleam
With frosty covering of sugar cream,
And little china figures decorate
In Polish dress the edges of the plate"

Pan Tadeusz by Adam Mickiewicz
Translation by Eliza Lewandowska

Pan Tadeusz, widely recognised as the national epic of Poland, was first published in 1834 in Paris. Adam Mickiewicz (1798-1855) was a thirty-five year old exile, who left his country nine years earlier, never to return.

CONTENTS

Principal Characters in Poland

Gdansk

Basia, my au pair, English teacher
Daniel, her husband
Ewa and Andrew
Ela who taught English in the medical academy with Basia and Ewa
Lucia and Andrzej, Ela's parents
Grzegorz, Ela's friend

Krakow

Janusz Walek, curator at the Czartoryski Museum
Dorota Dec, his colleague
Boguslaw Rostworowski (Boguś)
Chris Rostworowska, his wife
Leszek Sobocki, artist
Professor Jacek Waltos, artist

Colleagues at Wawel Castle State Museum

Jan Blyskosz, Head of Painting Conservation
Maria Leska, curator of Renaissance ceramics
Anna Kostecka, picture restorer/conservator
Krystyna Wanicka, conservator and translator
Anna Stolzman, scientist
Stas Michta, chief photographer
Krystyna Malcharek, Head of the Education Dept

Warsaw

Iwona Libucha, Education Dept, Royal Castle
Dr Agnieszka Morawinska, curator at the National Museum
Henryk Waniek, artist

Introduction

Perhaps an unconscious desire to escape propelled me to Poland in March, 1984. Facing personal anguish at home, a Christmas letter from my Polish friend, Basia, describing bitter cold and no boots to wear, galvanised me to leap into the unknown. I felt an unseen presence was guiding me as I booked my flights and hotels, packed much-needed provisions and clothes provided by friends, and secreted forbidden books I was asked to transport to a Polish publisher.

Born into an affluent family in post-war Britain, the Cold War seemed far away. Poland was hardly a popular tourist destination then. In my desire to help, I had no idea that this journey would change my perception of life and its priorities. In a country recovering from martial law I saw levels of material poverty coupled with generosity of spirit I had not believed possible. Despite living on the edge of their resources, the people who befriended me were not embittered by the injustices under which they lived. Their fight for human rights, democracy and freedom under Solidarity had, for the time being, been lost, yet somehow their strength of character and sense of community had survived, as I realised when I met Basia and her friends in Gdansk.

There were also riches to be found in Poland's ancient history and culture of which I knew little. Wandering around museums and churches I recognised Western influences as well as distinctly Polish characteristics in art and architecture. Through a mutual friend, the curator of the Czartoryski Museum, which was closed for refurbishment, laid out a little exhibition for me including Leonardo da Vinci's portrait of *Lady with an Ermine*. In Warsaw I was introduced to Polish art in the National Museum by the curator when she heard that paintings were an integral part of my life – both appreciating them with my eyes and working on them with my hands.

The courage and hope of these beleaguered but generous and friendly people were restorative. I felt I had stepped into an alchemist's crucible where I could discover my true self. On my return home I was no longer the same person. Within three months I had separated from my husband.

My training as an oil painting restorer helped me survive financially, both at home and in Krakow, where I returned each spring for the following three years – the first Westerner to be invited to restore paintings in the Wawel Castle Museum since World War II. It was a time of crisis both for the Poles and for me. They were coping with life post martial law; I was coping with divorce. The fortitude I witnessed there gave me a sense of proportion as I adapted to changed circumstances. I came to understand that the most valuable things in life come not from money or status, but from within the human heart and family solidarity. I found that love was stronger than fear.

Each of my visits to Poland faced me with intimate collisions between past and present, between life and art. Working on Polish paintings, I learnt about the politics behind portraits, the history behind battle scenes, the way of life in the countryside in landscapes. This is a story, taken from journals kept at the time, of my observations and experiences as a professional fine art restorer working among fellow conservators behind the Iron Curtain. It reveals a unique insight into a world few in the West understood.

After my divorce I drove with my two young sons to Poland, to meet my friends and show them the places I had described over the years. I hoped this journey to an unknown country would give them a fresh view of life and a greater understanding of the importance of solidarity and democracy.

PART I

1984

1

To Poland

PILING MY SUITCASE and bulging bags on to the scales at Heathrow Airport, I looked anxiously at the counter-clerk as the indicator bounced into overweight. He smiled kindly.

'Last week's plane to Warsaw had difficulty taking off,' he joked, as he replaced an errant orange, and handed back my holdall.

Others were not as fortunate. In the departure lounge for Gate 15, a bird-like woman, with a strong Polish accent, said tearfully, 'They charged me thirty pounds for a sack of tinned food I am taking to my mother-in-law. She's dying.'

Around me, relatives, friends and those with a sense of social responsibility were bringing vital supplies in their overweight luggage. Other women also carried coats. Though March had come, several months would pass before memories of the numbing cold of this particular winter faded. It was 1984. In the airport Party workers were dressed in new clothes. Heavily made up, the women looked superior; they were going home to dominate. These dull reminders of communist officialdom stood out among the more human, ordinary people. Who was to know that when a provisional government was sanctioned by Churchill, Roosevelt and Stalin at the Yalta Conference early in 1945, Stalin would ignore the Polish Government-in-Exile in London and make sure a Communist government took control?

Beneath the prevailing dread, unanswered questions hovered like wraiths in the artificial air during that two-hour flight on LOT airlines. I wondered what state Poland was in now, eight months after the repeal of martial law. At 9am vodka was brought to the passengers – to calm our fears, perhaps.

Beside me sat a tall, pretty woman, a genetic specialist, who told me that she regularly drove a lorry to her homeland with medical supplies for children. A Pole married to a Scot, Mrs Ferguson was flying to Warsaw to inspect an orphanage. She carried serum, and a teddy bear. The diet in Poland was so poor that many children suffered from rickets and anaemia and there were no vitamins or minerals to supplement. I thought of the few oranges and lemons in my bag.

'Every bit helps,' she said. I could feel the pain behind her words. 'I was one of the lucky ones that survived. Did you know nearly 18% of the population died in the war?'

I did not.

'My father was one of the million or two Poles sent to Siberian labour camps in 1940. When Stalin joined the Allies after Hitler invaded Russia, he granted an amnesty. The deportees were released. My father joined General Anders' army and fought at Tobruk and Monte Cassino.'

'Why was an amnesty necessary?'

'Stalin had to justify himself for sending Poles to Siberian labour camps. An amnesty assumed they were guilty of crimes, which of course they had not committed.'

She looked round cautiously, then leaning closer, whispered, 'Don't forget, Communism as practised is based on lies and deceit. It is utterly corrupt, utterly cruel.'

This intelligent, caring woman explained something of the mentality of this subjugated state. She spoke calmly and cautiously, for we were conscious of other ears. One word reported could cause her to be interrogated. Later, I wished I had listened more carefully. In our tolerant country, freedom of speech was an inherent part of life. I did not realise, sitting in that plane, how Poland would change me. Though nearly forty I had led a sheltered life – in a bubble of traditional privilege, though not a happy one.

As the plane descended, grey concrete blocks of post-war Warsaw jutted out of the plain-like rectangular rocks. The squat square airport building loomed nearer, resembling a cage. We touched down on the tyre-scorched tarmac and slowly taxied towards the airport terminal, crowned with huge letters: WARSZAWA. Young soldiers clad in pre-war khaki greatcoats and top boots stood at the foot of the steps gripping rifles as the passengers alighted, laden like tramps with their fat plastic bags. Some held bunches of flowers. We were escorted from the plane by armed police.

The first queue on Polish soil began, inevitably, with passport control. It took several minutes for papers to be scrutinised, a blacklist checked, the passport stamped and handed back. A uniformed woman noted down my hard currency, wedding ring and pearl earrings.

My palms were sweating and my solar plexus tightened as I waited for the luggage to go through; and breathed a sigh of relief as my suitcase was marked with chalk – as they were in England before automation. Underneath the piles of provisions were books I had been given to smuggle in to a publisher in Krakow. Grazyna Sikorska, who gave me the books, was a member of the Polish research staff at Keston College, where specialists on the USSR, Poland, Czechoslovakia and the GDR maintained basic research, and provided material for Keston's publications. The Library and Archives Department was open to academics and other researchers who wished to make use of the college's unique documentary records. Grazyna told me how the educational charity had been set up by Michael Bordeaux. As a student in Russia he had seen how Christians were persecuted, and wanted to provide practical help.

I had brought pitifully little for a nation that lacked everything, yet each gift had been given to me in London; each was a sign that someone in the West cared. This, I was to discover, was what mattered most in this seemingly forgotten land.

I huddled inside my fur coat and took stock. Basia's annual letter had arrived two months earlier. Reading between the lines I tried to imagine how this gentle girl, a gifted English teacher, had survived that winter, when the temperature dropped to minus thirty degrees, without boots to wear. Boots, even if they were obtainable, cost a month's salary. I heard about Basia through a friend, and had sent her an invitation to come and work for me. This enabled her to come to the West during her summer holiday in 1976. Two university friends had accompanied Basia to England: Ewa worked for friends of ours, and Ela pulled pints in a Norfolk pub. Good-natured, hardworking and uncomplaining, when I was ill Basia had run my large house and cared for my two young sons with resolute determination and quiet tact.

In the 1970s houses in London still suffered from wartime neglect or damage; many like ours were being restored. Iron railings round London squares had been removed for the war effort and replaced with unsightly chicken wire. My husband found some old railings outside London, and he installed them with all the residents mucking in with cash or muscle power. Frenchmen crossed the Channel to sell strings of onions from their bicycles. Joe, our milkman, had only recently exchanged his horse and cart for a little electric float. The bottles rattled in metal racks and there were gold, silver and red tin-foil tops to identify full cream from semi-skimmed. The King's Road was still a village street with a butcher, baker and greengrocer close at hand, but its Bohemian character also attracted entrepreneurs and designers like Mary Quant. I bought a black corduroy knickerbocker suit from her, a wide-brimmed black velvet hat and make-up that emphasised the eyes. I felt cool driving my white Mercedes 190SL around Chelsea with the top down.

I met my husband through restoring a painting for his mother, who lived near my parents. I was newly qualified. My commissions as a self-employed oil painting conservator came through recommendation. In this painting, a moonlit scene by Sebastian Pether, a man, looking very small, sits alone on a bank, watching as clouds part and a full moon lights a golden path upon the river that flowed into the distant horizon. Beside the lonely observer, ivy creeps up the west wall of a mournful church ruin, its Gothic windows bereft of glass. I learnt that the pressures of a large family forced young Pether to sell his pictures to dealers at knockdown prices. These unscrupulous men then had copies made and churned them out to an eager public. The artist died in Battersea in 1844, two years after the Royal Academy rejected three of his paintings. His genuine works are rare. This, a good copy, was left too close to a fire and suffered burns.

When I returned the painting to its owner after restoration, the client introduced me to her son who was staying. He had returned from farming in what was then Rhodesia and knew few people in England, so I invited him to join a table I was making up for a charity dance. A romantic looking couple in evening dress, we danced all evening and I was smitten. We were married on 1st April 1968 – five days before Martin Luther King was assassinated. Three weeks later students in New York protested against the Vietnam War, setting off a wave of student protests that challenged the status quo worldwide. Robert Kennedy was assassinated in June. The brief period of liberalisation and reform in Czechoslovakia under Dubcek, called the Prague Spring, was quashed in August when Soviet armed forces invaded and hard-line Communist rule re-instituted. On Christmas Eve the first men orbited the moon in Apollo 8. But decades were to pass before women had the same rights as men.

*

A glass wall separated new arrivals from the captive crowd. A sea of faces bobbed about the other side. Then one I recognised swam into view – slim, dark and pretty, she waved vigorously. I hitched the coats over my arm, lifted my bags, and staggered through the narrow gate. After it clicked shut behind me, I entered Poland. Basia hugged me close. Over meals round our kitchen table in 1976 this Polish girl had charmed us with her ready wit and lively descriptions of life back home. Everything in Poland had deteriorated sharply since those days when Basia had brought us chocolates. Her generation had seen the economy collapse. The woeful conditions led, in August 1980, to the foundation of Solidarity, a workers' movement set up to challenge the abuses of the government. For fifteen months the people tasted some freedom, until martial law was imposed. Solidarity leaders were interned, innocent people battered and killed, a curfew decreed, and tenuous threads with the outside world cut.

'Quickly Helen, we must take a taxi to the Central Station. There's only one express train to Gdansk at this time. I've reserved two seats. Thank God you were not delayed.'

Watching me peel off layers of clothing in the taxi, Basia giggled.

'This coat's for Daniel. I hope it fits,' I said, as I passed it to her.

Her eyes widened and began to fill with tears as she slowly took the coat, felt the cloth and began to stroke it, as if she was imagining her husband inside it, feeling warm. As we drove through the centre of the city there were few cars on its wide boulevards. With pursed lips, Basia pointed to a distorted derivation of pre-war New York.

'That monstrosity is the Palace of Culture. Stalin gave that to the Poles as a gift. We're lumbered with this landmark in the centre of our capital to remind us who's boss.'

Basia sighed.

WARSZAWA CENTRALNA signs announced the main station. Like everything else in post-war Warsaw it had been rebuilt. An escalator carried us underground to the platforms, where dark blue pillars grew out from the granite, stretching to the strip-lit ceiling before receding to further platforms. They looked like tree trunks in a dead forest. As we sat waiting on a hard wooden bench I began to absorb the atmosphere. Saul Bellow's *Herzog* was right: Poland could be drab and grey. This country, lying between Germany and Russia, had been a killing ground during two world wars and now its people lived in poverty. The rich agricultural land and material resources were systematically exploited by the Party.

The first-class compartment of the express train was spacious, clean and comfortable. Within half an hour it was barely possible to see the wasting, crumbling buildings that littered the skyline, the dirt and decay, the pockmarked roads which looked as neglected as the people who travelled on them. When darkness had enveloped the sky, an old steam engine hissed and roared by, gushing white smoke upwards. Glimpses of a fiery furnace evoked childhood memories. Poland lagged thirty years behind us. I took in Basia's well-cut tweed suit. Survivors obviously learned to look well-turned-out, even when there was nothing to buy in the shops. During the four-hour train journey I plied her with questions, and she answered patiently, with the shade of a smile hovering around the corners of her mouth. She had stayed with us in Chelsea. She was painfully aware of the differences between the worlds we lived in. Despite constant humiliations Poles are extraordinarily generous and kind, and Basia was no exception.

'How much do you earn as an English teacher? How much was the train ticket? Can't you buy shoes?'

Neutral questions. No political talk in this public place.

With quiet courtesy, Basia explained. The monthly salary of a teacher of English at the Medical Academy was about £60, the train ticket for two was £20. There were constant shortages, mainly due to incompetent distribution. If televisions, washing machines, soap, loo paper or anything else arrived in a shop, there was an instant queue. Demand was constant, supply intermittent. Goods with a built-in obsolescence in the West were investments here, as inflation, officially at 30%, was nearer 90%.

In Gdansk, Basia took me to the hostel for scientists, university lecturers, engineers and other intelligentsia, where Ewa lived with her husband Andrew, a brilliant electronics engineer. They had procured me the guest room there for five nights. Wooden sledges made a mountain in the outer hall, prams and pushchairs in the inner. The hostel was eight years old. It had not worn well. Cracks seared crooked paths along the walls, paint peeled, wafer thin curtains clung limply to plastic rails. Ten families shared a kitchen. Ewa and Andrew had to stow everything away neatly if they wanted space to move around in their tiny bedsit where, in Polish fashion, the bed converted to a sofa.

The room was warm and snug. One necessity few Poles forego is heating. Sub-zero temperatures may hover through the winter, sleet may follow snow, but inside, especially in State-owned buildings, the temperature was high. Heat came from two huge coal-fired central heating stations producing boiling water that was piped underground to radiators in public buildings like this, while local districts had their own stations. When a pipe cracked, steam rose like a volcanic eruption in the street. So different to the huge open wood fires we burned in the house in which I grew up – a focal point to sit round. Staring at the hissing logs, and watching the flames change colour from blue to red through a myriad of orange tones was, unconsciously for me, a form of meditation, as ancient as primitive humanity.

'I teach English to medical students,' said Ewa as we sat round a little table eating cold meat and potato salad, her round face pale from lack of sun, her large spectacles glinting in the light.

'The text books I use are written and published in Poland, but sometimes they're not available when the academic year starts. The students have to share copies and can't take them home. Like library books, they tend to get lost. I love teaching. Time spent with colleagues, though, can be tiring. I can't discuss my feelings as Party members infiltrate, usually among the administrators.'

I took out the books I had smuggled in. Among them was a copy of *The Captive Mind* by Czeslaw Milosz, winner of the 1980 Nobel Prize in Literature, who defected to the West in 1951, and three slim paperbacks of *Religion in Communist Lands* which included an article about Father Jerzy Popieluszko (of whom more later) by Grazyna Sikorska.

'Do read and note what you can while I'm here in Gdansk. I'm taking them to Krakow,' I said as the books were pounced on after we finished eating.

'Basia says you have to queue for food. How do you manage?' I asked Ewa later.

'When I'm working, I can't queue for meat, because even if I turned up at five or six in the morning it can take up to five hours to be served. I'm lucky because as an academic teacher I can fit my eighteen hours into three days, so I queue on my days off. Our neighbour's an angel. She doesn't work, so buys fish for us when she queues. Otherwise we eat potatoes, cabbage and carrots and sometimes just homemade soup and bread. It's a pity. We Poles love our food!'

*

Sleet turned the muddy snow into slush as we walked to the local market next morning. Peasants, bundled up in old coats with woollen scarves wound round their heads, showed off their wares: scrawny trussed-up chickens, mushrooms, cabbage and some thin leeks lay on wooden tables – and a goose, which cost 2,000 zloty – an unimaginable £13. Everywhere I went in Poland the ethos spoke of the 1950s: no plastic, no throwaway culture, and paper in pitifully short supply. Clothes, cars, and machinery were at least ten years old. Milk, even powdered, was hard to find.

'We share everything,' said Ewa. 'When a friend of mine gave birth and had no milk for her baby, it was wet nursed for a month by a friend whose baby was born at the same time.'

The biggest fear was illness. Malnutrition and diseases connected with dirt and deprivation were common. Later that day, Ewa's sister Magda, a pharmacist, arranged a short visit to the local hospital. Supplies were chronically inadequate and doctors and nurses desperately overworked. Patients lay in the corridors, queuing for dialysis. No painkillers were available for those giving birth. In an old people's ward the sadness was visceral. Visiting hours were restricted to four hours a week and tea arrived in the type of bucket you use to give horses water.

Yet wherever I was invited, I would not have believed there were food shortages. I first experienced the largesse of Polish hospitality in a gracious old flat in the centre of the city, where I was greeted by Ewa's parents, along with her sister and brother-in-law. Her father, Professor Romuald Szaba was a pioneer in children's urinary and kidney diseases at the child surgery clinic. Her mother was about to retire as secretary to the Medical Care Service and was preparing for a journey of a lifetime: a pilgrimage to Rome, Assisi, and Monte Cassino.

'The end crowns the work,' this dignified lady told me as she served up borsch soup, mince rissoles, veal cooked with wild mushrooms and vinegary pears, cheesecake, coffee and brandy. The lunch lasted three hours during which I discovered quite how much Poles love their food, and talking – especially to a visitor from the West. After the rise of Solidarity, when it seemed democracy and justice might prevail, every facet of life changed with the novel sense of freedom and renewal. Now, even though martial law had been repealed, they felt even more imprisoned by Communism.

'Now there is nothing to live for, to strive for. Every day new rules appear, all equally absurd. Highly educated people like us feel unwanted, for those in charge fear creative minds. All loopholes are closed and hope is draining away. During World War II we knew our enemy. Now we don't. The situation is tense and every day our people have to cope with survival and political problems. There is no energy left to resist. We only want to be ourselves. I haven't much money or material possessions. All my wealth is in the family. We visit every day after work to break bread together, and take it in turns to look after ninety-year-old granny.' These suffering Polish people were revealing riches I had never imagined.

Despite stringent rationing, this family could eat more meat thanks to a farmer they knew in the country. He turned up occasionally with joints, which went straight into the freezer. Oranges appeared from Cuba for Christmas; apples were the staple fresh fruit.

Ewa said, 'If we're sent food and essentials from the West, my mother usually shares them with others.' When we left, the old professor presented me with postage stamps commemorating the two visits to his homeland by Pope John Paul II.

Later, I understood why I was well fed wherever I went, and why, at the risk of repetition, meals figure largely in my story. They were a time of celebration and communication, mainly within the confines of the home, away from surveillance. Poles believe that 'when a guest comes to the house God comes'. In order to entertain me rations had been saved for weeks.

I thought of my family: how the importance of external show masked inner need. I grew up in a lovely old house on a farm with my parents and siblings, with ponies and holidays abroad. But my mother was unable to give her three children the love and emotional security we needed. My siblings and I were brought up competing for affection and now we rarely met. As a small child I suffered nightmares and would calm my fears in the quiet world of our large garden. I spent hours absorbing nature, marvelling at the greenness of moss, the clouds making pictures in the sky, the wind rustling the corn. I read voraciously and communicated little, for I was aware that us children should be seen but not heard.

*

There was hardly even standing room in St Nicholas's Church that Sunday as all ages crowded in to pray, undeterred by a trudge through sleeting rain and watery snow. There were gilded cherubs, and a carved Madonna and Child hanging from the vault in a gilded circular frame. Heavy baroque altars, carved in marble, looked back to a former age, when the Church was part of the Establishment. After 1948, it had acquired a new role – uniting society in opposition to the Communist state. Throughout Poland, priests proclaimed truth from pulpits to sustain the people, even if it got them arrested. Everyone knew informers also listened. The Polish Pope, John Paul II, elevated from the bishopric of Krakow, inspired them all from the moment he stood at the balcony in St Peter's Square in 1979 and exhorted people to 'be not afraid'.

Ela accompanied me to the service. She had worked in a Norfolk pub when Basia was with us in London. Tall and elegant, in a tweed suit remodelled by her tailor, she took over the task of my interpreter.

'Who is an honest man? What does an honest man not know?' asked the priest as he began his sermon. 'Evil is intelligent. The authorities cannot kill a man's soul, but how can we protect ourselves from evil? Be faithful. Bear witness to God's love. Don't be ashamed of your faith. When you see evil, don't hate the evildoer. Try by your example to change him. Jesus told us to love our enemies; one day that love may transform them.'

He stepped down from the pulpit and in the silence the congregation kneeled down. The priest prayed for a fair outcome at the current trial of a dissident. The words were enough to have the priest himself imprisoned for implying the justice system was corrupt. Poles understood Gandhi's words, 'You assist an evil system most effectively by obeying its orders and decrees. An evil system never deserves such allegiance... A good person will resist an evil system with his or her whole soul.'

*

The sand on the beach at Sopot was soft and white and stretched for miles. A hard, freezing wind lifted tiny specks and battered them into our faces, tossing the sound of our voices into the wide expanse of sky. The pier of this seaside resort was deserted and the lighthouse, nestling beside the casino, looked closed up. Well-clipped hedges separated sand from the roadside. Ela, Ewa and I had met up with Basia and her husband Daniel.

The elegant façade of the Grand Hotel concealed a drab, tasteless interior, which included a Pewex shop, where foreign luxury goods, from food to electrical items, could be bought with foreign currency. We sat down in the deserted ballroom and tried to re-create earlier, happier times, imagining the sound of jazz as the haute monde danced on the sprung parquet floor, the pop of champagne bottles, and laughter... I remembered the delicious Wedel chocolates Basia had once brought to London. She had not tasted chocolate for years, so I bought some in the local Pewex with US dollars. As her eyes lit up with pleasure I felt a spasm of guilt that back home I took so much for granted.

We walked to the edge of the forest where expensive houses were being constructed for party members and those with relatives abroad who sent hard currency. A dollar went a long way when exchanged on the black market. These houses, some glowing with finely carved pinewood doors and window frames, were a world away from the concrete jungles in which most of the population had to live – if they were lucky enough. Basia's sister waited fifteen years after she put down a deposit, before she could take possession of her slice of the Socialist dream. Basia and Daniel lived in one of three elegantly panelled rooms in her parents' flat, while they waited for their own home. They told me it was much worse in small country towns where it was common for three generations to live together in one room.

We ate another enormous and delicious family lunch with gusto. Later, over apple cake, coffee presented in exquisite pre-war Polish porcelain, and Daniel's homemade cherry vodka, a picture emerged of life under martial law.

'Initially,' said Basia, 'during curfew, we couldn't even leave town, and we required a passport to travel to other satellite countries. The West was closed to us so what incentive was there to queue for a visa?'

'Around Christmas time my mother started queuing at 4am for the twice-weekly shop for rationed meat.' I forbore to mention that Fortnum & Mason delivered our Christmas feast when I was growing up. We laughed as the inevitable Polish jokes were told:

'The Dutch ride bicycles and drive Volkswagens on Sundays, Germans drive Volkswagens and Mercedes on Sundays, the Russians drive Volgas and tanks on Sundays...'

*

I spent a night with Ela in her heavily mortgaged flat. The view looked on to a lush forest stretching to the horizon. The living green contrasted starkly with the concrete wasteland which had impinged into the virgin territory. Socialist policy was to build homes far out of town – an hour's commute leaves little time to stir up trouble.

'How do you feel being imprisoned behind the Iron Curtain?' I asked Ela.

'I don't dream of the impossible,' she said. 'We couldn't travel to the West, even to work, without an invitation. This was humiliating for us, but we got used to staying inside the Soviet bloc. It's not so bad. We ski in the Tatra Mountains, and go to the little summer house my father built in the Lake District north of here. I am happy with my family and friends.'

'Well, perhaps one day you will come,' I said

'When I have enough money not to be a burden on you, I would love to.'

The next morning Ela drove me to her parents' charming early 19th century flat in an old part of town. For several decades three generations had shared two rooms. Ela's grandfather fought as an officer in the First World War. His son, Andrzej, who later became an eminent professor at Gdansk University, suffered for his bourgeois background. He was forced to work on his knees in the mines at Auschwitz. They managed to move north before Ela was born – before that dreaded name could be in her passport for life.

Apart from his academic histories of German U-boats, which have been translated into several languages, Andrzej wrote seven children's books about twin boys who travelled the world in a ship with their father, carrying their young readers into other lands and cultures. Ela's mother, Lucia, spent some months in Cambridge in the 1960s and her English was immaculate, with an attractive accent. The glass-covered terrace where vines flourished gave a southern feel. Inside, where 19th century family portraits graced the walls, I was reminded of gentler times as we sat down and drank coffee from fine old porcelain cups and brandy in balloon glasses. I was taking to this habit of brandy with coffee and cake at 11am. Lucia's godfather, an eminent art historian, had just died and left her a pastel portrait by a well-known 19th century artist. She would try to collect it in Krakow while I was there. This was reassuring, for I had no friends in that city.

2

Gdansk

THE LITTLE BOY sitting opposite Ewa and me on the bus to the city centre wore red rubber boots. They looked like the ones I bought in London, and brought a spasm of yearning to cuddle my own sons, who were away at boarding school. Most clothes for children came from abroad because they simply had none. Young and old observed me with sad, questioning eyes, turning their heads as they heard us speak English. I wondered how many were reminded of World War II. Did they have fathers or husbands among those Polish squadrons who, by 1943, had been the fourth largest allied air force? Had they lost a son to Hitler's tanks? We drove past a wartime tank now serving in a play area for children.

We passed clusters of attractive houses with tiled roofs and white wooden shutters; and some rare relics of pre-war days: thatched-roofed one-storey wooden houses, the wood protected from insects by the addition of blue paint to the lime wash, surrounded by well-trodden earth with hens pecking about.

The beauty of the restored old city of Gdansk, where we met Basia, shone in the sunlight, in contrast to the drabness and difficulties of everyday living. Gdansk was founded a thousand years ago by King Mieszko I to connect the Polish State with the trade routes of the Baltic Sea. Throughout its history as a free city of the Hanseatic League, the city zigzagged between Poland and Prussia and had become the increasingly Germanised Danzig by the time the Nazis rose to power. The Nazis exploited the city's ambiguous political status and the tension culminated in the invasion of Poland. Clare Hollingworth, a young reporter with the *Daily Telegraph*, saw the German troops collecting on the border and warned the British Ambassador back in Warsaw. He did not believe her until she put the telephone out of the window and he could hear the tanks rolling.

Many Jews had already moved to Israel when the German battleship *Schleswig-Holstein*, lying in port, opened fire on the Polish garrison at Westerplatte before dawn on 1ˢᵗ September 1939, heralding the start of World War II. Over the next six years the Nazis virtually gutted the city. But Gdansk, like Warsaw, rose like a phoenix. Everywhere buildings were restored, and with them the national pride. Anti-Government demonstrations here precipitated the fall of the Communist leader Gomulka in 1970. A decade later Gdansk became the birthplace of Solidarity, a movement that played a major role in ending Communist rule in Central Europe.

The old ships' crane, constructed in 1444, was a landmark among cobbled streets and gabled brick houses, exquisite wrought-iron work and elegant fountains. In the parish church of St Mary's, the blue and silver Baroque organ glistened in its newly restored state, in contrast to a pile of battered carvings lying in a corner. They were surrounded by a group of conservators discussing their future.

Outside the church, little shops nestled between curving Baroque stone ornaments and facades. They sold amber jewellery and antiques, sporting guns and knives. I fell for an old silver boar bottle top but despite my pleas, the shopkeeper would not sell it, for sentimental reasons, even though his sick wife needed oranges. This was an opportunity to give away some of the vitamins I brought with me.

Near the church, the red bricks of the medieval town hall wore a coat of black grime. As we entered through two sets of stiff double doors, a different age emerged. Beside a beautifully carved wood spiral staircase a door led into the Council Chamber: the Red Room. Deep crimson damask hung on the walls and covered the cushions on the benches below. After a short absence the sun chose that moment to reappear, glinting through the mullioned windows, sharpening the black and white marbled floor and highlighting the enormous wealth of carving and inlay in wood, iron and paint. The room combined craftsmanship with an earthy simplicity. I imagined town councillors towards the end of the 16ᵗʰ century meeting here, dressed in a rich variety of colours and materials, sitting on their benches and leaning back against wood panelling inlaid with intricate hunting scenes, gossiping and discussing town matters.

A decade later Isaac van der Blocke painted the ceiling, including the central *Glorification of the Unification of Gdansk with Poland*. In this artistic representation of the function of the free port city within the economic system of Poland at this time, the crowned Polish eagle spreads protective wings over a panorama of the city, and below the bird an avenue of lush trees recedes to the sea: into a future full of hope. A magnificently wrought iron safe with several locks and large keys was inset prominently into the wall beside the door into the Little Council Chamber, called the Winter Room because the Mayor lived there during cold months in the 1690s. The inscriptions *Nec Timido* above the door and *Candide et Syncere* over the marble fireplace opposite were further reminders of a more chivalrous age.

We walked to a room showing a display of photographs taken in 1946. The medieval crane had gone, its rounded brick towers gaping like toothless old men. The Town Hall tower was half its size, rising above buildings reduced to their foundations, a rounded heap of grass-covered rubble. Photographic views of Gdansk in the 1890s, when steam barges and sailing ships ploughed her waters, struck a happier note.

Andrew had arranged to drive us back. On the way he stopped for petrol and I noticed graffiti had been painted out on the wall.

'Solidarity slogans are painted everywhere,' said Basia, 'but they're soon covered up by the authorities. Because of the shortages, the paint's never the same colour.'

*

An old monastery housed the National Museum. Vaulted ceilings and whitewashed walls provided a pleasing backdrop to paintings of the 16th and 17th century Gdansk school. A large oil of the *Building of a Church* by Anton Möller (1563-1611) was a superb example of perspective techniques. As I walked slowly from one side of the painting to the other, the vanishing point moved with me, pulling me into the bustle of activity – sawing wood with the carpenters, mixing cement with the masons, doling out wages with the foreman. In John Krieg's *View of Gdansk*, high grassy banks rose above moat-enclosing walls with the old town clustered around the church of St Mary.

The jewel of the collection is a large triptych of *The Last Judgement* painted by Hans Memling, one of the greatest Flemish painters of the 15th century. Commissioned by a Florentine banker, the galleon transporting the triptych to Italy fell victim in a sea battle between the English and the German Hanseatic League, and was captured by a captain who carried it to his home port of Gdansk. Not even Pope Sixtus IV, who commissioned the Sistine Chapel in Rome, could prise the masterpiece from St Mary's Church. Like so much else in Poland, *The*

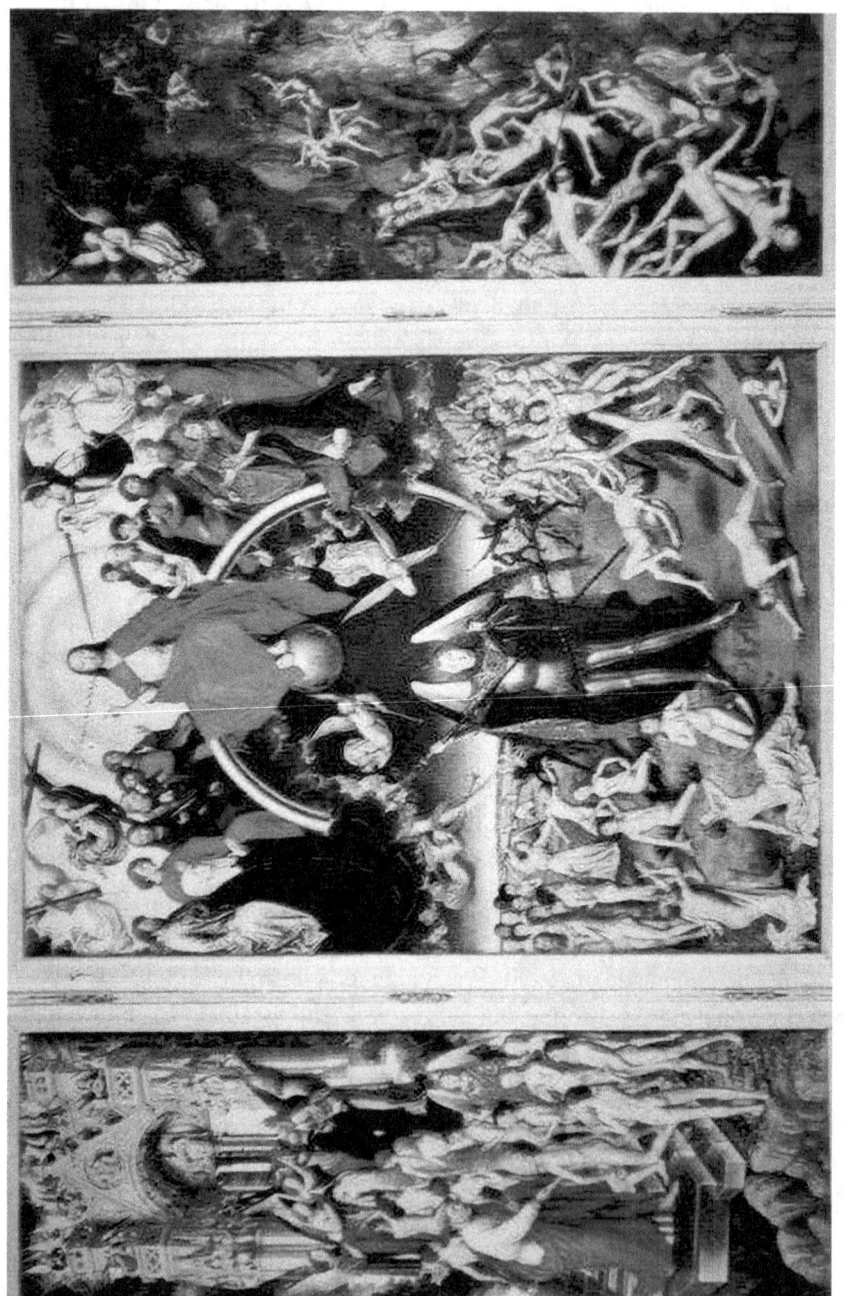

The Last Judgement by Hans Memling, 1473

Last Judgement suffered the vicissitudes of war. It was taken to Paris by Napoleon, to Germany by Hitler, found by the Russians in 1945 and taken to the Hermitage in Leningrad, where it hung for eleven years before returning to Gdansk. Looting great masterpieces, sometimes for their private enjoyment, but always for self-aggrandisement, was common practice.

In the central panel Christ sits enthroned in glory on a rainbow, his feet resting on a golden orb, his hand raised in blessing. Angels, with robes beautifully draped like Gothic carved figures, carry the instruments of Christ's Passion – suffering the Poles understood well– while those beneath his feet blow the Last Trumpet. St Michael, guardian of angels, stands on the broad, green meadow below holding scales in one hand, weighing souls. The righteous, waking from sleep and naked as the day they were born, are protected from evil as they move into the left panel of the triptych, where peace is promised for the redeemed. They wait patiently for St Peter to welcome them on the crystal stairs as they enter Heaven. In the right hand panel, the damned shrink and writhe in anguish as demons heckle them. They scream and gnash their teeth as they hurtle into hellfire. The scene reminded me of the inferno glimpsed in those black and white photographs in the Town Hall, taken in 1946, with their acres of rubble.

*

For more than a century Poland no longer existed on the map of Europe as Prussia, Russia and Austria carved her up between them. When she regained her political freedom after the Great War, the country was in ruins. Poles are survivors. With energy and enthusiasm they rebuilt the country. Gdynia was founded at about the same time as Tel Aviv. Both new cities were heavily influenced by Germany's Bauhaus school of modernist architecture. They represented the dreams, ambitions and aspirations of two nations: one that had regained its independence and the other on the road towards creating a new homeland. Within twenty years, the new port of Gdynia, designated as the site of Poland's naval harbour, was the busiest in the Baltic Sea. Ela drove me there. She wanted to show me the monument to forty workers shot by the militia in December 1970, at a time of unrest due to a hike in food prices. As she stopped the car and pointed, I saw four huge numbers: '**1970**', made from steel by their grieving fellow ship workers, that stood sentinel beside the road in the raw, cold air.

'No one told the workers not to come that day,' Ela said. 'They got off the commuter train at dawn and as they walked along that iron bridge above the road as usual, the police opened fire.' We looked up at the death trap. What memories were stirred, what emotions ignited, every time the workers still crossed that bridge? I took out my sketch pad and drew the letters.

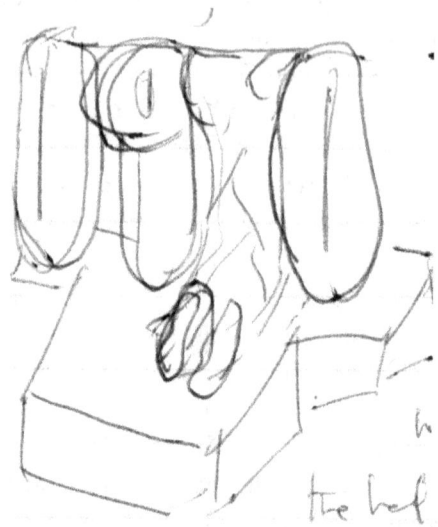

Steel monument – 1970 – sketch by author

A kneeling man replaced the '7', hunched between the nine and the nought, weighed down by that helplessness experienced in the face of gross inhumanity. It seemed appropriate to absorb this icon of faith, of the Polish unquenchable spirit, on my last day in Gdansk. It happened to be Ash Wednesday.

I told Ela about the strikes that raged in Britain during the 1970s. Rubbish was piled high in the streets, inflation grew, and a three-day week conserved energy. A quarter of wages went on food. The mineworkers union voted to strike after refusing a pay rise of 16.5%. In desperation the Prime Minister, Edward Heath, called a general election in February 1974. He lost. After two election victories within a year, the Labour government increased miners' wages first by 35% and another 35% a year later. The miners had won.

'How different to Poland!' said Ela.

'In 1976 the Party proposed changes to the Polish Constitution that gave the Communist Party a monopoly of power. Our citizens' rights depended on fulfilling our duty towards the State. Priests read a protest letter written by Cardinal Stefan Wyszynski from the pulpit in thousands of Roman Catholic churches. Then in June, overnight, the State nearly doubled basic food prices. We already spent over half our earnings on food.'

'Do you have social security?'

Ela laughed. 'Those who went on strike in protest lost their jobs. As in the rest of Eastern Europe, no State or other funds are available for the unemployed.'

'Everything changed when John Paul II became Pope in October 1978.' Ela's face changed from sadness to hope. I suddenly realised what we in England had not fully appreciated at the time – the enormity of the fact that the new head of the Roman Catholic Church was Polish. A man who had lived and suffered under both the Nazis and the Communists was now a serious challenge in the Soviet back yard. This much-loved priest had taken his flock skiing and organised picnics to give the young space to share their thoughts and feelings away from informers. When he became bishop, he made things happen against the odds, like the building of a church in the new Soviet city of Nowa Huta outside Kraków, despite the continuous refusal by the government.

When the Pope came to Poland for nine days in June, eight months after his election, he held his first rally in Victory Square in Warsaw. Vast crowds poured into this huge space more used to accommodating Soviet parades. As the Pope prayed, something pivotal happened, Ela told me. Barriers of fear were broken, and a sense of solidarity created. Even though the Pope mentioned neither politics nor economics during the nine days he travelled round the country, he talked about a revolution of conscience. People felt themselves to be degraded slaves to the system. He challenged the crowds to strip off this illusion and find their true selves which would empower them to resist evil. Here was a man of real authority whom the Poles could trust. He opened the way for the rise of Solidarity the following year. Exactly a thousand years after Mieszko I founded the city of Gdansk, Lech Wałęsa was David, leading the Solidarity strike against the Goliath of the Communist state.

'Were you here in August 1980, during the strike?' I asked Ela.

'Everyone was here and wanted to help. Numbers inside the shipyard grew to two thousand. There was a rota for providing meals for the strikers during those crucial two weeks. Peasants brought horse carts loaded with produce; taxis cruised around offering free transport to anyone bringing food; Father Jankowski from the nearby old church of St Brigid's celebrated Mass for about seven thousand workers on a makeshift altar erected just inside Number Two Gate.' St Brigid was the focal point of prayer, as well as being a store for grain and other necessities for the besieged strikers.

'Weren't you afraid of reprisals?'

'The memory of Gdynia's Bloody Thursday was very much in people's minds. We Poles need our monuments – to remember our victories as well as our losses. Do you know Solidarity's ideals?'

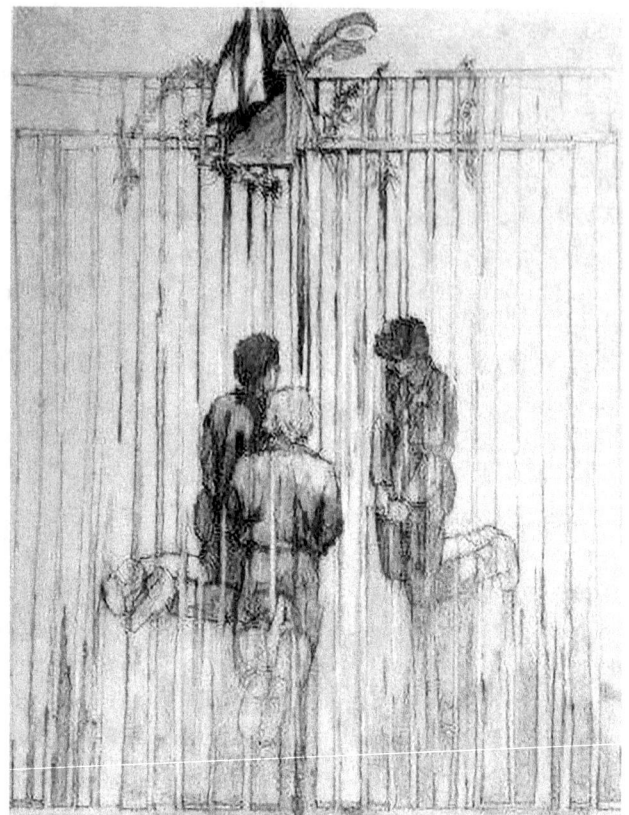

On Both Sides of the Gate, **J. Waltos, 1981 (pastel on paper)**

I shook my head. I knew nothing. Ela told me how, in their manifesto, the committee wrote: "The workers are not fighting merely for a pittance for themselves, but for justice for the entire nation. We have to oppose the authorities' attempts to break up the unity of our strike movement. We must live up to the words: *Man is born free."*

'The gates were ablaze with colour – people hung festoons of red, white, and gold flowers, pictures of the Pope, and the Polish flag, which was only allowed on official occasions. Even the sun shone. We'll never forget. Those fifteen months showed us what freedom was. The Communists imposed martial law because only force keeps them in power. Standing behind our leaders are the Russian tanks. Since 1939, we've been in bondage to two ruthless systems alien to our nature. The theme song of Solidarity is *Let Poland be Poland.* For a brief moment in 1980 it seemed there would be a bloodless revolution in the name of truth.' Ela shook her head, 'We got martial law instead.'

'What did you do to help?' I asked her.

'I worked in the press office as an interpreter. Sometimes I translated for Lech Wałęsa.'

'Was that dangerous?'

'After one interview with him, the militia stopped and interrogated me. My passport was confiscated. I didn't see it for several years.'

'Tell me what happened.' We walked to a café, and over steaming cups of coffee, Ela began my history lesson.

'Lech Wałęsa was a sacked electrical fitter. He climbed into the Lenin Ship yard on 14th August 1980 to lead a strike over the illegal dismissal of a fellow worker, Anna Walentynowicz. From his experience of strikes in 1970, Wałęsa knew workers out in the open were no match for tanks. He led a network of underground cells where a strategy was developed and goals defined. Realising the Government was in free-fall under the weight of economic disaster, he asked them to send representatives to the shipyard to listen to a list of demands which had the support of most of the country. Just over a fortnight later the authorities signed the Gdansk Agreement. But they never intended to honour it.' Ela sipped her coffee, and continued.

'The first independent labour movement in a Soviet-bloc country called Solidarity was formed. Before long it had 10 million members.'

'How did the ruling elite respond to this threat to their monopoly of power?'

'The Prime Minister of Poland, General Jaruzelski, faithful to his masters in Moscow, began a series of clampdowns. These came to a head on the night of 13th December, 1981. Communications were cut, and a state of war declared. Thousands of Solidarity supporters were dragged from their beds and taken to prisons or concentration camps, tanks patrolled the snowy streets, ZOMO storm troopers intervened at the slightest sign of trouble. There was a quiet, methodical purge of the academic world and a campaign against the Church. In October 1982, the courts dissolved Solidarity and introduced martial law.' Tears filled Ela's blue eyes.

'We are a proud people. It was hard to have to rely on aid sent by émigré Poles, among others, in order to survive.' Then she smiled ruefully, 'When police come, we're like mice, scrambling into our holes'.

'I'm sorry I didn't come sooner.'

'Helen, we're so happy to have you with us now.'

*

Mercy, justice and truth were values to fight for – values for which many had died or been imprisoned for during the latest round of Polish uprisings at the collapse of Solidarity; values that were encapsulated in the Lenin Shipyard monument. Shipyard welders made this work of art from sheets of cast iron, and erected it on the square outside the shipyard gates, on the spot where three of forty-five protesters were killed during street riots in 1970. Three elongated crosses with anchors rise into the sky like acrobatic jet planes. Penderecki composed the Polish Requiem *Lacrimosa* for its unveiling, at the request of Lech Wałęsa.

Inscribed on the base of the shipyard monument was a line from Psalm 29:11, "The Lord will give strength to his people", translated into Polish by the 1980 Nobel Prize winner in Literature, Czeslaw Milosz. This was followed by the penultimate stanza of Milosz's poem *You Who Wronged:* "Do not feel safe. The poet remembers. You can kill one, but another is born. The words are written down, the deed, the date." Milosz wrote these lines in 1950 when working in the Polish diplomatic embassy in Washington. On a trip home that winter, he fell under official suspicion and his passport was confiscated. Two months later he escaped to Paris, where he sought political asylum.

In 1981, after thirty years exile in the West, Milosz returned to Poland. When he visited the Gdansk monument, members of Solidarity unfurled a huge banner bearing the message: "The People Will Give Strength Unto Their Poet." The authorities dared not remove this reminder of where the Solidarity movement began, nor the poignant memorial at Gdynia. Within days of his visit the first official Polish publication of his poetry sold 150,000 copies, only to be banned and forced underground when martial law was imposed.

What a contrast to our much-loved poet laureate, Sir John Betjeman. During the last two years of his life, I used to walk over to the house where he lived a few streets away, and read to him over a glass of champagne. Despite ill health and a sense of insecurity, Sir John had an endless capacity to bring joy and happiness to others. His poet's vision was uncluttered by materialism, his simplicity a rare gift. Tennyson was his favourite poet and reading *In Memoriam* to him one day, we both felt transported to another sphere. When the front door slammed, I felt falling glass was smashing my illusions.

'Never lose your sense of wonder', he told me, and once, when walking up the King's Road as the sun was setting red on the horizon, I noticed a weed growing through the concrete pavement and my heart leapt at all that is.

One autumn day, Sir John's secretary, Elizabeth wheeled him over to our home for lunch. Rupert and Simon had read his autobiographical poem *Summoned by Bells* and sat spellbound at his feet as he talked. The small, mischievous boy within him lurked close to the surface and I watched as my sons revelled in the magic of his presence.

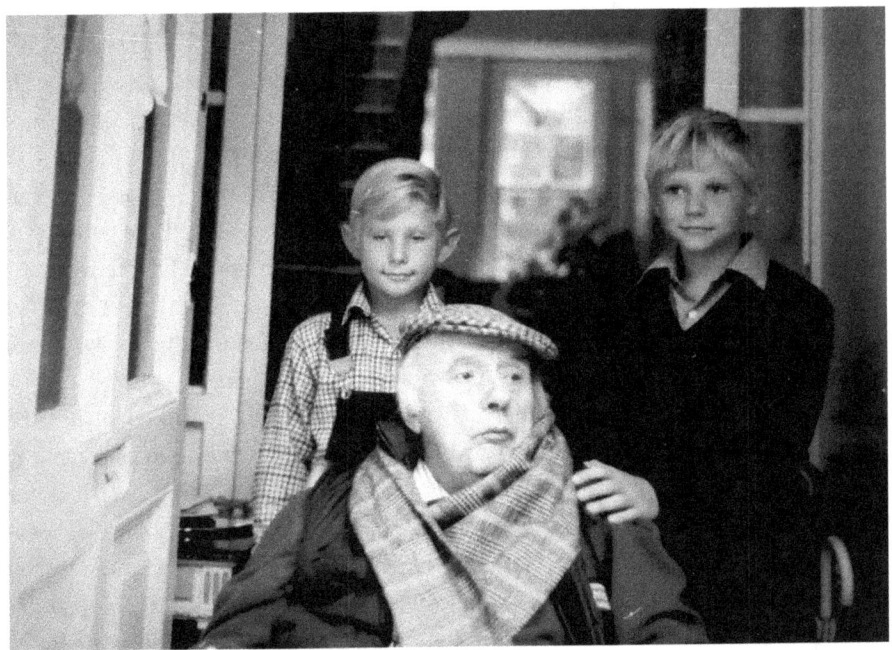

Sir John Betjeman with Simon and Rupert, 1983

*

Rich with dollars changed on the black market, I invited my five friends out to one of the best restaurants in town. *Pod Lososiem* (Under the Salmon) was Baroque in style, with brass sconces on the dark panelled walls of a staircase that rose in the centre of the house to the grand old dining room. A candelabrum squatted on each table, and the waiters were as stiff as the white damask tablecloths. Perhaps we were a bit underdressed in the formal atmosphere, for masks of politeness appeared on those dear faces and the discomfort increased when we looked at the menu. A plate of pork with salad and chips and a bottle of Bulgarian wine cost two weeks' salary.

Masks dropped as soon as we were back in Ewa and Andrew's room and they could entertain me. My week was reaching its end.

'We want to keep you longer. We'll hide you away among our English dictionaries to correct our mistakes and help with common usage,' said Ewa. Andrew spoke no English when I arrived. He was now almost fluent. The Poles have a facility with language, perhaps because few outsiders speak theirs, and my inability to grasp more than a few words was embarrassing. I fell back to German with the older generation.

My friends organised a party on my last evening– Shrove Tuesday, Pancake Day. In preparation for Ash Wednesday, when no meat is eaten, raw *Sledzig* (little herrings), Marynated overnight in oil and vinegar, are consumed with bread. Ewa opened tins since fresh herring was unavailable.

The next morning five of us crammed into Andrew's twelve-year-old car, after he removed a wheel stick, replaced the spark plugs, unlocked the petrol cap, removed special screws in the wheels and unset an alarm key. Theft was rife, the culprits usually Russian. We drove through a sun-speckled forest of silver birches and pine trees to the airport. My friends had given so much it was hard to say goodbye. I did not know when I would see them again.

There were two LOT Airline planes on the runway. I walked across the tarmac to the Krakow plane with a few businessmen and some couples travelling to the Tatra Mountains to ski. Everyone peered out of the windows to check the two engines as they started up and an air hostess offered sweets on a tray as we felt and heard the vibration in this ancient plane. As it rose into the sky I felt a sense of loss. The pilot spoke English for the sole British passenger: we were flying at 5,000 metres at a speed of 500km per hour. There was a great sense of space surrounded by blue sky and the odd trailing cloud, and freedom from the oppression of political bullying, of trying to exist with a mountain of difficulties.

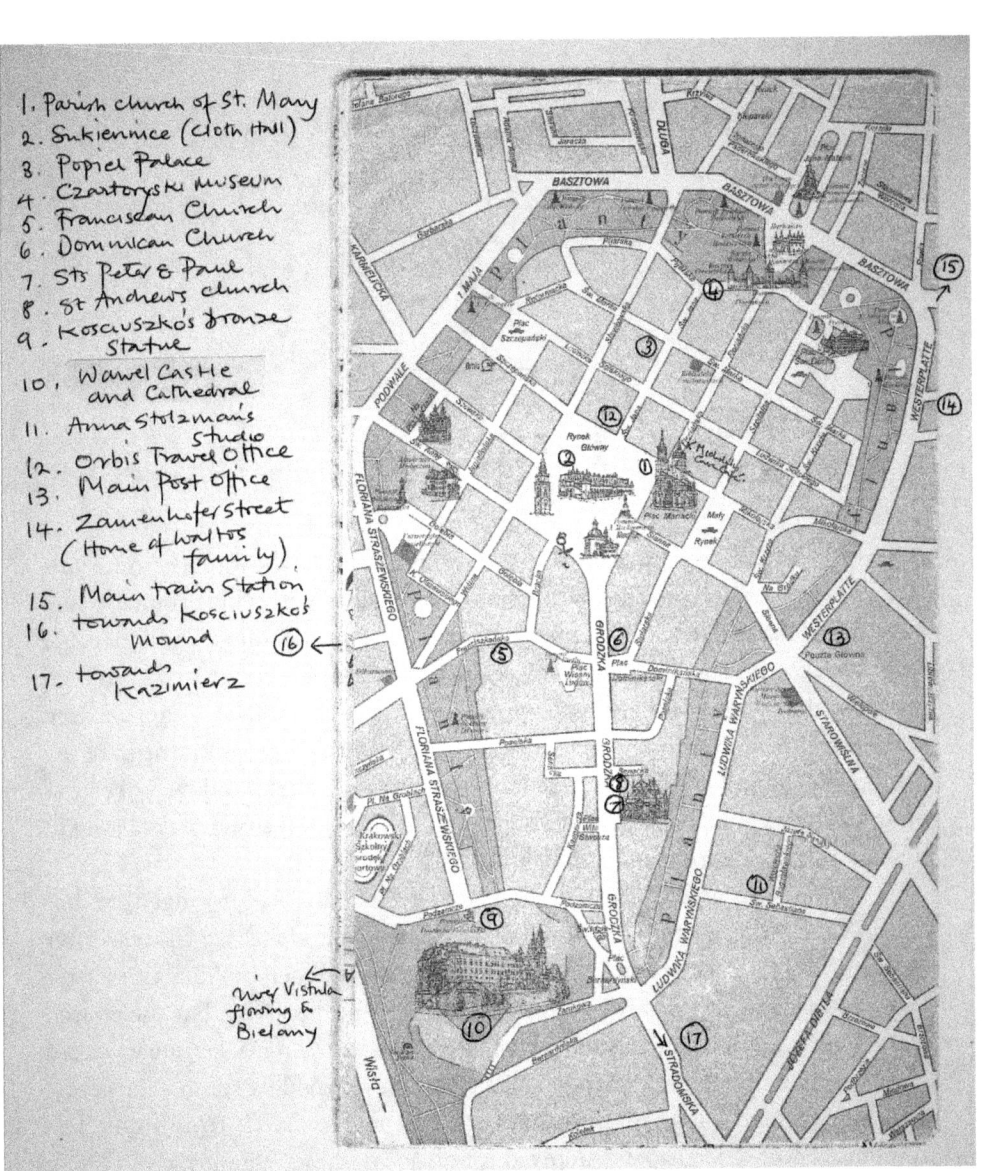

1. Parish church of St. Mary
2. Sukiennice (Cloth Hall)
3. Popiel Palace
4. Czartoryski Museum
5. Franciscan Church
6. Dominican Church
7. Sts Peter & Paul
8. St Andrews church
9. Kosciuszko's bronze
   Statue
10. Wawel Castle
    and Cathedral
11. Anna Stolzman's
    Studio
12. Orbis Travel Office
13. Main Post Office
14. Zamenhofer Street
    (Home of Wałtos
    family)
15. Main train Station
16. towards Kosciuszkos
    Mound
17. towards
    Kazimierz

river Vistula
flowing to
Bielany

Map of Ancient Centre of Krakow, 1984

3

Krakow

BUILT IN 1912, the Francuski Hotel was the best in Krakow. The front door opened to reveal a white marble staircase enriched with a blue runner rising majestically beyond the wide entrance, dividing on a half landing. The light came from a decorative stained glass window. I breathed a grateful sigh as a porter led me up to my room. It seemed enormous after my cubby hole in Gdansk. Large windows looked out on to the Czartoryski Museum and the adjacent Baroque church which blocked the end of St John's Street. The other window looked out on to trees and grass on the northern edge of the medieval city. I soaked long in my first bath since arriving on Polish soil.

It being Ash Wednesday, the first day of Lent, Ela had arranged for her cousin Grazyna to take me to Mass in St Mary's, Krakow's parish church. After the first Mongol invaders had entered and razed the wooden buildings on Easter Day in 1241, the city was re-created in a uniform grid pattern, but the church was rebuilt on its ancient site and stands askew on the main market square called Rynek. Inside the church, chandeliers and candles provide a sense of mystery. The blue-painted vault, speckled with stars, seem to stretch to infinity. The combination of side chapels endowed long ago by the city guilds, and Gothic vaults arching above Baroque altars, give a sense of continuity which historic troubles had not quenched.

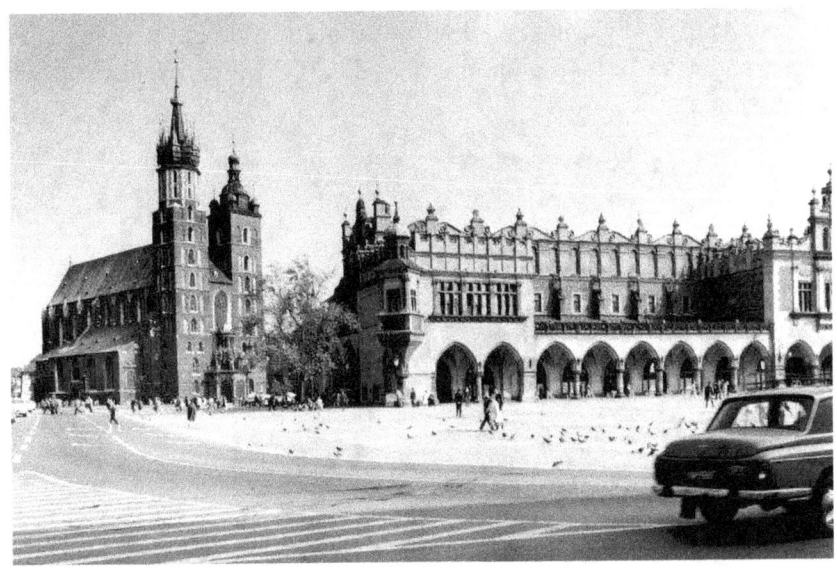

Rynek (Market Square) with St Mary's Church and the Sukiennice (Cloth Hall).
Photo by S. Michta, 1985

The great Mariacki Altar, carved by Veit Stoss, was completed in 1489. It took eleven years to create, and immediately became the pride of the city. Stoss was a versatile artist, but his genius lay in his chisel. Vasari described him as "miracolo di legno". Stoss, originally from Bavaria, moved to Krakow permanently in 1477 after being chosen by the City Council to produce the altarpiece. The great cost was paid for by the inhabitants of the town led by royalty, and from tithes and indulgences which the Vatican allowed to stay in Poland for this major endowment. Despite many adventures it still crowns the High Altar – a focal point for prayer. I gazed at the carvings of the story of Christ and his mother on the closed doors as I waited with Grazyna for our turn to kneel on the cold stone floor. The priest put his thumb in a bowl of ash and made the sign of the cross on my forehead with the words *you are dust and to dust you will return.*

The next morning I returned for the midday opening of the doors of the great gilded polyptych. A black-garbed nun with a microphone told visitors its history, as she pulled back each door in turn with an implement not dissimilar to a boat hook. Like many works of art in Poland, the altarpiece's survival was a miracle, from the decision not to replace it during the Baroque period, to World War II, when it was looted by the Nazis and shipped to Nuremberg Castle by the personal order of Hitler. Five years later, it was found hidden in the cellar of the heavily bombed Nuremberg Castle, lying crushed by the weight of other works of art, and damaged by damp and deathwatch beetle. Brought back to Krakow, it underwent major restoration in the Wawel Castle conservation studio before returning home.

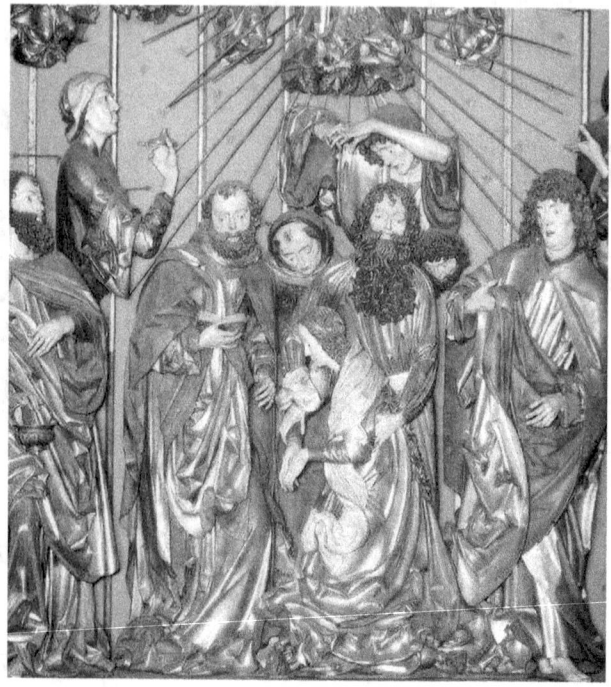

The *Dormition of the Virgin* by Veit Stoss (detail)

The doors opened to reveal the *Dormition of the Virgin*: her death and ascension. Each figure of Mary and the apostles was carved from one tree trunk. These portraits of prominent burghers of the day seemed to breathe, and their robes to move. The expressions on their faces as the apostles looked down on the dying Mary – pain, fear, awe, supplication – were mirrored in the faces of the people around me. Many were old women, up from the country, clad in head scarves and shawls. Young student priests in black soutanes knelt on the hard brick floor before the chapel dedicated to *The Black Madonna* of Jasna Gora, at the west end of the church. Fat, butter-coloured candles flickered light on the ornate silver frame of this eloquent copy, as old and young pleaded and prayed. They came like children to leave their burdens at the cross and be nurtured and renewed. One was prostrate on the iron railings. Here, all life's problems are brought to the altar; here, as in many churches throughout Poland, photographs of the Polish Pope with his would-be assassin were a visual reminder of the Church's plea to forgive and to love. I too lit a candle, strangely moved by the undisguised anguish and suffering I saw around me, deep in the fabric of this ancient house of prayer where people were not afraid to expose their innermost selves.

Every hour a bugle sounds from St Mary's higher tower. Outside, pausing to listen, I caught a glint of the brass rim of the instrument through an opened window. Suddenly, the bugler stopped dead, and I sensed around me a swift wiping away of a tear and a wisp of a prayer as he continued to play the hymn of praise to the Virgin – protector of the city since medieval times. He moved from window to window to play, viewing a different angle on life. According to legend, (which is well woven into the warp and weft of Polish history), the sudden silence is in memory of the watchman shot in the throat by an arrow while warning the citizens of the approaching army of Tartars.

As jam-packed trams trundled by outside the Gothic Franciscan church, peace reigned inside. Works by the artist, poet and playwright Stanislaus Wyspianski were a revelation. Around 1900 the artist painted William Morris-type pansies, lilies, leaves and patterns on the walls and proclaimed his joy in creation in the huge window above the west end entrance. God the Creator swirling with energy and colour – lilac and green, blue and pink – seemed caught in the breath of the Holy Spirit as he calls forth life, his gilded hand raised as in the Sistine chapel to *Let it be,* while the sea behind him and the sky above are bathed in light.

In a side chapel where Jozef Mehoffer painted the fourteen *Stations of the Cross* in the 1930s, a dozen brown-garbed friars sat in silence. As I turned to go they rose and began to sing. Then they re-enacted Christ's last journey, kneeling on the marble floor and praying in turn at each station, led by a young friar holding an ivory cross, followed by some old women. I did not understand the words, but the paintings spoke. A speckled spaniel standing beside Jesus looked on with quiet sympathy as the cross was thrust roughly on to the Saviour's shoulders by thuggish-looking men, the authorities holding back the crowds. Veronica, who according to legend wiped the face of Jesus as he staggered on his way, held the cloth on which his face shone. She was dressed as a bride in exquisitely wrought peasant folk costume and looked adoringly at her beloved, while he looked at us, his bare, bruised feet a contrast to hers, clad in pure white sandals.

As Jesus was laid in his tomb the sky was full of swirling Art Nouveau clouds, in the centre of which was the face of God, while a ram caught in a thicket referred to Abraham's sacrifice of Isaac. I was reminded of Father Maximilian Kolbe, a friar who served in this church after the Great War. Later he set up a printing press in Nagasaki, the main Christian centre in Japan and founded a community to carry on his work before returning to Poland in 1936. After the German invasion, Kolbe was arrested, released and then re-arrested because of his Christian activities, and sent to Auschwitz. There, he comforted fellow inmates and suffered beatings for his kindness. When, after an attempted escape, guards selected ten prisoners at random for execution, he offered to take the place of one of those condemned whom he knew had a young family. Left to starve in an empty barracks, guards finally gave Kolbe a lethal injection of carbolic acid. Word of his death spread through the camp and the *Saint of Auschwitz* became a living symbol of the triumph of good over evil. I looked closely at a portrait of this saintly Franciscan friar, (later canonised by John Paul II), wearing glasses and clad in prison stripes. Behind the quiet gaze he seemed such an ordinary man. Copies of this painting hang in many churches, the length and breadth of Poland.

Profoundly moved, I left the church. A century ago, when Krakow was occupied by the Austrians, the Town Council decided to pull down the ancient defensive walls of the city which had long been obsolete, fill in the moat and plant a park instead. Planty, as it is called, forms a ring of green around the medieval city. Its width is measured from the Florian Gate in the north to the Barbican, its outer fortress, which fortunately survived. Nothing much had changed over the years except the trees have grown.

Walking through Planty, I noticed that as protection from the icy winter, rose bushes and other tender plants were covered with tightly tied straw. Wearing their mournful winter dress, trees and shrubs seemed to weep with me. The atmosphere was evoked in Wyspianski's pastel painting *Capsheaves.*

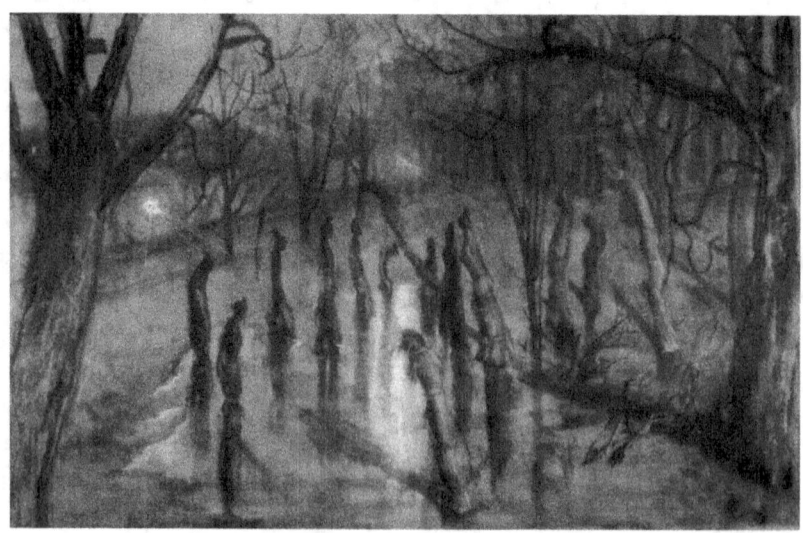

Capsheaves, **S. Wyspianski 1898-9 (National Museum in Warsaw)**

Lit as if by theatre lights, the straw dummies seem to wake once darkness fell and bow towards their reflections in the puddles. Beneath these straw dummies nature slept, ready to waken as the straw decayed and buds grew to reveal flowering rose bushes. Any Pole looking at this painting would recognise that just as goodness slept under the mantle of wretchedness, so the craving for independence lay dormant in the nation.

*

That night a terrifying dream engulfed me – someone unlocked my door from the outside, crept in, came to my bedside and stole my passport from under the pillow. I woke up shaking, checked my passport was safe and welcomed Lucia, Ela's mother, with a great hug when she arrived from the Gdansk train at seven o'clock. She had managed to arrange to collect the paintings she had inherited while I was in Kraków. We wanted to talk, but Lucia said my room was probably bugged. After breakfast we left the hotel and walked to Planty. It was safer to talk in the fresh air even though the level of pollution in the city was dangerously high. The Communist leaders had built Nowa Huta, a new centre of heavy industry in the 1950s, as their ideal town for Communist propaganda. The aim was to graft a large working class population on to an important artistic and intellectual academic city. Later, the factories became a hotbed for Solidarity.

In 1978 UNESCO included Krakow in its list of the twelve most valuable architectural heritages in the world. Yet everywhere in the ancient city black dust from the nearby chemical factories shrouded old carved stone, beautiful architecture, and finely wrought iron. Renaissance mansions, divided by the State into allotted spaces for families, stood proud. Plaster had crumbled to reveal original brick and stone in this jewel of Central Europe which had escaped destruction in the war. UNESCO withdrew the promise of funding restoration until the pollution was contained, but nothing much had been done. Lucia and I sat on a bench, wrapped up against the chill wind, and talked. I was glad to get to know this lovely woman a little better. A hard life had not quenched her spirit or her enthusiasm.

Lucia told me how over the centuries of foreign oppression, when Polish culture, language and customs were repressed, the underground press had developed into a fine art. During World War II, the Secret Military Printing Works was probably the largest underground publisher in the world. During the 1970s and 80s books of up to 500 pages long often exceeded 5,000 copies, and the Solidarnosc news sheet reached a run of 30,000 copies daily. The Movement for Defence of Human and Civic Rights and the Workers' Defence Committee organised printing in the 1970s which expanded as the years passed when small individual as well as several large publishers were created. Supplies were smuggled from abroad or stolen from official publishing houses. After the fall of the Soviet regime some of the underground publishers surfaced.

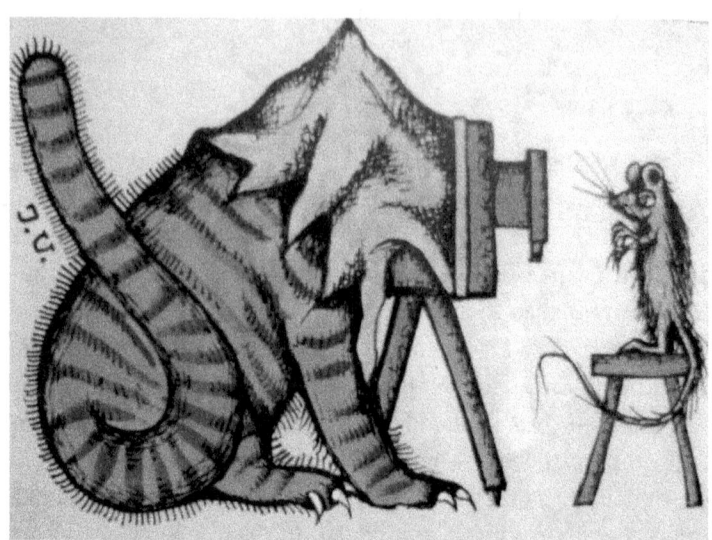

Political cartoon by Jerzy Urban, (presented by him to the author.)

I rang Professor Jacek Wozniakowski, writer and president of the prestigious publishing house Znak and old friend of Pope John Paul II. I told him that I brought greetings from friends of his in London and he invited me round to his flat five minutes' walk away. I arrived clutching the books I had smuggled in and handed them over. After settling me down in a comfortable sofa in his large salon this gracious, elegant gentleman poured me a brandy, then gently explained that my words had been enough to get a flat raided.

'You must be very careful what you say. Everyone's phone is bugged.'

As shame and embarrassment turned my face pink, he swiftly reassured me: 'Don't worry, they won't raid my home. Just be careful how you speak to others.'

I wished I had heeded Mrs Ferguson's words of warning on the flight from London. Professor Wozniakowski swiftly changed the subject. Had I been to Zakopane? The fashionable skiing resort in the Tatra Mountains had attracted artists and writers in the late 19th century. He talked about Polish painters and showed me photographs of their work. This made a big difference when I visited museums, since there were no guide books, let alone in English. (In June 1990,

Professor Wozniakowski was elected Mayor of Krakow, by the post-Communist Municipal Council.)

*

I negotiated a day trip to Zakopane with a taxi driver by writing in the dirt on the bonnet of his car. Five thousand old zlotys was a good day's wage for him; changed from dollars on the black market in the exchange kiosks called Kantors, it was about £10 for me. When he switched on the engine, I noticed before he mentioned it that the fuel gauge pointed ominously at empty. Petrol was rationed, and the ration card he showed me was filled with inky stamps, but with my foreign currency he made for a petrol station, filled his tank and an extra can with 38 litres and then did a detour home to tell his wife he would be gone for the day.

As we crossed the bridge over the Vistula he slowed down so I could absorb the beauty of Wawel Castle and the cathedral, where the Pope had been bishop, rising up above the river. The taxi sped on. Meandering suburbs melted into clumps of villages with strip-farmed fields between them, a thin veil of snow barely covering the tired earth. The occasional blue-washed thatched cottage with chickens pecking around outside reminded me of earlier times. How different these little farms were to the 17th century farmhouse, Lodgefield, where I grew up. In the '50s we had pigs and sheep as well as a dairy herd of Red Poll cows, though tractors had replaced horses. Ron, Charlie and Carey the bailiff worked the 250 acres. Over the decades my father increased the acreage by buying adjacent arable land. In Poland the Communists grabbed estates over fifty hectares and divided the land into strips for the peasants. Few manor houses survived.

Horses pulled wooden wagons filled with coal, bricks or bags of sand along the side of the road which tarmac had not touched, bringing materials to the many half-finished houses we passed. Poland seemed to be waking like the *Sleeping Beauty*, from a long sleep. Private enterprise was building as and when money from friends and relations arrived. The Communist regime turned a blind eye to this, for any foreign currency entering this beleaguered country was unofficially appreciated.

After an hour on the road, we reached a landscape where snow lay thick and forests appeared. There were few cars due to the cost of fuel and rationing. When we arrived at Zakopane my driver showed me the way to the funicular. We passed little booths where local peasants, wrapped up warmly, sold smoked goats' cheese, embroidered shirts and wooden toys carved during the winter months when their fields were frozen. I bought a pair of thick sheepskin slippers from a ruddy-faced, smiling woman.

In a few moments I was lifted up the mountainside to the Gubalowska, a high flat hill 3,694 feet above sea level in a cable train, which first carried passengers up to ski in 1938. It was overcast, and very cold. Horses hitched to sleighs stood in an ordered row like a taxi rank. The one at the front was a well-rounded chestnut that reminded me of my father's horse Square. Kennedy, our Irish groom, looked after my parents' hunters and our ponies when my sister and I were at boarding school. Much of our holidays were spent on horseback – riding round the farm or up the main road to Hammerwood where our local pony club met for lessons.

The driver settled me into the sleigh, threw over a pungent bearskin, climbed into the driving seat, and we trotted off to the jingling of bells. Snow lay undisturbed and hung heavily on drooping pine branches. Even the driver lifted his hands in wonder. Only the tinkling of the horse's bell and the thud of the runners disturbed the silence. Sweeping past mere mortals on foot I felt like the white witch in C.S. Lewis's *Narnia*. Poland was a country where, politically, it was always winter and never Christmas. A little wooden chapel and a house appeared. Both had carved beams and a parquet pattern on their walls – fairy tale buildings. Where were Hansel and Gretel? Then a farmhouse came into range, equally attractive, where two horses hitched to carts, filled with timber, stood waiting. The mare lifted her tail and whinnied excitedly, and the chestnut stallion pulling my sleigh plunged eagerly until the flick of his master's whip reminded him of his duty. The sleigh ride passed all too quickly.

Soon I was down the funicular and lunching on delicious trout fresh from the river, complemented by yellow boiled potatoes and cabbage, in a famous old café called *U Wnuka*. Here everything was carved pine, well insulated and warmed by an open log fire. In Poland it is customary to leave coats and clobber at the cloakroom where an attendant, usually a pensioner, relies on a small fee or tip. The lady here was delightful. She spoke to me in German as she sat eating a potato pancake by the range. I warmed to her immediately and was continually struck by how many people I met with whom I felt of the same mind, despite the occasional language problems. A silent look said much.

Replete and warm, I walked to the main shopping street named Zamoyskiego, and thought of Adam Zamoyski, who had advised me to take lemons to eat with caviar, which is cheap here on the black market. I had given my lemons away in Gdansk, and found no caviar. Zakopane is the Polish equivalent of St Moritz. This was my first sight of sophisticated women, dressed in fur from head to foot.

The shops were full, the houses most attractive – remnants from those gracious, gentler days, before Communism. I wandered round stalls examining intricately carved wooden boxes, rulers and other objects as I wanted to buy small presents for my sons.

*

The previous year I had met the Marchioness of Salisbury, known as Mollie to her friends. She was the chatelaine of Hatfield House, mother of six children and an international garden designer, who had taken Poland to her heart. Mollie arranged an air display at Hatfield House in aid of *Children of Poland* and my sons were roped in to sell programmes. No one could resist Mollie's entreaties for money and in eighteen months she raised £250,000 to buy medical supplies which she drove to Poland. This epic journey was one this late middle-aged lady was to continue to make for a decade, until the regime ended in August 1989. At Hatfield, Mollie flew in on a Micro-flex machine, landing dangerously on the bumpy grass to deliver a speech about the needs of the Polish people. A Spitfire flew over the ancient house and brought lumps to many throats, especially those who remembered the Polish pilots who fought so courageously with the allies forty years before.

Mollie had set up a foundation in Krakow with a friend, Professor Sofia Wlodek, to enable less privileged children to attend university. She suggested I call on another of her many friends in that city: Janusz Walek, curator of European art at the Czartoryski Museum. The museum, like most of the city, was an example of survival despite invasion, insurrection, pollution and neglect.

Though closed for extensive refurbishment, Mr Walek invited me round in two days' time. I stepped out of my hotel and crossed the road to the museum with no expectations. When I pressed the bell, the heavy door opened.

'Pan Walek, prosze! (Mr Walek, please!)' I said. At the name, the uniformed guard waved me inside and motioned me to wait in the hall as he clanged the door shut, moved back into his glazed office, lifted the telephone receiver and spoke. In the silence I observed the commemorative bronze shields and crossed swords of national heroes hanging on the walls. I knew little then of Poland's history, apart from the defeat of the Ottoman army at the gates of Vienna by King Jan Sobieski's cavalry in 1683.

Footsteps hurried along the passage and a tall, thin figure with flowing grey hair and a wide smile appeared. Janusz Walek welcomed me profusely, and led me up the stairs, talking quickly as our shoes clattered on parquet through a series of empty picture galleries where men were painting or lining walls with silk, specially made in the world-renowned Polish factories at Milanowek.

Janusz stopped at a mahogany door. He bowed me into the room with a flourish. He told me how Princess Izabela Czartoryska, during an extended stay in England in 1790, had caught her hosts' collecting bug. She bought objects belonging to famous people and among the works of art Janusz had removed from storage were some of these souvenirs such as part of Shakespeare's stool, Captain Cooke's sword, an exquisite ivory powder horn that belonged to Henry VIII, and some miniatures painted by Richard Cosway. Over the years Izabela accumulated works of art and in 1801 opened the first ever public museum in Poland in the grounds of Puławy, her country estate east of Warsaw.

Among the masterpieces laid out for me was Rembrandt's *Good Samaritan* and, in pride of place, a portrait by Leonardo da Vinci. Gripping the heavy frame, I lifted his *Lady with an Ermine* from the easel. Anxiety and excitement mingled as I drew the portrait close and examined this masterpiece with a conservator's eye.

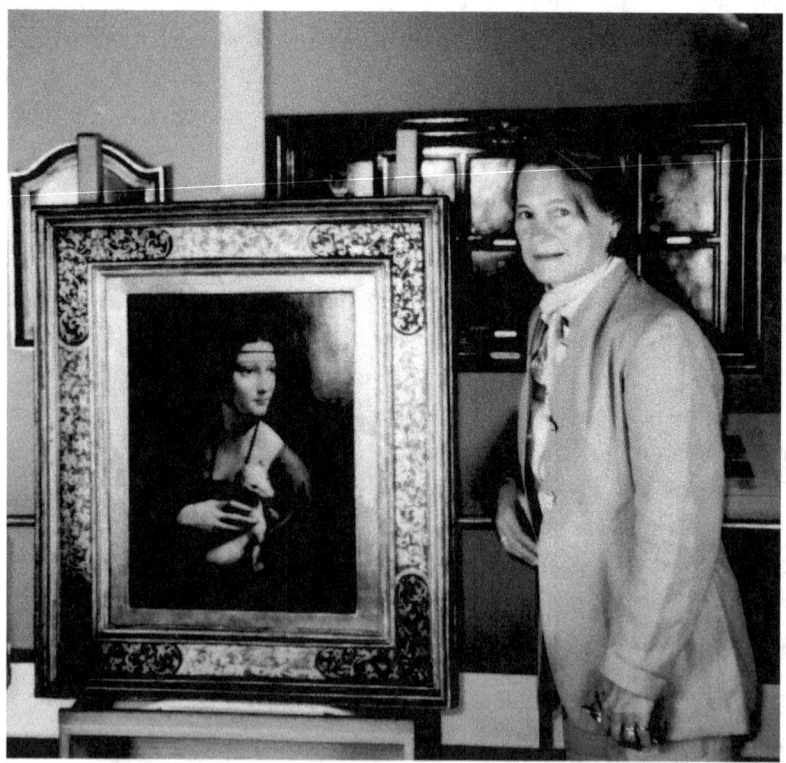

Author with Leonardo's *Lady with an Ermine*

The subtleties of Leonardo's painting were diminished by the varnish that had yellowed with age and the background, originally a harmonious shade of grey-blue, was later completely over-painted in black. Mastering my desire to clean it off, I was relieved to see the painting was stable, unlike several others by the master, for Leonardo liked to experiment with pigment and varnishes, not always successfully. I concentrated on the details of the portrait. It was of Cecilia Gallerani, mistress of Ludovico Sforza, Duke of Milan. The sixteen-year-old is modestly but elegantly dressed in a red gown and blue cloak. Her hair, parted in the middle and gathered in a plait, is covered with a gold-edged gauze veil so thin to be scarcely visible which is held in place by a thin black band. The rather broad-faced ermine, its coat no longer white, is a species of weasel in its winter coat. Whereas the weasel was considered a symbol of debauchery the ermine symbolised chastity. The Greek word 'gale' meaning ermine connects with the name Gallerani. Leonardo's contemporary, Bernardo Bellincioni wrote eulogistic poems at the Duke's court. This verse from a sonnet describing Cecilia, one of the most enchanting women at Court seemed prophetic:

"The honour is yours, though in his painting
He's made her seem to listen, but not to speak.
Think how very alive and beautiful she is,
To your great glory – for all time."

In order to avoid angering his future bride Beatrice d'Este, the Duke of Milan removed the pregnant Cecilia from the ducal palace. In her new home she gave birth to their son Cesare and kept a salon where she entertained musicians and artists. The portrait remained with Cecilia, perhaps as a reminder of happier days, until her death in 1536. Little more was heard of the painting, until Prince Adam Czartoryski purchased it in Italy around 1800 as a present for his mother.

As Janusz helped me replace the portrait back on to the easel, sunlight poured through the 19th century leaded windows, the centre of which bore the Czartoryski coat of arms. It featured a warrior in red, glass shield held close, mounted on a rearing charger flying over three towers, his right arm raised brandishing a sword. My eyes lingered around the little gallery, painted green. Each object had a story to tell, from exquisite early ivories to a copy of a portrait of Chopin – painted before the original was wrecked, along with the composer's piano, by marauding Cossacks.

Janusz led me to his office where we settled down with coffee brought by his colleague, Dorota.

'Why has the Leonardo not been cleaned?' I did not receive a clear answer, but Janusz suggested he took me to Wawel Castle to meet the restorers there. Like the custodians of the *Mona Lisa* in Paris, I think he believed in keeping the patina of age.

'Did you always want to restore paintings?' Janusz asked me.

'I wanted to study the history of art,' I told him, 'but I was very nervous and ill prepared when I went to the Courtauld Institute to be interviewed by the eminent director, Sir Anthony Blunt. He was Surveyor of the Queen's London Pictures, and a third cousin of the Queen Mother.' I paused to remember Blunt's gaunt, distinguished face which had struck me as rather sad and introverted beneath his patrician polish. How different to Betjeman, his contemporary at Marlborough College

'In 1939 he joined the British intelligence corps, saw service in France, was evacuated from Dunkirk, and worked for M15. In the final days of the war, he went covertly to Schloss Friedrichshof in Germany to retrieve sensitive letters from the Duke of Windsor to Hitler and other leading Nazis.

'Three months after my interview, Blunt confessed to M15 that he was one of the Cambridge Five, a group of double agents working for the Soviet Union from the 1930s to the 1950s. Blunt's full confession to the British Government came with the proviso that his spying career would be an official secret for fifteen years and he was given full immunity from prosecution. He continued to look after the Queen's paintings until 1972 and kept his position at the Courtauld Institute. Seven years later, his secret was publicly exposed and he was stripped of his honours.'

I looked at Janusz. Even though spies and informers were part of Polish life, he was shocked.

'It must have been very hard for your Queen,' said Janusz. 'Did you go on to study with him?'

'Blunt initially turned me down, but I discovered there was another door into the Courtauld Institute through the Restoration department. When I applied, the course was full. However, the idea of restoring old paintings took root, and on 18th June I found myself knocking apprehensively on the black door to the left of the main entrance to the National Gallery in Trafalgar Square. A young man led me along a stone-floored corridor into a large studio. Professor Helmut Ruhemann, Consultant Restorer to the Gallery since 1946, appeared from behind a painting. Tall and thin, he gazed with a characteristic calmness through horn-rimmed glasses as he sat me down beside him. During our conversation he noted my enthusiasm, and knowing how hard it is to draw a hand well, suggested

I drew my own and return with it.' Ruhemann had begun his career as an artist training in Munich and Paris and at the Prado in Madrid, during World War One. Later he became Chief Restorer at the Kaiser Friedrich Museum in Berlin, while developing his private practice. In 1933, when Hitler came to power, Ruhemann, being Jewish, was invited to London where his family stayed. While his private practice flourished, Sir Kenneth Clarke called him to the National Gallery and built him the studio where he interviewed me. Ruhemann became a pioneer of modern conservation techniques.

I lifted my square and workmanlike hands and showed them to Janusz before saying,

'Back home on the farm I took a new sketch pad up to my bedroom in the attic, sharpened two HB pencils, laid my left hand on the desk and observed it closely as if for the first time. I drew what I saw, noticing highlights and hatching in shadows. A week later, I took the train to London, and showed my drawing to the professor. He examined it carefully. Then, at the turn of a hand, my life changed. Professor Ruhemann said that he looked for talent, sensitivity, flair and a sharp eye – attributes he claimed he could develop as long as they were inherent in a person. He said that he would take me as one of his pupils in eighteen months' time, after I had done some further art training. That is how I became a picture conservator-restorer,' I said.

*

The next day Janusz walked with me from the Czartoryski Museum through the old city towards Wawel Castle, rising up above the Vistula River in the south. As we talked, I thought about my career sharing a studio with a fellow student, Anthea, after Ruhemann thought us competent to set up on our own. We shared premises but had our own clients, an arrangement that worked well for eighteen years. Is it worth having a picture restored? That nicotine-stained Victorian ancestor in the study; the modern landscape someone put their foot through when moving house; or the inherited 17th century masterpiece that needs attention?

A restorer, now entitled conservator, will give advice, an estimate of how much it will cost and how long it will take. No one wants to spend time or money conserving (if paint is falling off), lining (if the canvas is torn, or dried out) or cleaning (if the varnish has darkened enough to obscure the paint), an old pot-boiler of little merit. Misconceptions about oil painting restoration can lead zealous amateurs to attempt a do-it-yourself, before bringing a ruined picture for advice. A conservator is only as good as his last job. Clients came by recommendation, and through contacts. Being self-employed is a mixed blessing, but I preferred my independence, and once I was married with a family I was fortunate to be able to take pictures when I wanted them. Ruhemann trained us to work specifically on oil and tempera paintings on canvas, board or panel. They came in all shapes, sizes and condition, ranging from the 15th to the 20th century.

When we reached Wawel, Janusz led me up the dark marble staircase in one of the 19th century buildings, erected by the Austrians during their occupation, to the conservation department where I was profusely welcomed as an example of a species from beyond the Soviet bloc. Two of the restorers spoke English and we compared our various approaches to cleaning and restoring. Without access to Western currency they were unable to purchase much needed materials. Over coffee the Chief Conservator Jan Blyskosz invited me to come back and work with them another time.

*

I had language problems trying to buy a train ticket to Warsaw in the crowded Orbis Travel Agency on the corner of Rynek and St John's Street. This ugly, pre-war construction with its low ceiling and glazed, flat facade struck a discordant note beside its ancient neighbours. A tall, elegant lady wearing a green loden coat and dashing feathered hat asked if she could help. The ticket was soon purchased and we introduced ourselves. Teresa Rostworowska, who now lived in London, was visiting her son Boguslaw. She kindly invited me to lunch with them. The Rostworowski's Italianate town house lay on the way to the Czartoryski Museum. Nearly a third of the way up the street Teresa halted outside a Baroque doorway, wide enough for a carriage and horses to pass through, where 'heavies' held up the cornice on which cherubs appeared to be about to jump off.

She pointed to the Rococo cartouche in the centre, barely visible beneath the grime, and said, 'That's the Sulima coat of arms. It's shared by several families, including the Popiels, after whom the house was named.' Teresa opened one of the pair of 18th century wooden gates and we entered the inner courtyard. The paving slabs were knocked about and the decaying walls were as black as the high buildings visible around. We went through a door into a huge vaulted area, divided into two rooms by a screen, which had been the coach house.

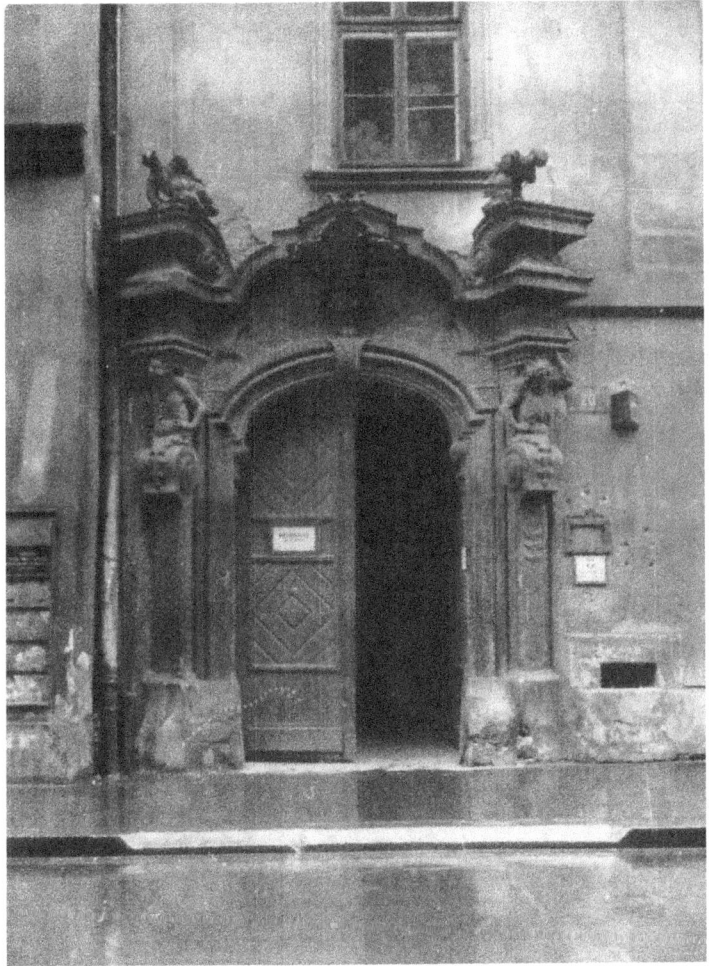

Entrance gate to Popiel Palace, 1980's photo (Rostworowski Archive)

'Oak planking muffled the sound of horses' hooves as they drove through' she said, then,

'I've brought a guest for lunch', as her son Boguslaw came to meet us with outstretched hand and cheerful smile. He was not much taller than me, with a well-trimmed black moustache and trimmed beard, which compensated for his receding hairline.

'Welcome!' he said in immaculate English, and with the casualness I had come to recognise as typical Polish hospitality.

'Your mother saved my bacon in the travel agency,' I replied to which he laughed and said 'lunch is ready' as he led me to a table and pulled more cutlery and plates from a cupboard. As he dished up pierogi I looked around. Antique furniture filled the space and old paintings covered the walls. As we ate I heard their story. Teresa's husband had been demobbed in Scotland where their children were born and raised, but he kept returning to his roots in Krakow, visiting an old aunt who lived in these two rooms with a servant. When the Communists took control of the country in 1948 the town council allocated the ground floor to barristers' chambers and housed families in the rest of the mansion. Eventually, despite the political situation, the family moved into these two rooms until her husband's death, when Teresa moved to London with her daughter. She worked tirelessly into her eighties, acting as an interpreter in Polish, French, Italian and Russian for hospital patients. When his British schooling was over, Boguslaw decided to return to his family home.

'Under Communism in Poland, title deeds weren't taken, unlike country estates over fifty hectares, about 120 acres, which were divided up and given to the peasants, or turned into state co-operatives,' he said. I gathered that writers, critics and poets trusted Boguslaw to translate their works into English with sensitivity and fluency. This scion of an aristocratic intellectual Polish family – his uncles were professors, respected internationally in their fields of art and history – had followed his father's footsteps and become a poet, and later, a sculptor. His uncle Marek was the Director of the Czartoryski Museum.

After lunch, Boguś (pronounced Bogoosh) showed me sculptures he had carved – elegant shapes revealing the beauty of white Carrara marble beloved by Michelangelo. (Bogus read some of his translations of post-war Polish poetry at the Richard Demarco Gallery, during the Edinburgh Festival of 1990). I admired his courage to reclaim an inheritance in a country where people of his class and culture were unwelcome.

Cheerfully, Boguś carried my suitcase to the station outside the city wall, for the three-and-a-half hour journey to Warsaw. There was time, bowling along on the train, for reflection. I felt more alert, more energised than I had for years – stimulated to the core by the highly intelligent, knowledgeable and friendly people I had met. I was not used to feeling so welcomed by strangers. In London, survival of the fittest meant making money. Here it was about keeping your integrity whatever the cost. I had seen something of this cost. The train trundled towards the capital passing strip-farmed land, horses pulling ploughs and wooden carts and thatched barns in the melancholic sandy flatlands. This landscape, over which armies had marched and fought for centuries, was described by the Polish artist Maksymilian Gierymski as 'a wayside inn for foreign armies'. And Warsaw had borne the brunt.

4

Warsaw

THE ORBIS GRAND Hotel in Warsaw where I had reserved a room was far from grand. Climbing out of the taxi I eyed an ugly, grey concrete rectangle, the unattractive sight amplified within by party members assembled for a Communist party conference choking the lounge. I wondered if constructing ugly buildings was a strategy for lowering people's sights, or a reflection of the mentality of the State. When I checked in I found I was the only tourist. The clerk handed me a pass to enable me to enter and exit this enemy camp. My tape recording of an interview with a Solidarity leader in Gdansk felt leaden in my pocket.

Now I was bereft of friends, I felt alone. Loudspeakers kept up continuous propaganda. By the tone I imagined the Party was praising its achievements. The members looked well fed and satisfied. They had their privileges including housing and the opportunity for their children to take the first places at university. They reminded me of the Party members I had observed in the departure lounge at Heathrow. Perhaps my bias warped my attitude but I could feel nothing positive about these persecutors of most of the population, with their sycophantic obedience to their Soviet rulers; who put their own ambitions and love of power before their conscience.

I watched a different side of Polish life in a short documentary film in the History Museum in the old town Market Square. This was a necessary introduction to the city. Only then could I understand what had happened to Warsaw: a bustling cosmopolitan city with a quarter of its population Jewish, its wide boulevards, stunning architecture and parks filled with children. It was a café society in 1939, when the Germans invaded. As the cine rolled on I watched as the ghetto, into which the Nazis had first corralled the Jews, was eliminated, the city reduced to rubble, and its people killed. The most furious fighting for the Old Town and the surrounding areas occurred during the sixty-three day 1944 Uprising, in which young and old, student and professional took part and 200,000 civilians died.

Jan Nowak, who delivered top security materials from occupied Warsaw to the Polish government in London in 1943, returned to Warsaw on the eve of the Uprising. On August 2nd he wrote: "Suddenly a captured armoured car appeared with the painted emblem "WP," "Polish Forces," covered with our soldiers. There was an outburst of enormous enthusiasm. People in the street stopped digging, put down their picks and shovels, and, as if by unseen command, began to sing the "Varovienne." The whole street...was now singing, those on the streets and sidewalks, on balconies and at the open windows. My old uncle raised a deep bass voice in the hymn of the 1831 Polish rising against the tsar:

This is the day of blood and glory
May it be the day of victory

I was filled with a sense of exultation that I had never experienced before and am not likely to experience again. I would have given my life to witness this moment. We felt free again in this small Warsaw neighbourhood re-conquered from the enemy with our own force". (Quoted from Jan Nowak's *Courier from Warsaw*, Published by Collins/Harvill, London 1982 p.348). Later Nowak managed to escape to the West to report on the city's destruction. The emblem P over W, called anchor, was daubed over walls during the Nazi occupation and stood for *Poland Fights.*

Manhole covers were a silent reminder of those survivors who fled from the centre of Warsaw through the sewage canals when the defence broke down. Civilians and the injured caught by the Nazis were shot. The film ended with the entrance of the Red Army, the so-called liberators, who had waited on the other side of the Vistula river until the Germans had finished dynamiting what was left of the city and retreated. Stalin's betrayal of Warsaw was one of the major infamies of the war. He too wanted, as its enemies had for centuries, to eradicate the Polish identity. By January1945 85% of the city was destroyed. When the people returned they rebuilt their old town, and their royal Castle, for Poles are a deeply patriotic people. Even little children helped clear the rubble, brick by brick. It is now impossible to distinguish the ancient buildings from the new as their stones have mellowed.

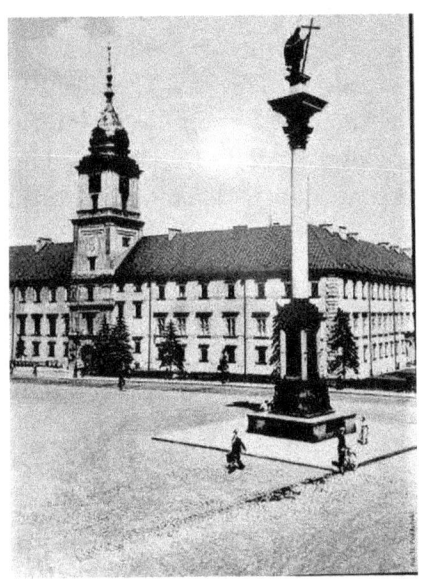

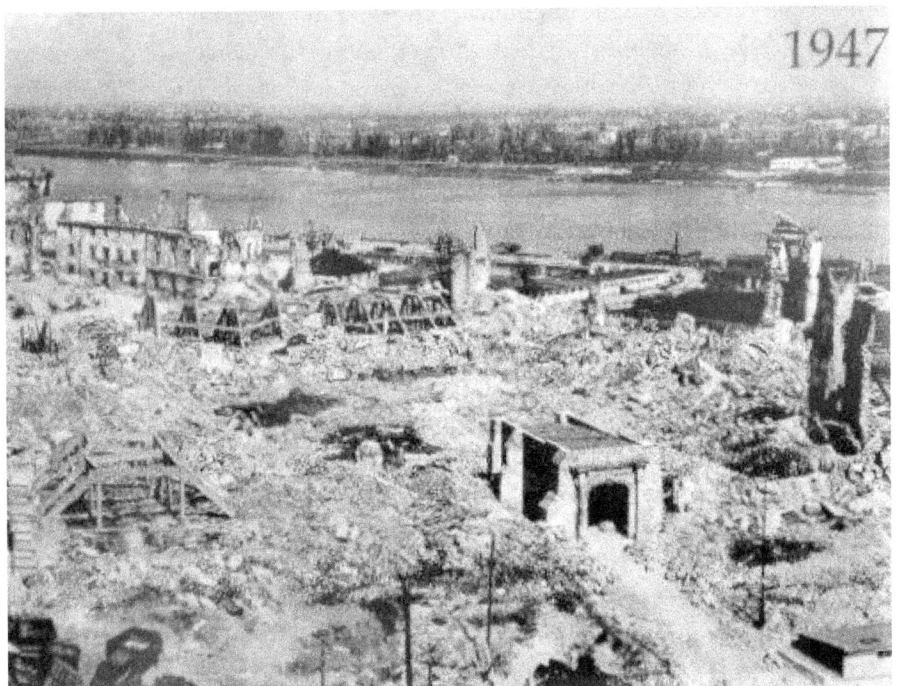

Warsaw Castle 1939 and Warsaw Old Town, 1947

I blinked as I came out of the gloom of the cinema into the sunlight of the large square. Marked out at the start of the 14th century this was the heart of Warsaw before the 19th century expansion of the city. The old town declined into poverty, until a campaign launched to protect historic monuments at the beginning of the 20th century led to the renovation of the finer houses. Eminent artists of the day decorated the facades in contemporary idiom which provoked heated discussions in the cafes around the city. Original fragments discovered in the rubble after the war, were incorporated in the reconstruction of the Market Square. This was undertaken by a team of dedicated researchers, designers, artists, craftsmen, technicians and workers, who traversed the narrow line between historic integrity and modern living. New painting and graffito graced the facades along with charming lattices, signboards, gargoyles and lanterns.

On the way to the castle, I stopped at the Cathedral Church of St John the Baptist which began life as the parish church six hundred years earlier. The cathedral experienced the same fate as its neighbours: attack from the air and the ground and eventual demolition by dynamite. Reconstructed after the war in its Gothic brick design, the builders incorporated fragments from the 14th century. Today, a member of the militia stood guard outside. Inside a soldier confessed to a priest. His cap and bag lay on the stone floor nudging a wall where plaques commemorated the great and the good, including Ignacy Paderewski, the world-famous composer and pianist, turned politician, who became Prime Minister and Minister of Foreign Affairs in the newly independent Poland in 1919. In the ten months of his leadership Paderewski achieved democratic elections to the Sejm, ratification of the Treaty of Versailles, protection of ethnic minorities and the establishment of a public education system. His government also tackled border disputes, unemployment, ethnic and social strife, the outbreak of epidemics – and averted the looming famine after the devastation of war. Fluent in seven languages, and gifted with diplomatic skills, he was able to negotiate thorny issues with Poland's Ukrainian and German neighbours and gain international respect in the process.

Peace was soon threatened by the Red Army, determined to link up with the burgeoning Communist cells in Germany, and advance further west into a Europe exhausted by war and the Spanish flu. Reaching the outskirts of Warsaw, Tukhachevsky, Commander-in-Chief of the Bolshevik forces, issued his orders:

"Soldiers of the Red Army!

The time of reckoning has come. The army of the Red Banner and the army of the predatory White Eagle face each other in mortal combat. Over the dead body of White Poland shines the road to worldwide conflagration."

Once more, against all odds, a Polish victory saved the Christian West from invasion. Few are aware of what became known as the Miracle on the Vistula.

*

Since the late 16th century, Warsaw castle had been the seat of the monarch as well as housing the Polish parliament, which is called the Sejm: a dual function unique in Europe at the time. I bought a ticket and walked across the large entrance hall to start my tour, when English voices halted me. An enthusiastic young woman was just setting off with a group of Swedish restorers, friends of the artist painting the coat of arms in the Senate room. She invited me to join them. Our little group of five stopped to watch their friend at work. The Germans had dynamited the castle; now forty years later the rebuilding was almost complete and the final, finer details were being put in place all over the interior. Gold leaf glinted and the smell of varnish hung thickly in the air. Contributions to furnishing the interior flowed in from all over the world. Princess Alexandra of Kent gave four tapestry-covered fauteuils and Pope John Paul II a 16th century painting of St John for the chapel.

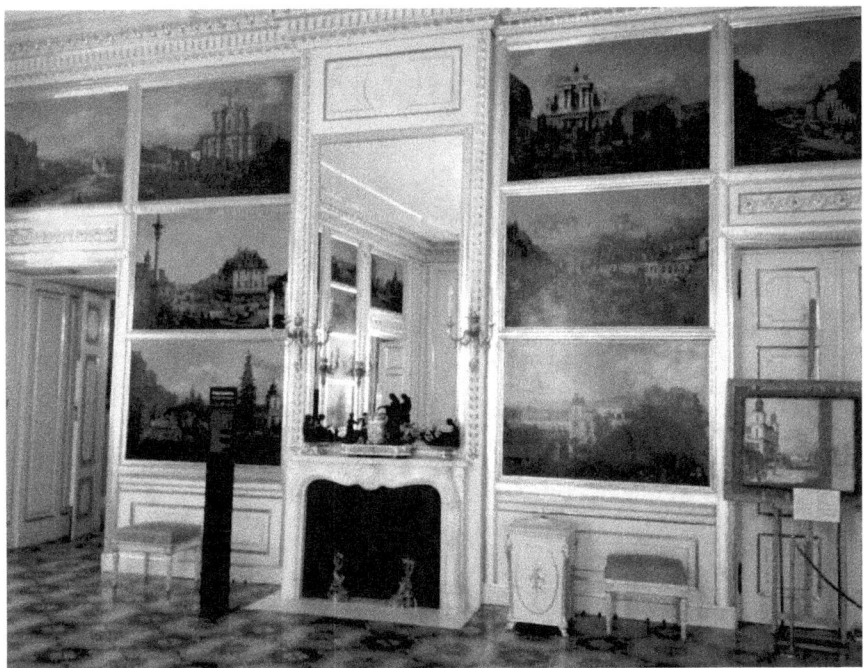

Views of Warsaw **by Bernardo Bellotto, 1767-1780**

In the Senatorial Antechamber, where those expecting an audience with King Stanislaw II Poniatowski waited, views of the city by Bernardo Bellotto plastered the walls. I happily spent a considerable time exploring these paintings. They are rich in detail like those by his uncle Canaletto with whom he trained before becoming court painter in Vienna, Munich and Dresden. Bellotto spent the last thirteen years of his life working in the artistic climate of Stanislaus's court. The King also invited Marcello Bacciarelli from Rome to be the first Director of his newly established Academy of Arts.

While Bacciarelli taught young Polish art students the techniques of portraiture, Bellotto introduced townscape into Polish painting. His series of twenty-two views of Warsaw and its environs, all of which survive, is a valuable source of knowledge of town planning and architecture in late 18th century Warsaw, its history and customs. The pictures are also full of life: of people and animals. They were so accurate they were used as a guide during reconstruction of the city after the war. As well as the views, Bellotto painted the *Election of King Stanislaus Augustus 1764* which gives a fascinating insight into how these functioned: there is the 'shed' where the Senate debated, a circle of Deputies who sat in the lower house, crowds of gentry and the Primate Wladyslaw Lubienski, who went round the election field collecting votes. Polish kings were elected after the Jagiellon dynasty died out in 1572.

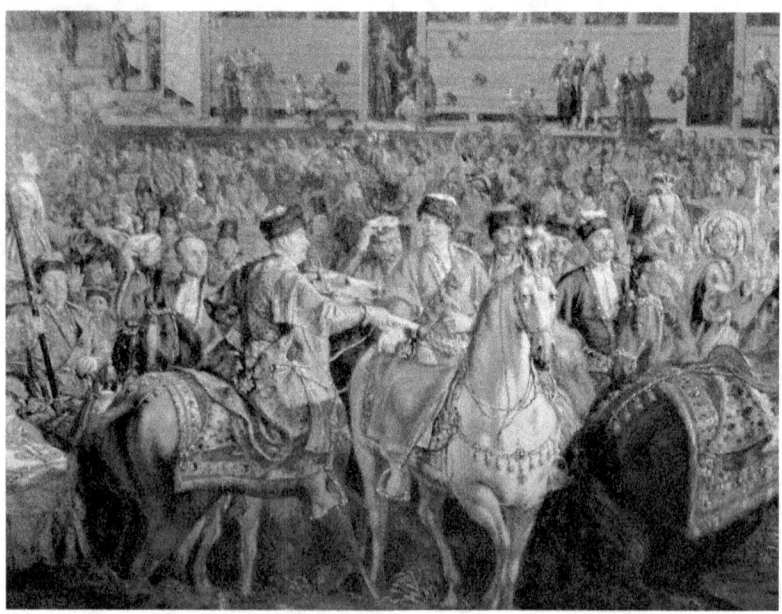

Election of King Stanislaus Augustus, 1764 (detail) by Bernardo Bellotto 1760's

The king's former lover Catherine the Great of Russia, who saw him as a useful pawn, had used Russian troops and Russian influence to ensure his election in 1764. As King he sought to strengthen the parliamentary system, reforms which were opposed by some Polish nobles and by Catherine. In 1772 Russia, Prussia and Austria annexed portions of Polish territory despite the King's appeals to Western powers. Stanislaw saw his own personal power cut away and limited by the partitioning powers. Fighting back he temporarily strengthened his position and achieved a full reform of Polish education. Constitutional reform followed with a new constitution, approved by the Sejm on 3rd May, 1791. This was too much for Catherine, who invaded and crushed the movement. On 25th November, 1795 as Russia, Prussia and Austria annexed the entire country, Stanislaw was forced to abdicate.

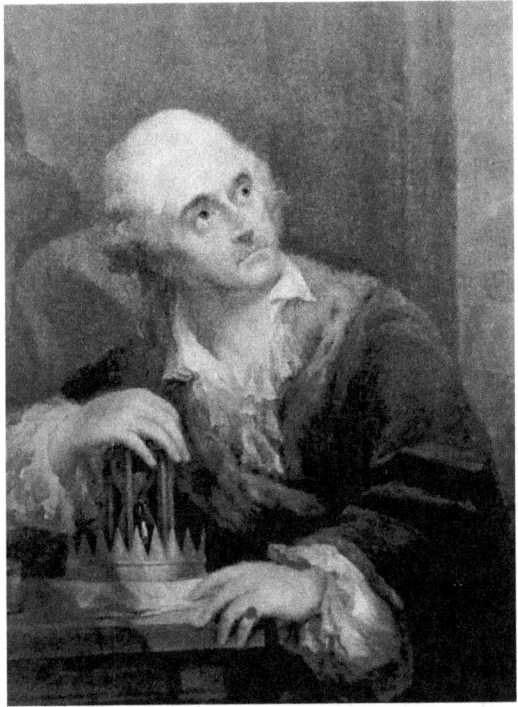

The Last King of Poland by Marcello Bacciarelli, 1793

The art collection Stanislaw amassed in England never reached Poland. After the King's removal to St Petersburg as a semi-prisoner, the collection was purchased and hung in the Dulwich Gallery, the first purpose-built public art gallery in England designed by Sir John Soane and opened in 1817.

After the tour, I invited our guide Iwona to lunch. Slightly shorter than me, she had brown hair and a determined look. Like others, the difficulties of everyday life in this Soviet satellite had etched lines in her face. She led me back to the Market Square, to the Basilisk House, built in the 15th century, but re-modelled two hundred years later in the Classicist style for a banker, who had made it his home. The five-storey façade with its gilded stucco survived the War, and was now a restaurant called Basilisk. On the signboard outside is the monster with a fatal eye, which according to legend guards a hidden treasure. Here, the treasure was an excellent meal. Questions bounced back and forth about painting, history, politics, and Iwona talked about her work in the education department at the Castle, as we tucked into wild boar cutlet with chips and salad and a glass of Hungarian bull's blood wine. I could not resist Polish 'lody' which compares favourably with Italian ice cream. I was conscious, as in Gdansk, how restaurants like this catered for tourists, Communist officials, and those with US dollars to spare.

'Why not spend the afternoon at the National Museum?' she said. 'I'll see if I can fix something for you.'

After our feast, Iwona took me back to her office on the ground floor of the castle where dark wood and cream walls predominated. After introducing me to her colleagues she picked up the phone, dialled and said, 'Agnieszka, have you time today to introduce an English restorer to Polish painting?' There was a pause as she listened. 'Excellent. She's on her way.'

Iwona turned to me, smiled enthusiastically and said, 'Dr Agnieszka Morawinska, curator of Polish art, is one of the most intelligent women in Poland. She's waiting to meet you!'

I thanked Iwona and hailed a taxi. We drove down Krakowskie Przedmiescie, past former palaces, churches and the university, into the elegant Nowy Swiat street built in the neo-classical style in the 1820s and rebuilt after the war, towards the Poniatowski Bridge – which had become a symbol of Polish survival. After ten years of work, the bridge was finally completed in 1914. Within a year the retreating Russians had blown up part of it to slow down the German advance. Thirty years later the Germans destroyed it during the Warsaw uprising, and though it was hastily rebuilt after the war and widened in the 1960s, only after the Wall came down was the bridge returned to its former glory.

Everywhere I went every building told a story, a silent drama. The National Museum was not exempt: built in the 1930s in an elegant unadorned style, this too suffered Hitler's hatred of anything Polish. In 1937 a Nazi historian compiled a meticulous list of the most valuable artefacts in preparation for their first opportunity to loot the museum. I found my way to the staff entrance, where a guard escorted me to Agnieszka's office and invited me to make myself comfortable. I looked around. A 19th century portrait of a young woman hung above a Beidermeyer settee and chairs set at a round table. Lovely inlaid furniture completed the drawing room atmosphere. Agnieszka arrived a little late and rather harassed. She was off to the USA in a couple of days to organise an exhibition of Polish art, but despite the rush, she willingly shared her extensive knowledge. She took me round the gallery and into a new area of art, beginning with some history.

After the failure of the November Insurrection of 1830-1, many Poles escaped abroad and continued the struggle for national liberation in exile. Polish culture lived on in the music of Frederic Chopin, who captured a timeless peasant culture in his Mazurkas, and the characteristics of courtly life in his Polonaises. Literature dealt with the problems of survival under foreign rule. Indeed, Polish Romantic literature was more preoccupied with national existence and the struggle for independence than any other country in Europe. Three great poets Mickiewicz, Krasinski and Slowacki expressed the ideal of national liberation in their works. Mickiewicz shone poetic light on the Polish people's despair and sense of abandonment by the rest of the world and suggested that Poland was a martyr in the cause of righteousness. He was considered to be, with Alexander Pushkin, the greatest Slavic poet, but was little known in Europe where the Polish language was not understood.

'Here, after the death of the great Romantic poets, 19th century artists took over the mantle of Guardians of the Polish Soul,' Agnieszka said and continued, 'These late Romanticists succeeded through their art to convey a patriotic message in an accessible and attractive way. They also provided a visual lesson in Polish history for many generations to come. Farewells and welcomes, the former more joyous, have always been a striking paradox of the Polish lot,' this shy academic explained. 'In his depictions of the January 1863 insurrection, Artur Grottger extolled both private sacrifices and experiences common to all Poles. He reached a wider audience by having photo-reproductions printed of his drawings.'

She stopped at *The Saxon Garden* painted by Grottger shortly after the second failed insurrection. The cripple was lucky to be here in Warsaw, unlike Agnieszka's stepfather Arkady's grandfather who was exiled to Siberia after that uprising.

'My mother's family was also sent there. My great grandfather was chief architect of bridges and did well. They returned to Poland before the Russian revolution and bought an estate in the east of our country. Exiles were allowed to work, and even to flourish – unlike in the gulags under Stalin.'

We entered a room and were confronted by a seething mass on canvas.

'This is probably the most thrilling depiction of a battle before the invention of the cinema,' said Agnieszka. I saw what she meant. The *Battle of Grunwald* spilled out of a canvas half the width of a tennis court. It certainly needed a room to itself.

On 15th July 1410 the combined Polish and Lithuanian forces under the Polish king Ladislaus Jagiello won an important victory over the Teutonic Knights. Jan Matejko painted as one possessed, placing his picture in a cross-section through the swirling mass of knights and horses entwined in mortal combat. Three parts of the battle, one of the largest in medieval Europe, merge in this writhing tableau where some characters stand out like the Grand Master Ulrich von Jungingen, dressed in white and charged by Lithuanian peasants. They attack him with St Maurice's spear, a gift from Emperor Otto II to Boleslaus the Brave, crowned Polish king in 1025. The Grand Duke Witold gallops in vermilion velvet towards us with arms raised, eyes blazing, ready to deal the final blow. Others present include the one-eyed Bohemian Hussite leader Jan Ziska and the famous Black Knight. Glimpses of the green forest, Grunwald, breathe a space between stormy clouds and the seething mass.

'To create an authentic picture the artist Matejko studied source literature, visited the site, sketched and collected fragments of textiles, armour and inscriptions. So all the people are recognisable, all details are accurate, and'... Agnieszka paused in what I sensed was a painful moment... 'Matejko painted it after the Franco-Prussian War when France's defeat enabled Bismarck to tighten his grip on Polish culture. The painting was so important that when it was unveiled in the Krakow town hall in 1878, the Mayor presented the artist with a sceptre as a symbol of spiritual rule over the nation during the interregnum'.

In 1910 Ignacy Jan Paderewski took up the baton. He funded the Battle of Grunwald monument in Krakow to commemorate the battle's 500th anniversary. His passionate speech after the unveiling inspired his audience to rally to the political cause just as his music had stirred their hearts. His status as an artist and philanthropist, independent of the many Polish political factions, enabled him to legitimately appeal to higher ideals of unity, sacrifice, charity and work for common goals. During the Great War he spoke to Americans and the British in public speeches and on the radio, appealing to them to remember the fate of his nation. He founded the White Cross Society in the USA and the Polish Relief Fund in London. Edward Elgar used a theme from his *Fantasie Polonaise* in the

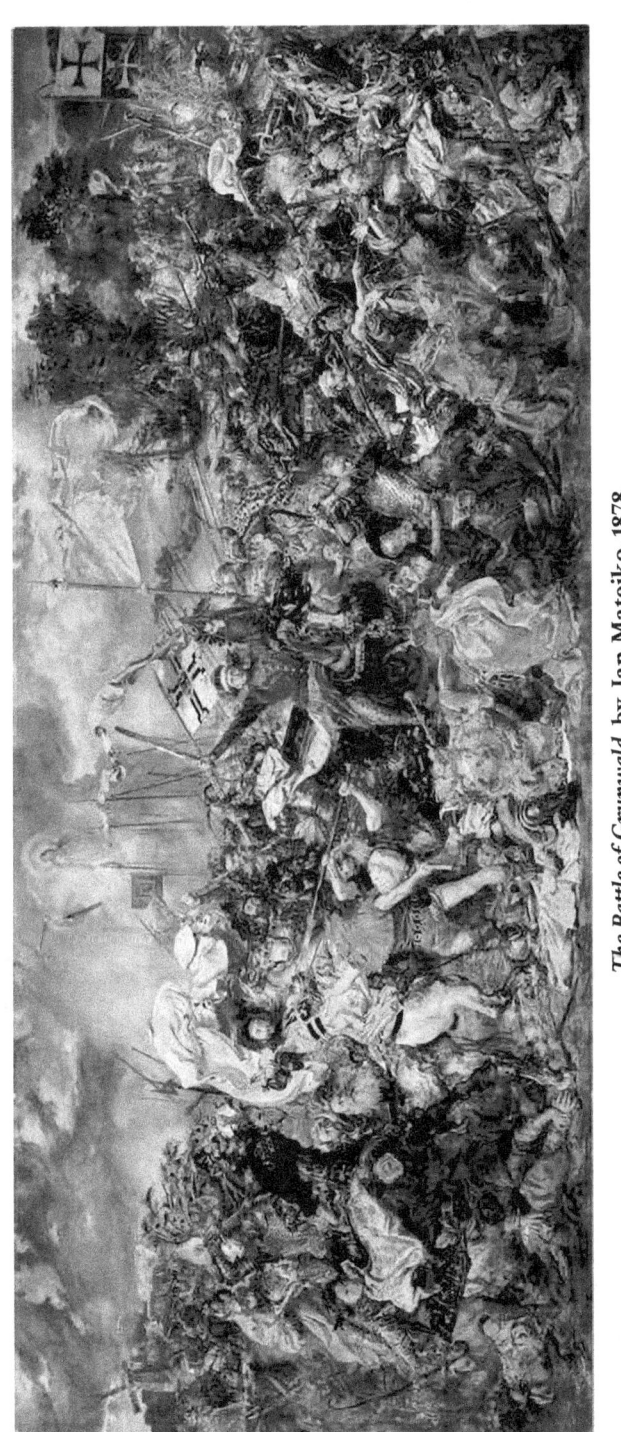

The Battle of Grunwald, by Jan Matejko, 1878.

work he wrote for the fund. Paderewski kept up such a demanding schedule of public appearances, fundraising and meetings that he stopped concert playing for several years. In the United States he met President Woodrow Wilson, who came to support the creation of an independent Poland at the Paris Peace Conference in 1919.

No wonder German propaganda chief Joseph Goebbels was determined to destroy Matejko's huge painting when Germany invaded Poland in 1939. Goebbels put a price of two million marks for its capture or information of its whereabouts, which rose to ten million marks. He tried to bribe Professor Woyda, then in charge of Lublin Museum where the painting was hidden, first with money, and later promising him German citizenship and a German passport. When this failed, he threatened to kill him. Only when Polish radio in London broadcast the news that the painting had arrived in Britain did the Germans cease searching. Woyda had cleverly broadcast this false information before removing it to its final hiding place. Restored after the war, the *Battle of Grunwald* has hung in its own room in the National Museum ever since.

Paderewski returned to his musical career, until duty recalled him in 1939, when the Polish Government in exile was set up in London after the Nazi invasion. He gave numerous concerts to raise money for the Polish cause, until he fell ill on tour in America, and died in New York – aged eighty. He was another example of intellectuals and artists being respected as politicians in Poland because of their integrity.

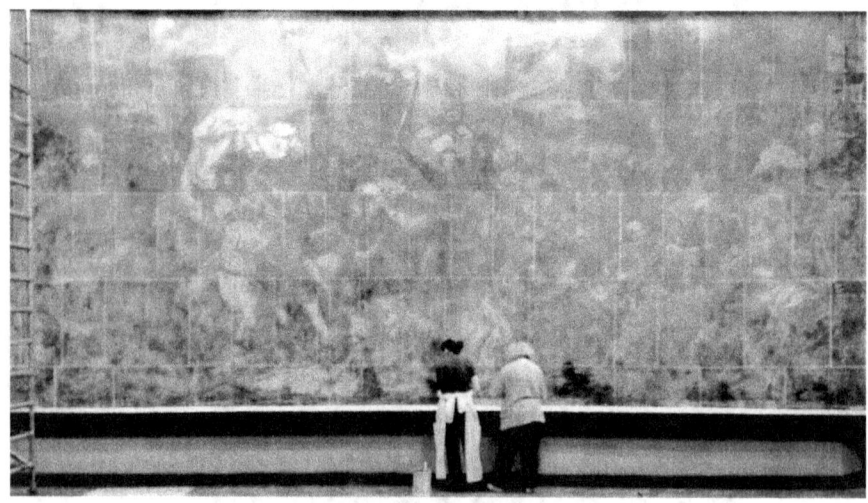

Restoration of The Battle of Grunwald

*

Agnieszka was born in Warsaw at the time of the Uprising. After the war, her father, an art historian, helped track down paintings looted by the Nazis. After the two hours we spent together I knew that, like the others I had met on this journey, she would become a lifelong friend.

The image I carried out of the museum with me was of *The Insurgent Patrol,* painted by Maksymilian Gierymski (1846-74) who loved to paint horses. He studied in Munich, one of the leading art centres in the 1860s and 70s, where the Polish artists were the largest foreign contingent. Gierymski, who was to contract tuberculosis and die aged twenty-eight, created a modern school of genre, historical and landscape painting. He expressed the new Polish Realism mainly through painting landscapes and episodes from the 1863 January Uprising, in which, as a seventeen-year-old, he had taken part. The experience left a permanent impression and affected him deeply as a man and an artist, and he renewed his memories by annual visits to Warsaw.

Agnieszka explained that *The Insurgent Patrol* with its greys, blues and ochres was one of the most Polish pictures ever painted. Composed with a low horizon where the cloudy sky and diffuse light take up half the canvas, a patrol receives information of the enemy from a barefoot vagrant dressed in a long coat and hat, with a satchel slung over his shoulder. He leans on a stick, his face in shadow. Perhaps Gierymski disguised himself as the tramp, owning only the possessions he carried – the staff, instead of a sword, a hat, and greatcoat – reliving a remembered incident where he had given vital information to his compatriots as he re-created the colours, texture, and tense atmosphere. Three of the mounted insurgents watch intently, one twisting round on his saddle to look into the distance, listening to the young artist a decade after the event, as he pauses to reflect with both his outer and inner eye. They wait uncertainly in this empty, sandy place, a place no doubt Gierymski knew well. He re-created it to symbolise the pattern of oppression and uprising he saw repeating itself, remembering the loss of friends as he breathed the very air.

'This landscape is like a failure, a smiling melancholy', he wrote.

*

When I returned to the hotel, the Party delegates were still making merry into the small hours. The weather had been grey, the countryside looked tired and

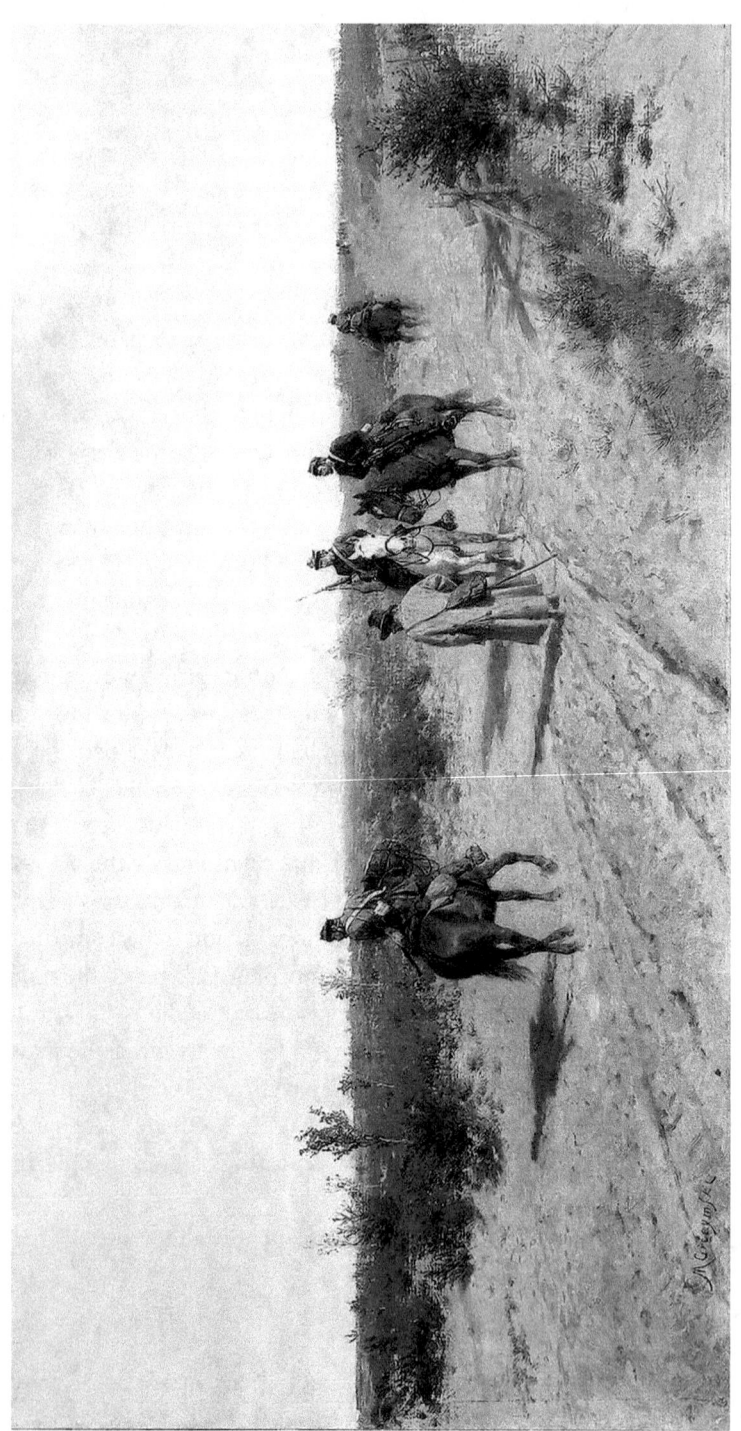

The Insurgent Patrol by M. Gierymski, 1873

dead after the winter snow, but the spirit of Poland shone through. "We do not suffer persecution", I wrote in my journal. "Instead, in our prosperity fears and phobias, selfishness and greed all seem to work to undermine our confidence and self-worth". On this journey, despite the difficulties, I found open-hearted love and generosity, family solidarity and the courage to speak out against oppression. My experiences on this first visit to Poland, half a millennium after Leonardo painted Lady with an Ermine, encouraged me to change course. As I entered the LOT plane for the flight back to London, I understood better why some Poles were described as *polot* – they flew through hardship with panache.

I drove down to see Rupert and to watch his school play. After the performance, I tried to answer the questions he plied me with. When I mentioned the lack of citrus fruit in Poland, he took my hand and led me into the school kitchens in search of tangerines.

'Here you are, Mummy,' he said triumphantly, lifting a little orange ball into the air and passing it to me with a flourish. He watched as I carefully removed the peel, sniffed the pungent sweetness, parted the fruit into segments and shared them with him. Never has a citrus fruit tasted so good.

5

Separation

A NTHONY BLUNT, THE art historian, concealed a double life until he confessed; Ruhemann, the picture restorer, used x-rays to reveal fakes. Lies and truth exposed. During those two weeks in Poland I began to see art and life with new eyes, though perhaps with still half-closed ones. There, stripped back to basic necessities, people could only be themselves, with few distractions from the reality of the system and their situation. I was valued for myself. Not someone who fitted into preconceptions of who others expected me to be. In Poland, love was projected to friends and family. Here, in my English world, possessions and privilege too often masked a fear of loss.

Rolls Royce cars swished up the King's Road as I walked to my local supermarket, soon after my return home. Instead of simple, shabby shops with a few tins stacked, and buy what you could, the shelves were, as usual, full of everything anyone could need or want, with a wide choice of teas and coffee, bread and cheese. Piled-up fruit and vegetables glistened in their freshness – red peppers about to tumble out of their neat stacks, round yellow pears lying beside their long conference cousins, bunches of bananas in various stages of ripeness from green to yellow with brown spots, cauliflowers and cabbages, oranges and lemons – the whole area a rich variety of colour and smell. At the meat counter, no ration cards were required. Well dressed women waited impatiently to be served, a world away from those meat queues I had seen. The contrast between the value of life and the value of money sharpened.

I wandered round the shop with Polish eyes, imagining I was Ela or Basia, Iwona or Agnieszka. I wanted to shout aloud,

'Do you realise how lucky we are to have a constant supply and plenty of everything here in Britain?' Later, the 1980s were considered dreary in England, but at the time yuppies were driving Porsches and the 'get rich quick' opportunities were beginning. How very different to Poland!

Guilt welled up inside; I felt ashamed to be privileged. How easy it is to take material riches for granted, as if by right.

And of what worth was my life, beneath the facade of wealth? My unhappiness had leaked out in poems:

'Surrounded by people, noise, activity,
alone – cut off; in a desert of misunderstanding,
a silence that cuts deep....'

Is courage contagious? I felt the Poles had sowed a seed of it in me. If they could survive under those conditions I had witnessed, could I climb out of my marriage and start again with our sons? Despite the difficulties my friends in Poland faced, I had felt a student again, relaxed in mind and body, enjoying the freedom to be myself.

For several months my husband and I had attended regular sessions with Paule, a psychotherapist who specialised in marriage problems. She opened the way for a trial separation, since it was obvious the marriage had broken down. Three months after my return to England, the moment arrived.

'Isn't it a lovely evening?' I said, gazing up at the sky streaked with crimson and orange and patterned with gun metal clouds, hoping for help to manage these last moments. My husband was leaving after sixteen years of 'for better, for worse', for an unspecified time to an unknown place.

'How can I contact you?' I asked, nervously,

'You can write to my office in Pimlico, I will collect my tools, clothes and anything else when I need them.'

I owned nothing except a few paintings and books, and the money saved from my picture restoration work. When everything was packed my husband drove away.

'Come on Bilbo!' My black pug wiggled with excitement as I clipped on his lead, picked up my keys and opened the front door. Walking always helped. We turned right and walked to the Albert Bridge which links Oakley Street to Battersea Park. The old notice warning troops from the nearby barracks to break step while they crossed this Victorian bridge brought a smile to my lips. There were few people in the park, it was too hot. I released Bilbo and he trotted to a favourite tree; only when concentrating on sniffing an interesting smell did he cease panting. I wandered down the cherry-lined path towards the lake and noticed a large white rabbit hopping complacently in a banquet of spacious greenness, infinity nearby beyond a cage. Where had it come from? Would I follow Alice into a wonderland of highs and lows and unexpected consequences? I called Bilbo and left the rabbit to its feasting.

We walked through the small park gate by the river and on to the bridge. I love its icing cake colours: pastel pink, blue and white and its thousands of bulbs waiting to spring into light when dusk descended and the park gates were locked. Halfway along this painted iron latticework a man walked towards me with a large bird perched on his gloved hand. I looked up into his face and feeling anxious about the rabbit said,

'There is a large white rabbit grazing under the plane trees. Your bird won't hurt it, will it?'

'Don't concern yourself,' the young American replied gently. 'My hawk is only two years old, her feathers are brittle and she needs protection. I take her to the park to get some exercise, and I like to fly her near the adventure playground so the kids can see some wildlife. She is the vulnerable one, not your rabbit!'

I left him, feeling a curious sense of relief that this creature was being nurtured and loved with patience and kindness, and stopped again to embrace that breadth of vision rare in Central London – the Thames to the right and to the left endlessly ebbing and flowing, crowned by the dome of sky. 'In the beginning God created the heavens and the earth'… which rose from the ocean. And in the chaotic depths, according to Babylonian myth, the evil dragon Apsu and his consort Tiamat ruled. Waters below, heavens above and the endless battle of good and evil fought on terra firma.

'Come on Bilbo!'

He looked up at me and then, despite the heat, we made purposefully for home.

I cleared up in a fever of busyness, determined to vacuum away the accumulated dust left by the clutter of our marriage. An ordered life, at least on the outside, kept those fears at bay. Didn't chaos end in darkness and oblivion? For the first time since moving in eight months earlier our home looked tidy. I poured myself a glass of wine, and as I sank into the leather sofa, Bilbo leapt on to my lap. He seemed to sense my sadness. The study was separated from the drawing room by four panelled doors which we kept shut: the patina of antique pine brought warmth to both sides. It had taken several years to transmogrify this Victorian double-fronted house from bed-sits into three units. The basement flat and top half had been sold, and six months before we had moved into the ground and first floor with its wide staircase and sash windows. The future should have been bright. Instead, the marriage had failed. The moment my husband left I felt relief.

Divorce would give me independence, and the opportunity to discover my own resources, though I felt frightened at the thought of having to provide for the boys and myself, for I had never earned a living. Paule asked me to examine what was of each of us in our relationship. Separation would help see that more clearly.

In those days parking in Central London was easy and we rarely used public transport. Since my husband had the car, I had to use my legs. Claws of anxiety deepened their grip with each stride as I walked down the King's Road into Belgravia, preparing to face my mother with the news of our parting. I pressed the bell at the top of the marble steps, heart thumping. She opened the door and I followed her into the dining room and sat down on a hard Regency chair: a Trafalgar chair, so called since the design became popular after the famous victory.

While my mother busied herself in the kitchen, an 1830s Meissen porcelain pug on the chimney piece looked at me with large brown eyes. The bells in its blue and white collar sat comfortably on a sleek, pale neck. I inherited my mother's love of pugs, real and porcelain. She had given me this one's pair to place on our wedding cake. Our first pug, Gimli was dead, but the porcelain one was still with me.

Although my mother grew up in Montreal, both her parents came from Saxony, which was not far from the Polish border. I realise now, decades later, that perhaps she received comfort collecting Meissen because this was her one remaining contact with the land of her ancestors, from which she had been cut off, first by World War II, and then by the Iron Curtain. Her only relation I knew was her mother, who died when I was sixteen. I remember staying with my beloved Oma in Kufstein where she lived her final years. I was the last of the family to see her alive.

I smiled as my mother returned and handed me a glass of white wine.

We have separated, I said.

She sat in her upholstered chair and digested this information. I braced myself. There was no divorce in our family.

'I'm not surprised. You know we tried to put you off marrying him. You were always headstrong.' I tried to explain that I had been very young and immature, and had little knowledge of men apart from my patient, hardworking father.

'Like you, I need order around me, not brick dust'.

'Don't exaggerate Helen. You like making dramas out of the smallest thing. You will have to get a job, won't you?'

She didn't mince words. She once said she preferred her pugs to her children because they did not answer back.

'Well, I have got some pictures to restore, and hopefully they'll keep coming. I thought I might try for a job in the journalist world now that my articles on Poland are being published. The problem is the boys' holidays. It would be difficult to get a full time job.'

'Won't the boys' father have them some of the time? What's he going to do?'

'Mummy, I don't know. And he's got the car.'

'Well you will have to buy yourself another one.'

My mother had no idea of money.

I hadn't seen her since my travels in Poland three months earlier. She loved culture so I filled the strained atmosphere with descriptions of the architecture and art of Krakow and Warsaw. My mother listened politely, with a German ear, brought up with a Poland obliterated from the map. She had no concept of the courage of the Poles or the conditions in which they lived. She rose from her chair.

'Thank you for telling me your news. I have to cook your father's supper now.'

I thanked her for the wine. She gave me a peck on the cheek as she ushered me out of what had once been my home.

I walked round the corner to St Peter's Church where I had taken my marriage vows. Since then the church had been burned down by an arsonist and rebuilt; another phoenix arising from ashes. Sixteen years later, I slowly lit a candle and knelt down in a pew. Silently, the cross on the altar calmed me. How young and artless I had been; sheltered by my privileged life I grew up appreciating the beauty of our world – the shape of a horse, the proportions of a house, the panoramic views from my attic windows at Lodgefield. I believed people were essentially kind and good, and was unaware how I lacked mothering. My Polish friends had shown me the true measure of wealth in their family relationships. I could not imagine sharing two rooms, as they did, with siblings, parents and grandmother.

Words that Betjeman said with candid honesty came to me, "Lord I believe. Help thou my unbelief". I reflected on the story of Jacob's dream, during his flight from his brother Esau. When the sun set, Jacob settled down and put a stone under his head. During the night he had a vivid dream: a ladder stretched from earth to heaven with angels ascending and descending upon it. It has taken me ages to climb one rung, and sometimes life seemed more like snakes and ladders.

*

In a utilitarian environment suitable for cut and dried facts and figures, the solicitor elicited information for an hour and a half until my mind was buzzing. Remembering was difficult, but the lawyer managed to squeeze out facts. At the end of the interrogation she gave me homework: a list of my living expenses, which meant phone calls to the London Electricity Board, British Telecom and the bank.

It was pouring with rain when I left. After the heat it was like walking in a tepid shower, and I remembered how, as a child, I loved sitting under the canvas cover of our garden swing, listening to the rain plopping on the puddles outside, while I stayed dry.

Old friends who lived nearby in Chelsea, welcomed me into their home whenever I felt the need of their support. I was heartened by the judge who reassured me that 'a woolly memory is more bona fide to a judge than exact dates and descriptions'. On one occasion when I felt very low – the boys were at school – I lay on the floor in their boudoir while stories by Damon Runyon were read to me. He spoke in a similar voice to his actor cousin whose recordings of the Narnia stories had given my family endless pleasure on long journeys.

Woken one night by the sound of rain racketing against the window, lightning reaching through closed eyes and thunder boosting the orchestra, I felt a yawning pit of fear, fear of losing our home and having to fend for myself for the rest of my life. Questions hurtled round in my mind, adding to the noise outside. As the trees shed their leaves, I knew I must let the breeze blow away my fears.

The next morning I noticed that a geranium in the garden had flowered. Staunch in the wind, it had taken its battering with dignity. A small rosebud seemed uncertain whether to shed its inhibitions and protective skin and surrender its beauty to fate. As I walked to the library, the sun glinted through the yellow leaves transforming them to burnished gold. A gang of sparrows fluttered and squeaked in the garden of the Phene Arms Pub nearby.

I went to the Tate Gallery to look at Mark Gertler's *Merry-Go-Round* painted in 1916. The electric blues and oranges transfixed me. Sitting upright on rigid horses, soldiers, sailors and civilians were carried around screaming – powerless against the forces of prejudice, fear and violence. The world was closing in on life as more and more died in the trenches or suffered shell shock. "Stop the world I want to get off!" But they looked as helpless as I felt. I returned to the solicitor to discuss the final details of the petition.

*

I needed a break so decided to drive to Clare Priory in Suffolk, which I had discovered the year before.

'I am Anglican and female, but may I come in?' I had asked then. I bowed my head to walk through the narrow, low door into the old Cellarer's Hall, where, with a mischievous smile and a soft Irish lilt, Father Billy Baldwin, of the Order of St Augustine, assured me I was very welcome to stay as long as I liked. He had spent his life in the service of God teaching mathematics. When his health failed in Africa, he came back to Britain to serve as Prior here, in what some considered a white elephant.

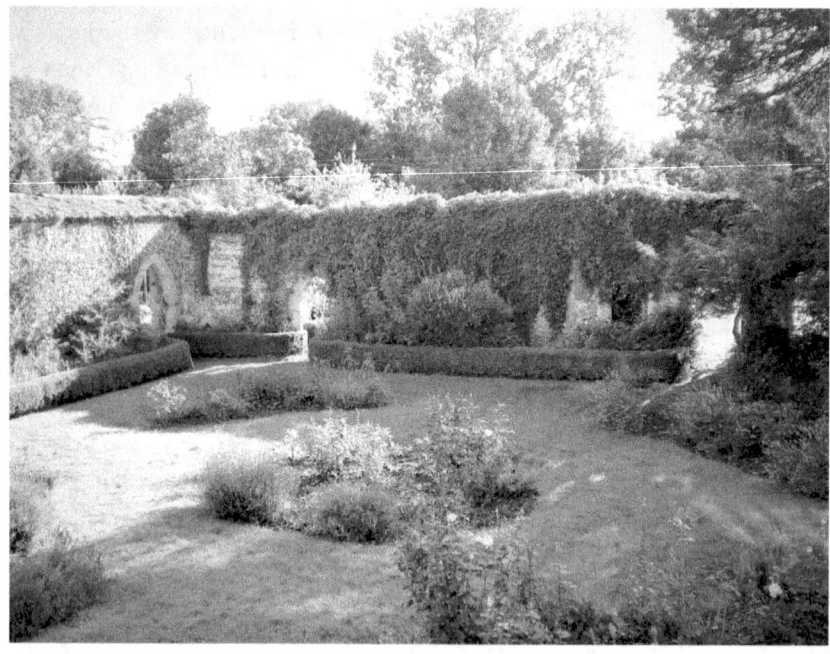

Cloister at Clare Priory

'God's love for the individual is greater than his law for the general,' said Father Billy when I showed him the critical letter I had just received from the rector of the church we attended, which lacked any understanding of my predicament.

'Don't justify the divorce. Keep in God's will. Don't let the hurt disturb your peace. Above all, forgive. This does not mean going back into the marriage.'

He would not let me be downcast for long. As we prepared lunch, he dropped a bag of frozen peas on the floor, faced me with mock horror and said, 'Oh, I've pea-d on the floor!'

The next day he gave me more of his time. We sat in the orchard in what had been the 14th century church, surrounded by apple, pear and plum trees and two original flinty walls.

'Justice is seeing others as they are, made in the image of God. We are not judged by what we do, but what we are. Listen to your conscience. Risk and insecurity are compatible with life.'

Perhaps this is what I learned in Poland without realising it. He told me he was going to the Vatican next month with priests from all over the world for a week's retreat led by the Pope and Mother Teresa.

'Look with loving eyes, enlarge the field of vision and understanding of life. Test thoughts and consider the significance of an action, the impulses of our whole being. Ask – is my will really orientated towards God?'

*

After we told the boys at the start of the summer holidays that we had agreed to separate I took them to see Paule, the psychotherapist. The boys, who knew and liked her, were attentive as she helped the three of us try to understand what was going on.

'You boys will be better off with your parents living apart with the space to be themselves.' I hoped they understood the logic of this. After our session we bought some cherries and sat on a park bench to eat them, competing over who could spit their stones furthest, giggling with the fun of it.

*

I was very fond of my husband's uncle Bob and his wife who lived in an old farmhouse near Penshurst in Kent, not far from my home. When I drove down to see them Bob took me out to the garden, and after settling ourselves down on a bench, he took my hand.

'Helen, my dear, you know we love you. But blood is thicker than water, and we have to stand by our nephew.'

We sat sadly in silence for a while letting the fact that we may never see one another again sink in. Bob told me that his nephew started planning in August to take the boys to his mother in South Africa for the Christmas holidays. Paule told me there was little chance of stopping him.

When my father retired and my parents spent winters in Germany, we celebrated a traditional dinner with Uncle Bob and his family, a party of ten round their circular Regency table every year. There was smoked salmon, turkey with all its trimmings and Christmas pudding with a generous quantity of whisky butter, since their son, whose task it was to make it, used whisky rather than brandy. Thus are family traditions created. When we were young and my father's parents joined us for Christmas, our habit was to guess the amount of leaves on the pineapple. Each number was written down and a sixpence added to the pot, then Grandpa would pull out the leaves one by one with every eye watching, the tension building as hopes were dashed until the last leaf left a winner.

Celebrating Christmas was a happy occasion. Separation carried connotations. As I wondered where we would all be this Christmas, a sense of bereavement crept up on me. For someone naturally energetic, getting out of bed in the morning became harder. I lay looking out of the sash windows at the walled garden that had been part of Henry VIII's manor house and pondered my future.

My father came for lunch.

'Rely on your gut feelings, Helen,' he said. I proudly showed him Letter from Poland – my first piece printed in *Arts Review*, and lent him Nowak's *Courier from Warsaw* for a different side of the German/Polish story. We discussed Betjeman and agreed how important security is to the inner man.

*

I only had Rupert and Simon home for two days before they left for South Africa. After collecting their malaria pills, and washing and mending their clothes, Simon helped me ice the cake. Over a relaxed evening we played cards, consumed steak, and packed for their holiday. At 3am Simon crept into my bed. Rupert joined us later and we opened our stockings, and exchanged presents. This was our Christmas. Godparents turned up for our turkey dinner, helped pull crackers and don paper hats. Much laughter and fun ensued. The boys left early the next morning.

*

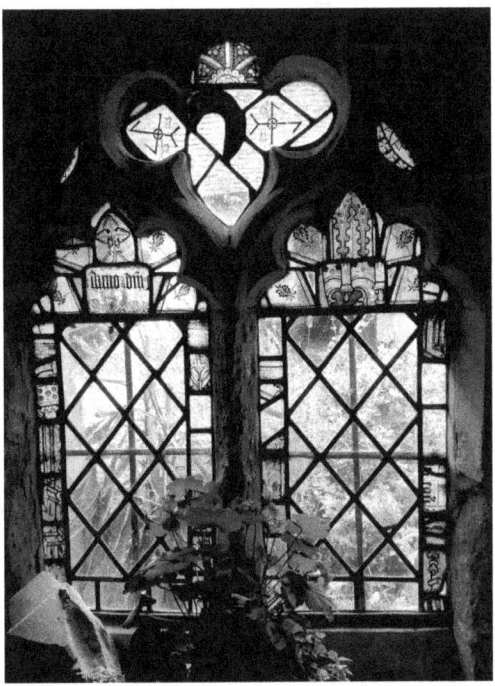

14th c. window in Clare Priory

I had no heart to share the festivities with friends, so asked Father Billy if Bilbo and I could join the friars at Clare Priory after the boys had left. Windscreen wipers swept back and forth like a metronome. 'Gone, gone, gone', they told me as the miles left London further behind. I arrived at Clare in time for a hearty welcome from Father Billy as food was placed on the dining table. Later I walked through the late 14th century Little Cloister, (cleaned up by young men doing Community Service), which was now a shrine to Our Lady of Good Counsel. I sat on a chair. As I gazed at the carving of the Mother and Child my need to experience the warmth of a mother's love surfaced in tears.

In this ancient, tranquil house of prayer I could ask – why was I born? What is life for? Whatever my faults and failings, I began to realize that they did not matter, for God loved me and accepted me as I am. He would help me become the person I was destined to be, if I let Him. Those pious voices who said divorce was unacceptable however bad our marriage was, who put ideology before care about children living in an unhappy atmosphere, faded. I was cleaning off the tarnished background and moving into a clearer place. Here I had the space and security to think about my decision to divorce. I took comfort in Father Billy's counsel,

'Jesus looks at the intentions of our hearts, not the mess we make of our lives.'

I walked Bilbo in the twilight. There was a huge silver star – only one – above black silhouettes of bare branches that cut into the pink horizon. An owl hooted as if to welcome the sliver of moon that rose out of the dying embers of the day and moved towards the Christmas star as night covered the sky like a tent. All was still and silent. Silence quenched the noise in my head and allowed the still, small voice in the heart to speak. Gradually other stars appeared, glinting brightly.

Birds sang for joy on a cold and frosty Christmas morning. I heard Father Larry singing in his room next door, while the other friars celebrated Mass. I attended the 10am service in the narrow church with its thick, flinty medieval walls, and thought of Mother Teresa: "Ponder these things and let God work on you in the silence". It was easier here to believe that God is love. I was fortunate to have many loving friends. As I lit a candle at the foot of Mary and Jesus I prayed for light to shine on our families – and a great light in my boys' hearts at this difficult time. Later, in bed, I cried for the world – for the fear and oppression, the loneliness and pain, the lack of love.

After Father Billy left for Ireland, Father Malachi settled me down beside him by the warmth of the log fire and talked about grief. His brother had died three weeks before aged forty-eight.

'You need to experience a situation before you can truly empathise with others,' he said.

On my last morning I felt weak and vulnerable, fearful of leaving the security of this beautiful place for the busyness of London, or lose the sense of peace these few days had given me. Until I was able to buy a car, I had been lent an old one by a school friend. The car only started with jump leads, and the ice on the bonnet took half an hour to melt. A cobweb on the rear window was encrusted with ice. How soon had the frost encroached after the spider spun?

I gave Father Larry a lift to London. During our conversation he said, 'Do you know Helen what a gift you are to us?' I felt blank as I stared at the road in front of me.

'What do you mean, Father?'

'Here we were, four Irish friars, rather closed up in our priory, and you fly in like a wild goose, an exotic creature from a different world.'

'Well, that's thanks to Father Billy, who allowed me stay last year and then again this Christmas, even though it's your private time after all the festivities.' I paused and then asked, 'Why a wild goose?'

'That's a Celtic symbol for the Holy Dove. You've opened up for us a wider world. Even in those wonderful meals you cooked for us. We have never eaten anything like it! I think you've inspired Father Billy to be more adventurous in his cooking as well.' I pictured the fillet steak in a mushroom sauce, the potato dauphinoise, the chocolate mousse...

'Did you know Father Billy is halfway through the four years he was given when he took on Clare as prior to turn the place round?' When I shook my head, Father Larry continued,

'It's a white elephant draining money from the poor. It may have to be closed down, unless he can make it viable. Maybe now he'll feel able to open it up to others who need the spiritual succour we can offer.' He did. Within a few years a block was built to house visitors and the priory became a retreat centre.

*

My empty house was so cold that I read my mail in bed. I opened an envelope from Iwona who had tucked a piece of wafer into her Christmas card. The Poles share this wafer on Christmas Eve as a symbol of reconciliation and fellowship.

Janusz Walek had sent me his latest book translated into English, *A Panorama of Polish History* with paintings to illustrate events. He was pleased with the piece I had written for *Arts Review* on the Czartoryski Museum, and wrote "Thank you for those kind words about me. It was nice to read that I had laid on an exhibition not for a restorer, or journalist, but simply for someone from Britain interested in art. You forgot only to add that it was laid on for Helen de B!" He wanted to discuss his work with me when I return to Krakow in the spring.

The New Year opened in brilliant cold sunshine. I worked in the garden, clearing away dead leaves and generally tidied up. A red rose blossomed in isolation. And under dark, soggy leaves, new spring bulbs were thrusting through the soil.

*

PART II
1985

6

Warsaw

"LET LIVE THE Brotherhood between the Nations of Poland and Russia" proclaimed a red banner stretched across the Opera House. En route to Krakow, I was staying in Warsaw with Iwona, who had shown me round the Royal Castle on my first visit. The day after I arrived we took a bus to the centre, alighted at the Palace of Culture and walked – with difficulty, for streets were barred by the police – to Saxon Square. All over Poland the red and white national flag fluttered beside the plain red flag on State buildings and lamp posts, and flapped one either side of elderly trams. Police patrolled the area for the victory parade; the peripheral streets were lined with military machines and water cannon. The first of May was cold.

Saxon Square, the largest in the capital, was renamed Victory Square by the Communists. I tried to visualise the neo-classical palace enlarged by the Saxon kings in the early 18th century that had once graced one side. Later the palace housed the Warsaw Lyceum, in which Frederic Chopin's father taught French – the family lived in the garden – and faced the Alexander Nevsky Cathedral, built under partition by the Tsarist overlords, and demolished after World War I when the palace became the headquarters of the Polish General Staff.

I remembered Grottger's poignant painting of the soldier in the Saxon Gardens, crippled in the 1863 Uprising, that Agnieszka had shown me in the National Museum last year. Accompanied by his faithful hound the one-legged soldier looked beaten but not cowed as he hobbled along on crutches. Beside him, in the garden transformed into an English park in 1816 by the English designer James Savage, a family rest in the shade of a tree. Mother and daughter

gazed sadly at him. The old man looked down, perhaps remembering the horrors of the previous insurrection. He stopped his granddaughter from running to pick up her doll, which lay helplessly on the ground, its red dress lit up by the sun. Who will rescue Poland now?

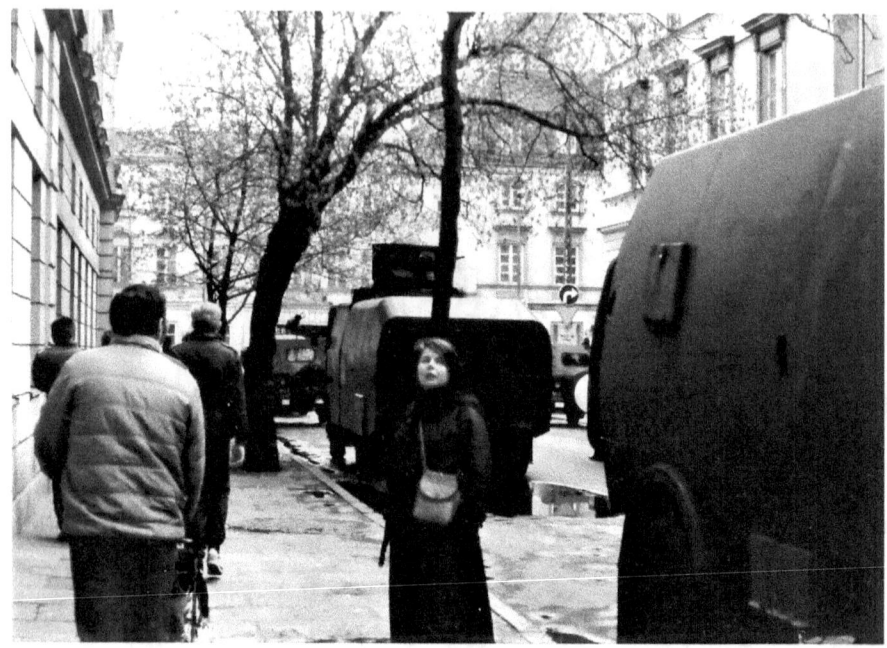

Iwona by water cannons, on May Day

During the inter-war period of political freedom the Tomb of the Unknown Soldier was established in the colonnade-topped arcade that joined the palace's two symmetric wings. A guard of honour had been continuously held by the tomb, changing ceremoniously at midday, except during the German occupation. After the Warsaw Uprising in 1944 the palace was blown up by the Germans as part of the planned destruction of the city, but they left the sections of the colonnade that sheltered the tomb. Old photos show two arches remaining among the rubble. A third arch was restored and the memorial stands proud, though rough-edged and out of scale, with stubs of pillars resting on the balustrades above the arches. The flame burns.

General Jaruzelski and high-ranking officials stood on a balcony and took the salute. All workers had to take part in the celebration and acknowledge their leader, or risk losing their jobs. First the military, then, like soldiers in mufti, teachers, air hostesses, steel workers and members of other State institutions marched past their leader. The May Day parade in Warsaw lasted most of the morning. Jaruzelski wore dark glasses. They lent him a detached look, as if he could not bear eye contact. In fact he had contracted snow blindness in 1939 when, still a teenager, he was sent to forced labour in the coal mines of Siberia. He wanted to join General Anders' army but by some quirk of fate joined the Polish units being formed under Soviet command. He rose through the ranks to become Minister of Defence and ordered the 2nd Army to invade Czechoslovakia in August 1968. Ruthless and cruel, he was responsible for the massacre of steel workers in Gdansk, Gdynia and other coastal cities in 1970. Later, in February 1981, he was the only professional soldier to become leader of a ruling European Communist party, as Prime Minister of Poland. That winter, in an attempt to suppress the Solidarity movement, Jaruzelski introduced martial law.

After watching the May Day ceremony we joined the crowds trudging through the streets towards Father Jerzy Popieluszko's church five miles away. Public transport in this direction had been cancelled to discourage people going there. The atmosphere was restrained and tense. Many felt uncomfortable at having shown official loyalty to their political master. The people felt that honouring this much-loved priest might salve their conscience. Seven months earlier, this brave spokesman for Solidarity during martial law had been murdered.

In contrast to the drab streets, the confines of St Stanislaw Kostka Church were ablaze with the red and white Polish national colours. Red and white flowers and Solidarity banners from all over the country covered the stone walls of the churchyard. The authorities had no power to quash this statement of brotherhood as it took place on Church property. A long queue had formed at the entrance. Everyone wanted to walk past the young priest's flower-laden grave. In the centre a stone cross was illuminated by hundreds of candles placed in short red glasses. Women wept. Men looked grim. They had come to pray for a man they loved and missed; to wash their souls after the hypocrisy of their salute. Some had come earlier – for communion with Christ before giving forced acknowledgement to worldly power.

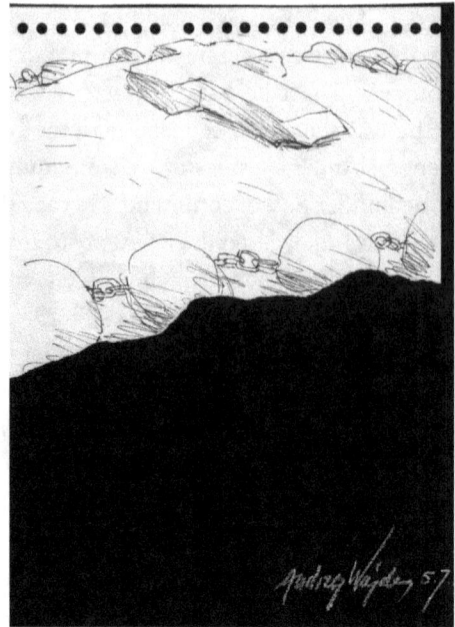

Fr Jerzy's Grave by Andrzej Wajda, 1986

Fr Jerzy was chaplain to the ten thousand men employed in the Warsaw steelworks, during the memorable Solidarity strike in August 1980. The workers loved their spiritual and compassionate young priest. During martial law, Solidarity members were often unjustly sentenced to long prison terms. As they received their sentences, Fr Jerzy would sit in the courtrooms among their families. Incarceration was easier to bear knowing Fr Jerzy would take care of their children both spiritually and financially

Every last Sunday of the month Fr Jerzy had celebrated Mass for the Fatherland. His sermons were broadcast by Radio Free Europe. Thousands from all over Poland came to hear him speak about Christian ideals of social justice, of freedom, truth, love and the need to defend basic human rights and the dignity of every man as God's child.

"Fight evil with good", Fr Jerzy begged.

In July 1984, he was accused by the Warsaw Public Prosecution Office of defamation by imputing in his sermons that the authorities used "falseness, hypocrisy and lies, that they abuse human dignity by anti-democratic law, that they deprive society of freedom of thought and action". These accusations were dropped, but a campaign of attack and accusations against him continued in the State press.

On Saturday 19th October Polish television and radio announced the kidnap of Fr Jerzy Popieluszko by unknown assailants. Banners went up immediately on the fence of St. Stanislaw Kostka saying, "Give us back Fr Jerzy!" He called his dog Tajniak, meaning secret agent; a humorous gesture of defiance against the secret police everyone knew were tailing him; and who had thrown a brick with explosives through his window. When the news of the priest's kidnapping was announced, day Masses were held every hour attended by thousands. Lech Walesa came. At the end of the service the Solidarity leader stood up. His voice quivered as he spoke:

"Dear Countrymen! There is a big danger hanging over our Fatherland. I appeal to you, please, do not let anyone provoke you to bloodshed! I beg you to maintain peace and to pray constantly for Father Jerzy". (Quoted from *The Grave of martyr Fr Jerzy Popieluszko,* by Fr Antoni Lewek.)

Steel workers, lawyers, doctors and students prayed day and night. Tension grew. Many were exhausted. Father Jerzy's body was found in the Vistula Water Reservoir eleven days after his kidnap. At seven that evening, with thirty priests at the altar and the congregation overflowing into the courtyard, the news came through:

"Today Fr Jerzy's body has been found in the Vistula". At once there was shouting and crying and people falling on to their knees in anguish. The worst had happened.

On 1st November, All Saints Day, it was announced that Fr Jerzy's funeral would take place two days later. While bells tolled, steelworkers carried the coffin from the car into the church where it was placed on a catafalque. All through the night Poles waited in long queues to pay tribute to him. The funeral was celebrated by the Archbishop. There were delegations from embassies, universities, factories, and social organisations. Such a funeral had not been seen in Warsaw in living memory, except for that of the late Cardinal Wyszynski who also suffered persecution by the authorities.

Two days later Fr Antoni said to his congregation, "The Holy Father once said that the heart of the Polish nation beat in the Jasna Gora Sanctuary: the heart there, the conscience here. Every man who stands at this grave – unless he is senseless and with no conscience must ask himself: "Whose side am I on? Good or evil? Truth or falsehood? Love or hatred? Who killed him? Why?"

If Father Jerzy's driver had not escaped from the kidnapper's car, the trial of the priest's murderers might never have taken place. And with it a real-life drama of manipulation and disinformation of the sort Fr Jerzy constantly warned against. The hero of Ronald Harwood's play *The Deliberate Death of a Polish Priest* at the

Almeida Theatre in London that autumn was his driver Waldemar Chrostowski, played by Brian Cox. From his answers in the witness box and comments to the audience, Chrostowski filled in the gaps and related the rumours. Much of the play's script was taken from verbatim translation from the records of the original twenty-eight day trial. It presented a chilling picture of a totalitarian mentality fighting justice and truth whatever the cost.

Harwood set the play in a stark and gloomy courtroom. The three security officers on trial were perplexed. Seemingly accountable to no one, they had expected praise not punishment for ridding the State of a troublesome priest. Captain Piotrowski justified kidnapping Fr Jerzy, and subsequently killing him by beating, gagging, and throwing his heavily weighted body into the Vistula, with the comment, "the lesser evil is necessary to avoid the greater evil". His subordinates were more concerned with advancing their careers. Under Kevin Billington's direction the bitter tale was retold by a powerfully convincing cast. The prosecution made sure that the defendants in the dock, who described their actions in gruesome detail, took the blame. The mixture of arrogance, weakness and fear contrasted sharply with the gentle priest who, we were reminded at the beginning, spoke of fearing "not those who kill the body but the soul."

Iwona and I were squeezed tighter than sardines in a tin in the bus to her home in the suburbs. I bought a bottle of Bulgarian wine in her local shop and we walked down the sandy road to her bungalow, where Rudy welcomed us with energetic wags of his tail and lots of barking. We slipped through the gate set in the chicken wire fence that surrounded the property, and walked down the track shaded by oak, spruce and a crab-apple tree, past her little Polish sandy-coloured Seat 600 car, to the front door. Grandfather greeted us with equal enthusiasm but less energy than Rudy. Tall and thin, he stood straight-backed despite his ninety-three years.

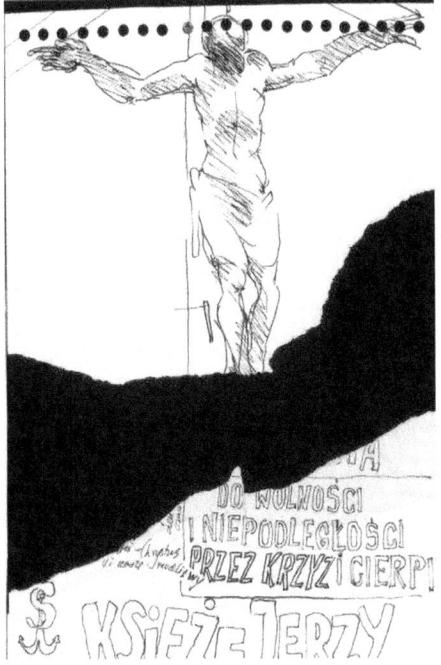

Homage to Fr Jerzy, **by A. Wajda, 1986**

*

The bungalow which my hosts shared consisted of three bedrooms, a bathroom, and a living room with French windows opening on to the garden. This was large by Polish standards. Valuable foreign currency paid for the plot and the building work, for Iwona's mother had married an Englishman and lived in Sussex. She helped to keep them both afloat. In the tiny kitchen I opened the wine and mixed a salad while Iwona heated up the braised beef she had prepared earlier and poured yoghurt flavoured with fresh mint from the garden over the cucumber she had thinly sliced. All the water used in the kitchen was poured into a bucket and placed beside the lavatory to flush it. Nothing was wasted. While we ate in the charming living room with its wood floor and antique furniture, Iwona translated as grandfather reminisced over his experiences in a Siberian prisoner of war camp during World War I. Because Poland was partitioned until 1918 Pole had been forced to fight Pole. He married a Russian woman and they returned to a free Poland. Everyone worked hard to redevelop their country after one hundred and twenty years of occupation – until Hitler marched in his troops in 1939.

*

Like Iwona's grandfather decades before, I was now discovering new challenges. He returned to a country ruined by war. For me it meant earning a living for the first time as a single parent in Thatcher's Britain. I too had adapted to changing circumstances. Soon after our separation my husband stopped our joint account. I left the studio I shared with two colleagues and started working from home. Not ideal, but it reduced my expenses. The Citizens Advice Bureau in Chelsea Town Hall helped me with my accounts and the council reduced my tax. Fortunately Helen Ward, a sought-after young family lawyer had agreed to take me on legal aid when she heard my story, which meant I had no fees to pay.

*

A century ago Jan Matejko wrote: 'Art is a weapon not to be separated from love of our country.'

In his historical painting, discussed earlier, he created a vision of Poland's patriotic past to inspire depressed hearts. Art was still a weapon in Poland. Living on a knife edge seemed to have heightened perception, and images were often harsh, sometimes angry and usually sad. These feelings were expressed in an exhibition called *Apocalypse* organised by Professor Bogucki in the crypt of the Church of the Holy Cross in the centre of Warsaw, where an urn, immured in 1882, contains Chopin's heart. Art critic and gallery owner, Bogucki taught at the celebrated Academy of Art in Torun, the birthplace of Copernicus. Like many artists in the 1950s he started out from a Marxist viewpoint. Over the years his awareness of spiritual values grew. He encouraged artists to restore the crypt of the church on the edge of the ghetto in Zytnia Street so they had a permanent exhibition centre. It was a provident move. After the introduction of martial law in 1981 most artists left the Union, thereby cutting themselves off from State support. When Iwona and I visited the church, a strong smell of wet concrete and the sound of water pelting down complemented the skeletal sight of bare breeze blocks, charred bricks and trailing electricity wires.

We were invited to visit the professor in his flat on the fifteenth floor of a concrete tower block. Small, rather portly with a modest air and smiling, crinkly eyes, he showed us slides of the exhibitions he had organised. Over the years he had become an important rock for artists, who trusted his integrity and relied on his *critique*. Shortly after the Pope's visit to his homeland two years earlier, Bogucki organised an exhibition in Zytnia Street called *Sign of the Cross.* Variations on a theme produced art for everyone in a cohesive setting. Artists used the fabric of the church – the burnt brickwork, the scars and character of the walls and spaces – as part of their work. New leaves entwined Jalowczyk's beautifully painted *Cross of Life.*

This sense of hope was utterly absent in the *Apocalypse* exhibition. Fr Jerzy had been murdered shortly before it opened and the artists expressed their own grief. Brzozowski slung ropes from six columns into the shape of his interpretation of the nightmare, spattering red paint like blood on to a mirror on the floor. Henryk Waniek arranged black soutanes to signify death robes. Documentary photographs ranged from naked women on their way to the gas chambers at Auschwitz, to the White Mass held in Krakow's Rynek after the attempted assassination of the Pope. This art was not meant merely to shock or to manipulate emotions for political or religious ends. Bogucki warned me that too often simplistic answers can overshadow truth. But these exhibitions proved what an important role art can play in a world filled with materialism and poverty, increasing violence and injustice. They encouraged people to think and search for deeper reality.

*

In Warsaw Castle Iwona took me to the Conservation department for paintings, wood and fabrics on the second floor. This used to be President Gierek's apartment as Head of State until 1980 when, under Solidarity, an agreement was made to separate the Castle from the State Museum. Fabrics were restored in the kitchen. The picture restorers worked everywhere else including the marble-clad bathroom which became their science laboratory. Apart from a spray gun for varnishing they seemed to have everything they needed.

That evening we were invited to dine with Agnieszka who, on my last visit, had introduced me to Polish art. She lived upstairs in her father's house with her husband Andrzej, in a suburb of Warsaw called Mokotow. Her mother and stepfather Arkady lived downstairs. There were parquet floors, fine wood bookshelves and lovely old Beidermeyer furniture. Agnieszka gave me a copy in English of her illustrated book on 19th century Polish painters. As well as looking after Polish painting in the National Museum, she wrote art reviews for a prestigious newspaper and taught in the drama academy. Heating bills were high. Times were hard. I wished I could arrange lecture tours in Britain for her. We continued our discussion from last year about the artist's role in society. I understood more clearly now why, after composers like Chopin and then the poets, painters like Matejko took on the role of Guardians of the Polish soul – a mission passed on through the decades to contemporary artists.

*

Ela took the night bus from Gdansk, a five-hour journey, to spend a day with us in Warsaw.

The harsh weather on May Day gave way to warmth. The three of us sat in the sunlit garden and talked. Words may cost lives if the wrong people are listening but here we were safe to talk as we pleased.

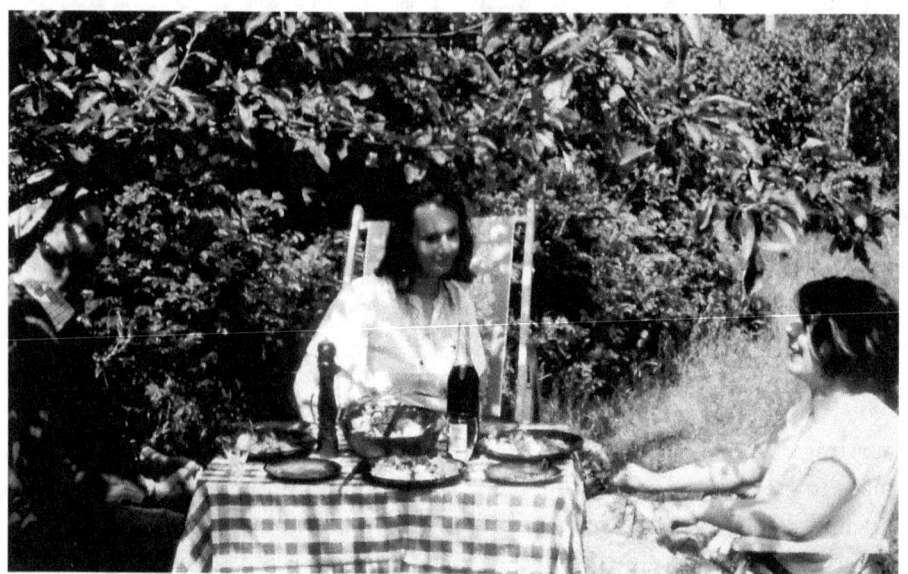

Grandfather, Ela and Iwona in the garden

They wanted to know about the tumultuous happenings in my life since they last saw me. I began with Christmas, a family affair in Poland wrapped up in faith. I knew they put bits of straw on the table to remind them that Jesus was born in a stable. As a symbol of reconciliation and fellowship, wafers blessed by the priest, are eaten on Christmas Eve before the carp is served. According to tradition, the youngest child keeps watch for the first star to appear, and then the family sits down to celebrate the mystery. What a contrast to London where the real meaning of Christmas was pushed into the background by frenetic consumerism beginning with decorative lights put up in November.

'Last Christmas I had no children for the first time since Rupert's birth thirteen years ago,' I told Iwona and Ela gloomily. 'Without telling me arrangements were made to take the boys to stay with his mother in South Africa.'

'How horrible,' said Ela, putting her arms around me.

'Your kindness to me was deeply felt,' I said, remembering how Ela, like Iwona, had tucked a piece of wafer into her Christmas letter. 'You understand the pain of parting as well.'

Malczewski's painting *Christmas in Siberia* which I had seen in Krakow sprung to mind. Exiles after the 1863 Uprising against the Russians sit at table holding empty plates thinking of home and their loved ones. Their beards are streaked with grey now as one old soldier drops the holy wafer from an envelope sent from home to share with his seven fellow exiles. This and straw peeping out from under the tablecloth are all they had to celebrate the ancient festival. Their plates are empty. A small crust of bread lies beside a knife on the white cloth.

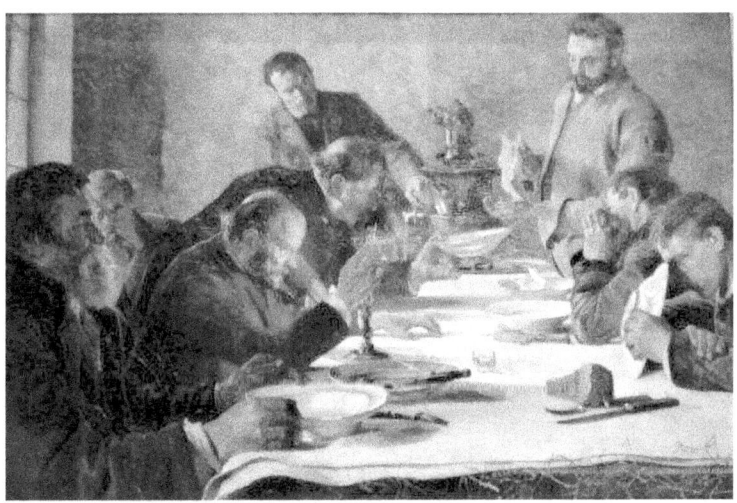

Christmas in Siberia by Jacek Malczewski, 1892

'I couldn't face spending time with other happy families after my sons had gone, so on Christmas Eve I drove to the Augustinian priory in the town of Clare in Suffolk.'

I told them how the priory was founded in 1248 by the Lord of Clare, who invited the Augustinians to build their first foundation in England - one of the oldest religious houses in the country. The Priory remained a house of divine worship, prayer, and service to the community until 1538, when it was dissolved by an agent of Henry VIII. After nearly four hundred years in private hands, it returned to the Austin Friars. A place of worship and prayer needed coaxing back into life – buildings restored, statues cleaned, books unpacked and sorted. The friars' infirmary, which had survived due to its usefulness as a schoolroom and barn over the centuries the house was in private ownership, became the church. I was glad to help, cleaning and waxing centuries-old statues and a Dutch chandelier that hung in the library.

'Father Billy comforted me as Father Popieluszko comforted his parishioners,' I said, popping a piece of quiche and salad into my mouth.

'You understand why our faith is so important. After the crushing of Solidarity, it keeps us from despair.'

'Let's drink to the future, full of hope,' I replied raising my glass, suddenly aware of the attitude that made Poles perennial survivors. We drank deep.

7

Krakow

A s I sat in the first-class carriage from Warsaw to the 'Jewel of Central Europe', and watched the snow-scattered flat land speed by, I thought about the challenges that lay ahead. I had responded to the invitation from Jan Blyskosz, the Chief Conservator at Wawel Castle State Museum, to work with them for a few weeks. Maria Łeska, Keeper of Renaissance tiles at Wawel, was due to meet me and drive me to my lodgings. After three hours the train ground to a halt at the down-at-heel station. The soldier who shared my carriage carried my suitcase out of the train and I trundled it along the platform to the exit. Remnants of past elegance peeped out from a crumbling brick and stone façade. Rain-filled potholes and indented tyre marks scarred the tarmac.

Maria was waiting for me, peering anxiously among the mass of passengers streaming out. She was neatly dressed in a thin blue suit and white blouse. Her nervous manner, lined face with deep-set blue eyes and greying short brown hair, revealed a woman aged by suffering beyond her fifty odd years. She smiled with relief when she saw me and was delighted with the tulips I presented to her. Giving flowers when you meet someone is an old Polish custom, even if you could only afford one, for they are expensive. Maria immediately divided them up and gave me the bigger bunch.

We dragged my suitcase along a soaking platform to her little 2-stroke plastic-coated Trabant, made in East Germany. It looked very frail, and spat out toxic black fumes when she started the engine. We left a black trail as we drove through the suburbs to the apartment she had found for me on the eastern side of the city near her home.

My new landlady, Pani Jadwiga showed us the room. It bore no relation to the apartment advertised. She hadn't mentioned that I was obliged to share it with her cakes. This was a commercial business and there were plenty– cheese and chocolate, apple and fruit. They smelled delicious. How could I resist eating them? Clearly she exercised self-control, as she was surprisingly thin, considering her occupation. Her sharp white face and black hair were softened by the flowered overall that covered her tall frame. She showed us the bathroom. The bath was full of dirty washing. Pani Jadwiga said the other lodgers were not allowed to use the shower. They had to wash in the basin. She handed me a list, in Polish and English:

"Please take off your shoes.
Please turn lights off.
We have no toilette paper.
Take shower connector to your room."

Maria and I looked at each other in dismay. Then she drove me up the road to her home for supper.

Maria lived in a street of private houses where red and white Polish flags fluttered from the beams. There were no all-red flags to match, as in public buildings and on trams. We walked up a few covered steps and she opened the front door into a lovely room. Sunbeams patterned the floor, and birds sang as if for joy of sunlight after the rain. Maria, whom I had only met briefly before in London, told me her story as we tucked into salami and bread, washed down with Cinzano, which seemed to be the only alcohol in the house.

Maria studied in Lvov, in Western Ukraine, then part of Poland, where her father was a professor. After the Nazi-Soviet invasion, Maria was forced to watch as he was shot by the Nazis during their purge of academics. Renamed Lviv, the country became part of the Soviet Union. After the war, as boundaries were changed throughout Eastern Europe, ethnic cleansing followed. Over a million Poles and Polish Jews were moved west to replace Germans, and Ukrainians were moved east. When Maria later reached Krakow with her husband and daughter Agnes, they took her mother with them. They began renting two rooms in this old suburban house, with its parquet floor and panelled double doors.

At first they shared the house with eleven families. Now there were four: the owner, an ancient Russian count, a wrinkled old Polish lady with a sweet smile, who spoke French, and Maria. Despite her doctorate and expertise, Maria's salary was that of a restaurant chef, half as much as a steel worker. She had heart problems but there was no time to consult a doctor for you wait in a long queue to be seen, nor had she the money for a holiday away from the polluted city. Her second husband lived in London, but it did not sound like a happy marriage. At the end of the evening Maria drove me back to my filthy lodgings.

I narrowly escaped sitting down on a chair covered with dog food.

'Pani Jadwiga, please may I have a bath?' I asked tentatively, aware she lived up to her name which means contending battle. She scowled, told me to wait an hour, and within half that time called me in. She was cleaning her teeth in the loo. The bath water was tepid and well below the Plimsoll line.

'Don't turn the key,' she said as she departed. I wondered about the male lodgers.

'Was it good?' she asked when I appeared partly clean. I had no energy to answer. I smiled weakly.

The next morning, after Madame's dachshund leapt on to my bed and licked me awake, I noticed Madame's false teeth lying on the sideboard, as I breakfasted on bread and butter with jam supplied by Iwona, washed down with the coffee I had bought in a Pewex shop in Warsaw. As I ate, I couldn't help but reflect how little of the Polish hospitality and kindness my landlady embodied.

How relieved I was when Maria arrived. I smiled gratefully and hugged her with relief. She drove me first to a police station where I had to register my presence. I showed my invitation from Professor Szablowski and received a stamped paper that exempted me from paying $10 a day for living in a private home rather than in a hotel.

*

In September 1939 Hitler's troops entered Krakow; in November his secret police began to implement his Ostpolitik by arresting university professors and putting them in concentration camps. The ex-Bavarian Minister of Justice and ruthless Governor General, Hans Frank, selected Wawel Castle as his residence, and made the most of his stay by stealing priceless works of art.

Maria drove me to Wawel via the local market and bakery. A few eggs and some old bottles full of beetroot juice sat on trestle tables. Vegetables lay on ground sheets below – carrots, turnips, lettuce and spinach. Fluted tin bowls held the produce on scales. Maria bought six eggs, spinach, four tomatoes and 200 grams of mushrooms, carefully measured with brass weights. As we queued for twenty minutes in the private bread shop, I contemplated the small stained glass of the Madonna and Child hanging on the window behind the counter. I missed my boys. Communication from here was not easy, but as last year, I would write postcards. Boguś, whom I had seen in London, had kindly offered me the use his telephone. When it was our turn, I asked for two brown rolls and one white, which the baker's wife put into a paper bag.

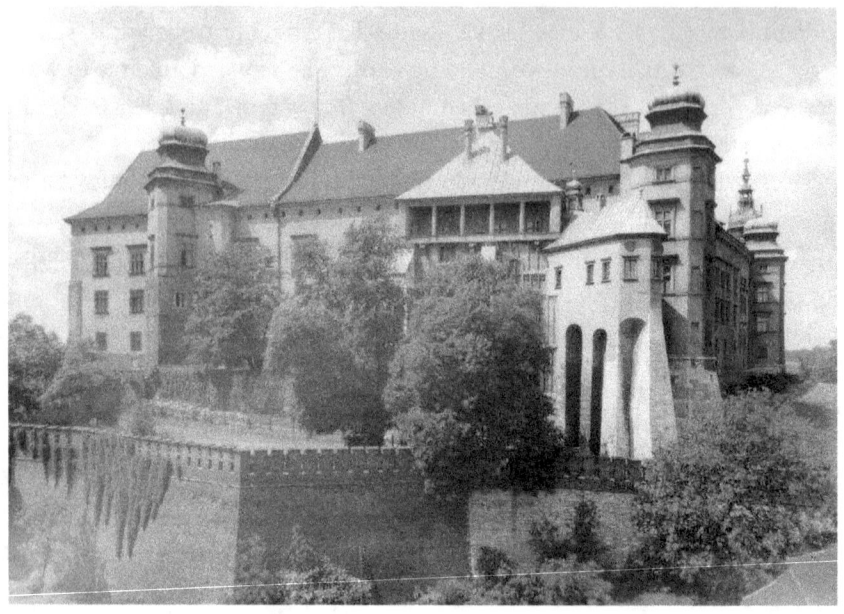

Wawel Castle. 1985 (photo: S. Michta)

'Special treatment for foreigners,' whispered Maria, as she put her bread straight into her basket, after making room between the eggs and vegetables.

On the way to Wawel, the car stuttered to a stop and Maria switched on the reserve tank.

'I'll queue for petrol later,' she said, 'my coupons are at home.' Petrol, like meat and other staples, was still rationed, and continued to be until 1989, when the Soviet Empire collapsed. We reached the southernmost part of the old city, where the road curved round the limestone hill rising above the Vistula River. Maria related a popular folk tale. Long, long ago in the days of Prince Krak, a dreadful beast appeared in an empty cave under the castle hill. This enormous monster, covered in green scales, spitting fire from its horrible mouth, devoured cattle, sheep and even heedless young people who came too near its cave. It became hungrier and hungrier. Prince Krak sent out a proclamation saying whoever killed the dragon could marry his daughter and have half his land. Many brave knights from near and far tried, and failed, to kill the beast. Then a skinny young Krakovian cobbler came up with an idea. He filled a sheep's carcass with salt and left it at the mouth of the cave. When the dragon saw the carcass he devoured it in one gulp. Suddenly his stomach felt as if it was burning and he ran to the river to quench the fire. The more he drank the greater the pain until he burst. The cobbler married the princess and received half the kingdom. The town was rid of a menace and the cobbler cut a few pairs of wonderful boots from the beast's hide.

'The dragon's den has become a major tourist attraction,' said Maria with a grin, as we passed the Senator's tower, one of three Gothic bulwarks. She brought the Trabant to a halt under an arch, portcullis raised. A guard waved her through. Round the last bend, past the Sandomierz bastion, and soon the sight of the Thieves Tower welcomed us into the open area within the castle walls. Maria parked outside one of the 19th century blocks built by the Austrians during their occupation. I looked across at the cathedral – at the cupola of the 16th century Sigismund chapel, with its golden tiles that glittered in the sunlight. During times of war the gold was protected from theft by a covering of tar. But this was not the time for sightseeing, or musing on the past.

'People like to believe the huge bones above the entrance to the cathedral come from the dragon, but in fact they belong to some prehistoric animal,' Maria said as I followed her into the administration wing, which curtains the castle from the grassy thousand-year-old foundations of the early settlement. I was signed in, given an identity card, and followed her up the grey marble staircase to the second floor where restoration work was carried out in a series of large rooms with parquet floors and ordinary lights dotted around the ceilings.

About twenty people worked on metal and ceramics, textiles, pictures, framing, chemical analysis and photography. For them my presence was significant. I was the first guest restorer from the West since the Iron Curtain separated us from Eastern Europe.

Jan Blyskosz welcomed me and introduced the ten restorers of various disciplines who were gathered round a large wooden table during a break for 'second breakfast'. Over coffee and sandwiches, they explained how difficult it was to get supplies. The economic shortages in the country inevitably affected conservation and they had to rely on ageing equipment and erratic delivery of such materials as the ministry was able to provide. There was no spray gun. Pictures were varnished by brush. Pigment was unobtainable. The few odd jars of old colours were of pre-war vintage, and sat rather disconsolately in a cupboard.

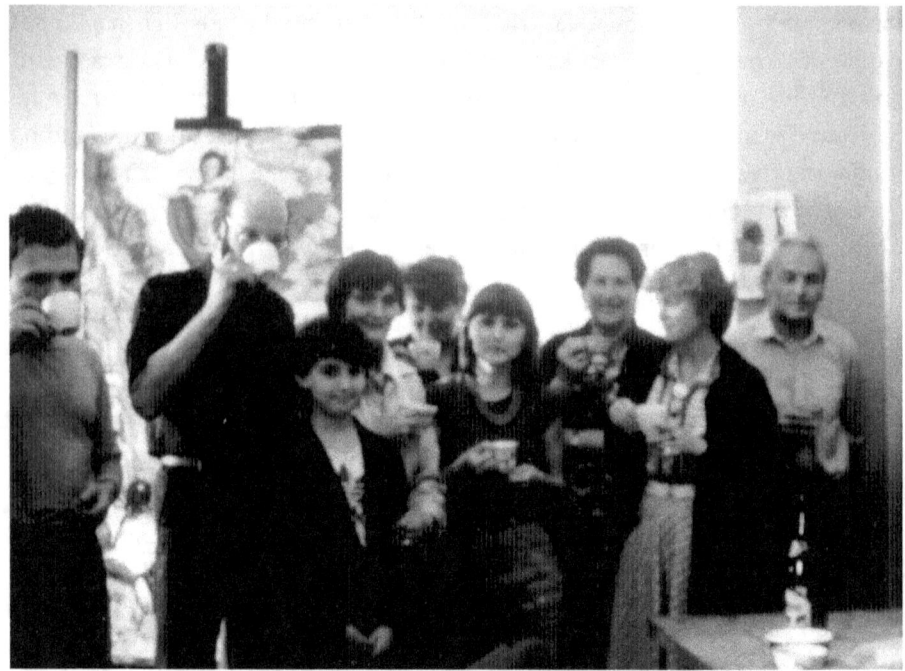

**Conservator's congregate for 2nd breakfast. Jan Blyskosz is far right.
Krystyna Wanicka, my interpreter, in the centre**

The State provided Rembrandt and Le Franc oil paint. Polyfiller was not available so they made their own, as Ruhemann had taught us, from chalk, Venetian turpentine and stand oil (heat thickened linseed oil which does not darken over time and helps to form an enamel-like surface). They inserted it after animal glue was brushed into the holes. Shellac was painted on the smoothed-off filling after it had dried to prevent absorption of paint and varnish. Both glue and wax resin were used for lining pictures to consolidate the canvas, but there was no vacuum table here. Instead they used an iron, which, if it was too hot, could flatten the impasto, (thickly applied paint loved by the Impressionists). The spatula used to lay flaking paint was very advanced when Professor Kozlowski designed it in the 1950s. The controls fitted neatly into a cube-shaped wooden box with fittings and switches for two spatulas. The temperature was gauged by the level of light produced by a little bulb. It still worked well.

The three older restorers were pupils of the professor, who was known internationally for his research into the origins of wood panels and their repair. A fine portrait of a man by Lucas Cranach, which the professor restored and wrote about in *Studies in Conservation* in 1962, had begun to split again. The Cranach sat in the picture restorer's studio while Jan Blyskosz and his team considered how to treat it. Lack of foreign currency prevented them subscribing to foreign journals, and lack of opportunity to discuss problems with colleagues in the West increased their sense of isolation. They called me their Window on the West. By good fortune, one of the *National Gallery Technical Bulletins* I brought them contained a report on repairing splits in the panel of Rubens' *The Watering Place.*

I had packed powder pigments, sable brushes, paints, varnish, linseed oil, spatula, scalpel, blades and sketch pads donated by suppliers and friends in my suitcase. They were accepted with relief and gratitude. The restorers poured over a catalogue of laboratory equipment trying to decide what to choose with the £50 donated. This led to a discussion of techniques.

'When I trained with Professor Ruhemann he taught his students that a conservator's job was to restore a painting as close as possible to the artist's original intention,' I said, remembering how the *Lady of the Ermine* had not been touched.

*

I became aware of the restorers' shortages of equipment during my visit last year, and wrote to suppliers on my return home. Lady Salisbury, who drove vital medical supplies to Poland, had brought the first 125 litres of solvents I was given, on her last lorry trip out. The first journey out for these amateurs in 1982 was a steep learning curve, Mollie told me. They continually ran into trouble as they had filled in no paperwork.

'The professional driver I'd engaged let us down, so a friend of the family, Charlie Mortimer, stepped in to drive the 32 ton goliath we'd been lent. Charlie held an HGV licence. The first problem arose when the laden truck was too heavy to cross any of the bridges leading out of Hatfield House. Everything had to be unloaded, the lorry driven to the main road, and reloaded.'

Mollie took the ferry from Harwich to Hamburg. Her friend Ginny went in convoy in a smaller truck driven by her son Tom. When they reached the Eastern border German guards searched the two vehicles.

'Das ist für kinder?' one asked, finding a box of whisky.

'Alles ist für kinder', Ginny firmly replied, anxious not to lose their sustenance. Rather than take the usual lorry route round Berlin, Mollie decided she would save time by going through the centre. Her son Valentine was stationed there with the Grenadier Guards and sent a message through to the border guards to facilitate his mother's passage into the DDR. Unfortunately, Checkpoint

Charlie was not designed for lorries. If you visit the site now, you can see the entrance is narrow. Charlie got the lorry stuck. They finally made it, with Ginny slipping through after them. The French guards collapsed in laughter, while the American, British and Russian border guards glared.

Mollie continued, 'We were making really good time once we reached Poland until we came to a wooden bridge. There to our consternation was a notice which said "9 tonne limit". Well, we certainly didn't want to drive back forty kilometres to look for another way over the river.'

'What did you do?' I asked, suspecting the answer.

'Even though the lorry was three and a half times overweight, I decided to go for it, so Charlie drove across at speed after Ginny. The bridge survived. When we got stuck under a low bridge another time, Charlie had to let the tyres down and back out. Lots of adventures, but we came through.' There were unpleasant brushes with the militia, and they once got arrested and were interrogated for some while before they were released. Over the following years professional drivers steered the lorry to Warsaw, Lublin and Krakow where supplies were distributed. On arrival they slept in church rooms, dormitories, and even a bishop's palace. Derek, a fire engine driver, was a regular. Solid and reliable, he was trained to cope with every eventuality.

They transported supplies of solvents that had been donated by the British Drug Company, for use in the Wawel and Czartoryski museums. They arrived safely, but not without extensive grilling from the authorities, since these chemicals were also useful to the underground press.

'I loved my lorry life,' Mollie told me. 'I looked up companies in the Yellow Pages, and when I explained I needed to hire a lorry to drive vital supplies to Poland, every company I talked to offered me a vehicle free of charge. They remembered the vital part Polish pilots played in the Battle of Britain.' She chose a truck lent by Lord King who was CEO of British Airways at the time.

*

I invited Maria to lunch. It was apparent she rarely ate out, but after pausing to think, her face lit up and she led me to a restaurant off the Rynek. As we entered and sat down at a table, I looked around at the décor, suspecting nothing had changed since the war. Silver-plated cutlery, beakers and white plates with dark age-cracks, not unlike the craquelure on old oil paintings, were laid out on damask table cloths. The arched vaults were attractive, if in need of a coat of paint like everywhere in this polluted city, and the waiters were polite. I had rarely eaten out in restaurants since my separation, but felt quite rich, for the dollars I brought with me, exchanged on the black market, gave huge purchase power.

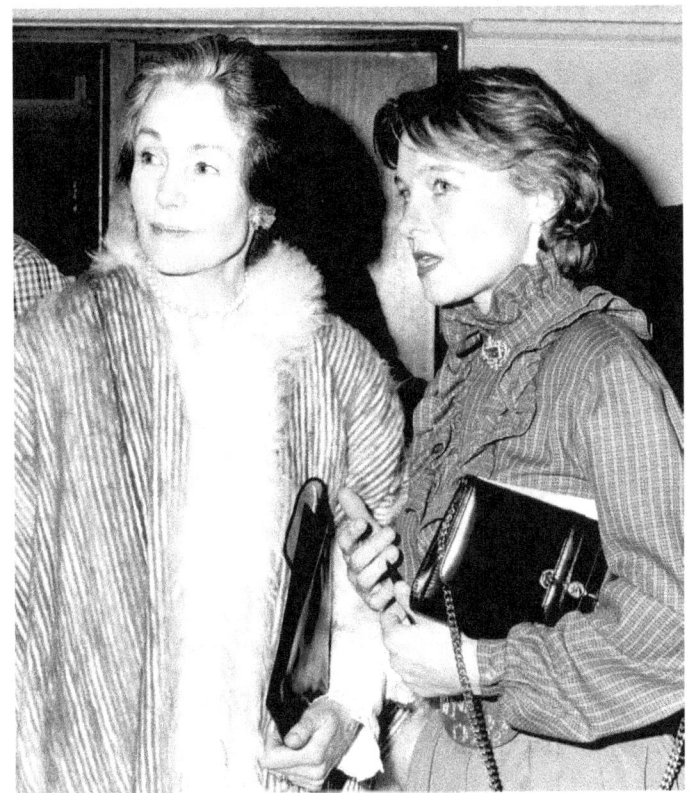

Mollie and Author in London, 1983

'What do you recommend, Maria?' She looked at the menu, much of which was 'off', and plumped for goulash.

'And two glasses of red wine, please,' I said to the moustachioed waiter. He returned swiftly with the wine, just as it started raining.

'Why are names engraved on plaques covering every inch of the retaining walls on the way up to Wawel?

Maria replied, 'That path has been the main route from the town since the Middle Ages. The names are those who paid for the renovations when the country received back its identity after World War I.' She filled me in with more history before changing tack.

'I'm not very happy with your lodgings', she said gently. 'I'll drive you back after we've eaten, and have a plain talk with Pani Jadwiga. I had no idea you would be so uncomfortable.'

'Don't worry, Maria, I'll get used to it. And perhaps I can have a bath at your flat sometimes.'

At that moment the goulash arrived, steaming hot. A pungent smell of paprika wafted from the serving dish. The waiter ladled portions into our plates, followed by a hill of rice and a side salad of grated carrot, beetroot and celeriac, each occupying a third of the plate. It was all delicious.

Maria had made up her mind. When we reached my lodging she had an argument with my landlady, which I realised was not easy for this self-effacing soul. The two women's voices became increasingly staccato and high-pitched as words were exchanged, none of which I understood.

'I think she's mad,' said Maria finally. 'Pack up your bags. It will be a pleasure to have your company in my home.' I sighed with relief, paid the landlady, and we left.

Maria donated me her sitting room, where, as in most Polish homes, a sofa doubled up as a bed. Several Renaissance stove tiles were stacked in a corner. Their wonderfully vibrant greens and turquoise were as fresh as the day they were fired. Some had finely wrought faces or figures sculpted into the clay. They were more attractive than cakes.

After dropping my suitcase, Maria took me to a room in a house nearby where she and a colleague, Andreas, sorted, restored and reconstructed 16th century stoves tiles.

'Why are there are many more green tiles?' I asked.

'The blue, orange and yellow colours are more expensive and were only used in homes of the wealthy; so many more green tiles were made.' We walked back to Maria's flat, past endless chicken wire fencing, softened by white and pink blossom and red tulips – flowers growing haphazardly in mounds of deep brown earth. A boy washed his hands in a rain barrel and scrubbed them with soap in the yard of a dilapidated house, where a chained dog barked fiercely.

'This house belongs to some Christian organisation,' said Maria, pointing to our right beyond a well-tended garden. Slates had slipped from the roof of the old wooden house, painted green, with a carved door lintel. Further on we passed allotments, where primroses and rock gardens enlivened seeded earth. Opposite was a drab four-star Orbis Hotel which, Maria whispered, acted as a bordello frequented by Arab and Italian workers on cheap holidays. Two tarts with spotted stockings, primped hair and jewelled bags tucked under their arms walked out, looking for custom. Maria pointed to a leaking water pipe in the road. 'That's been broken for six months, but we're told there're no materials to repair it.'

*

During those weeks I stayed with her, Maria often left for work before me so I took the tram into town. There was an air of resignation about the people I observed around me. They all looked tired and worn, cold and ill from lack of proper nourishment during a long winter. Shopping baskets were meagre – filled with bread, milk and root vegetables. Sometimes I noticed a woman holding a container of water and a flower vase full of lilac that seemed to lift the spirits with its fragrance. I wondered if it was to place on a grave or to celebrate a First Communion, for I had seen little boys in white suits and girls in white dresses clutching posies, walking to church with their families.

After working at Wawel, I enjoyed walking across the Rynek and often stopped at the Sukiennice, which dominates the centre of the square. This Renaissance cloth hall was once the centre of international trade, where travelling merchants met and bartered exotic imports from the east – silk, spices, leather and wax, in exchange for textiles, lead and salt from the Wieliczka Salt Mine (of which more later). The covered market now sold handmade wooden toys made by the farmers during the winter months, beautiful embroidered blouses, leather and glass goods, sheepskin jackets and slippers.

Outside the market, curving stone steps led up to the National Gallery, opened in October 1879, which stretched the length of the first floor. The gallery immediately became a major cultural venue with its four huge galleries exhibiting 19th century Polish paintings. Poland is well-known for its love of horses, and they became a subject artists frequently painted. In conflicts against invading Turks, pure-bred Arabians were taken as spoils of war until Poland's truce after the victorious Siege of Vienna. Poles travelled to the desert to purchase Arabians from tribesmen to upgrade their own stock and breed animals suitable for use by the cavalry, farm work and carriage pulling. From 1817 when Janów Podlaski Stud was set up in Eastern Poland, the farm has bred some of the finest Arabian horses in the world.

The greatest of these horse-loving artists was Piotr Michalowski, landowner and industrialist, who produced arms in the steel mills he supervised during the 1830 November Uprising. When the Polish troops were defeated, Michalowski was forced to leave Poland briefly. He fled to Paris, where he worked in the studio of the much respected painter of battle-scenes, Charlet. When he returned to Poland four years later to look after the family estates, and work for various charites and societies, he set up a studio in the country and in Krakow.

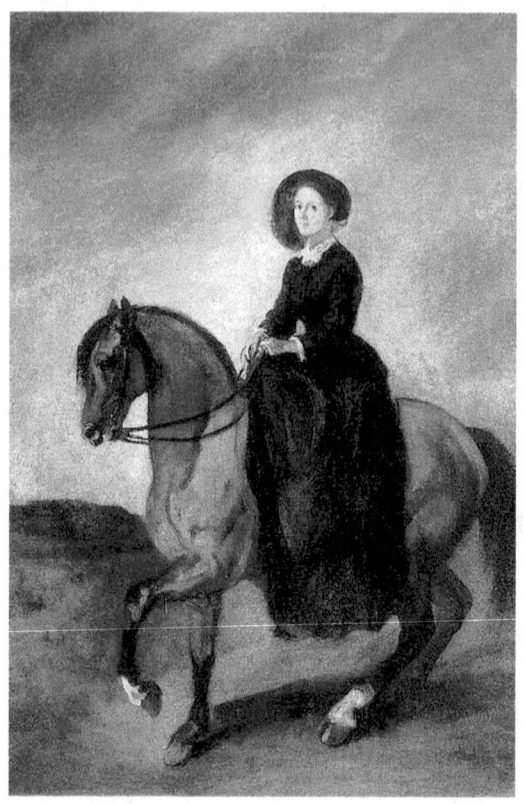

Portrait of his daughter Celine on Horseback by Piotr Michalowski
(National Museum, Warsaw)

Inspired by Theodore Gericault, Michalowski's painting is instinctive, spontaneous and romantic. He focused on three main subjects: the Napoleonic epic, the likeness of past military commanders, and the world around him, both people and animals. In a room devoted to his work there are portraits of Napoleon, of Polish officers, of battle scenes. I preferred the closely observed portraits of the "family": farm hands, friendly old peasants, old women, beggars on the doorstep, Jews from the local inn, and his children on their ponies. Rare among his contemporaries, instead of telling stories, he captured a moment or a likeness in a glance, with sweeping brush strokes and limited detail and colour, using an elegant palette of browns and silvery-greys, mixed with blues, blacks, whites and reds, employed with exquisite skill.

Michalowski regarded horses with the same insight as humans, each with their own personality. From his own experience he knew how horses, whether thoroughbreds or work horses, helped Poles become perennial survivors. In skirmishes with invaders and flight from captivity, to re-working the land and rebuilding homes, villages and towns, horses were their partners in starting again.

In London later, I met a descendant of Michalowski, an elegant old man who told me how his landowning family, like many others, escaped both the Russians and the Germans in 1940 thanks to their horses. He was fourteen when a horse was shot under him, but despite tortuous, death-defying adventures, part of this family made it to Britain. This old man was a living example of *polot.*

I didn't want to think about the fate of the Polish cavalry charging German tanks in 1939. More than 80 percent of Janów Podlaski's horses perished in the war, and the stud was severely damaged. Later, Hungary sent Arabian mares to help rebuild Poland's decimated breeding programme.

*

The last King of Poland, Stanislaw II Augustus Poniatowski, supported the freeing of peasants on some estates, and some landowners turned their farms into peasant co-operatives. One founded the Peasant Commonwealth of Pawlow in 1769, a self-governing village with its own school, hospital and citizens' militia. The King also encouraged Poles to travel abroad and foreigners to come to Poland.

Among those who travelled was Tadeusz Kosciuszko, who went to America. In 1777 he joined the army of General Horatio Gates in northern New York. His work fortifying all the roads along the Hudson River helped defeat the British Army under General Burgoyne at Saratoga on 17th October. He spent the next two years fortifying West Point, before active service in the South including conducting the blockade on Charleston. At the end of the war he was given U.S. citizenship and made a brigadier general in the U.S. Army. After their victory, Washington's General Charles Lee was the King's guest in Warsaw.

Sharing space in the National Gallery in the Sukiennice is Matejko's iconic historical painting, *Kosciuszko at Raclawice.* The 1794 battle against the Russians was won, but Kosciuszko's forces were too small to pursue the retreating troops of General Denisov, who continued to attack in the south east of the country. The campaign was lost, and Poland finally partitioned a year later. In this painting Matejko celebrated the brotherhood of all classes, for this was the first time that peasant-volunteers, armed with scythes, were invited to join the fray, inspired by their leader. This began the evolution of the Polish peasantry from serfs to equally entitled citizens of the nation.

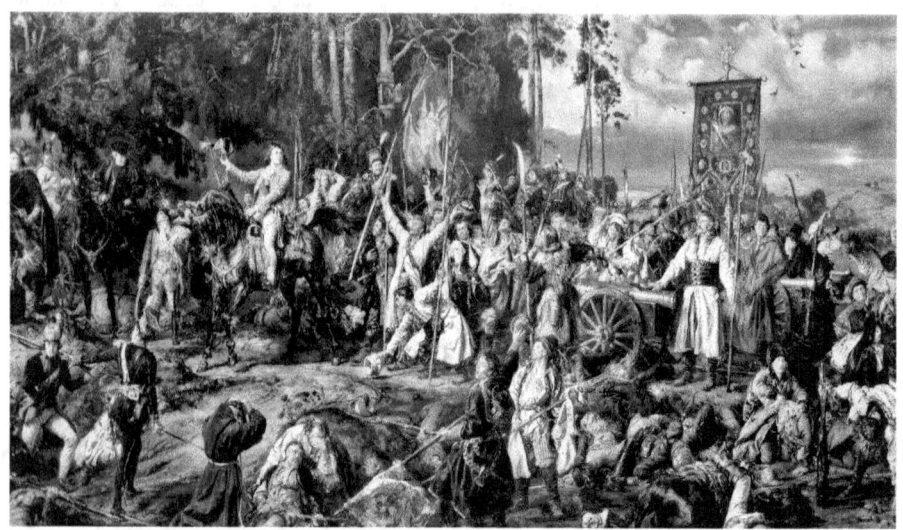

Kosciuszko on the Battlefield at Raclawice **by Jan Matejko, 1888**

Across the valley from Wawel, the Kosciuszko Mound rises like a green hill. This mound, nearly thirty-five metres high, was created on a voluntary basis by patriots of all ages and social class to commemorate their hero's victory at the Battle of Raclawice. For three years, as the mound grew, urns containing soil from all the Polish and American battlefields where Kosciuszko fought, were buried. One Saturday I walked up this landmark. At the summit I noticed the pall of pollution hanging over the city and the castle, and beyond, the chimneys of Nowa Huta factories belching shades of grey smoke.

Back in Maria's home I could gaze at Kosciuzscko's Mound from my window as I wrote, and listen to the birdsong. When the artist Wyspianski became ill during the winter of 1904 he painted his view of the mound over and over again, in pastel and paint, in different light and colours; as Claude Monet had repeatedly painted the same subject, like Haystacks, to show the light and atmosphere across time and seasons.

*

The focus of the pedestrian walk up Wawel hill is Tadeusz Kosciuszko, lifting his cap from astride his horse on a plinth near the summit. The bronze statue of the hero was melted down by the Nazis, and this cast was taken after the war. Nothing in Poland rests easy. Like his close friend, Thomas Jefferson, Kosciuszko valued human rights. Indeed, the Pole dedicated his American assets to the education and freedom of slaves there.

I saluted Kosciuszko and continued under an arch and past the bulk of the Romanesque cathedral which abuts the castle, where Renaissance chapels have rounded out the original walls, into the open space which contains foundations of an earlier settlement. I made time to stop here today and look. History in the form of architecture assailed me from four corners, from the extant Gothic walls and towers to the 19th century blocks. I listened for the noise and bustle of trading and craftsmanship, of eating and laughter, as the population grew over more than a millennium; until the rulers of Poland took up residence here and Krakow developed into a rich trading city. Then I walked to the administration building. Even as I took out my credentials, the guard recognised me and waved me through. I walked up the stone staircase to the second floor, wondering what pictures Jan would give me to restore.

8

Wawel Castle

MARIA'S HAND SEEMS to ward off the trees that loom menacingly around her. Angrily she ignores the peacocks' enquiring look. They may be symbolic protectors of women, but they had not shielded her, or her country, from treachery. Like the light, her house, which was no longer a family home, is receding into the distance, diminished by grief and loss. Her husband had betrayed her beloved country – refused to fight with the Poles against the encroaching Tsarist army. Now Poland was like a prisoner in chains, occupied by its neighbours, Prussia, Russia and Austria.

It was fortuitous in many ways that Jan Blyskosz, the chief conservator, had given me this portrait to restore. Janusz Walek's enthusiasm and knowledge of Maria's mother, Princess Izabela Czartoryska, had fascinated me on my visit to Krakow last year. In 1790, during a crucial period of upheaval in Polish politics, Izabela, a seasoned traveller, was asked by her husband to accompany their twenty-year-old son, Adam Jerzy, to England. They wanted him to complete his education in the country synonymous with constitutional liberty and industrial progress. They wintered in London, but Izabela was homesick and found the weather depressing.

During a three-month summer tour round England and Scotland, the Czartoryskis were wined and dined by the most prominent inventors and entrepreneurs driving heavy industry and luxury manufacture, They visited many of the great houses and gardens, including Castle Howard, where Izabela admired Nicholas Hawksmoor's Tivolian temple. The centre of aristocratic display had shifted from London to the country, where great houses became the

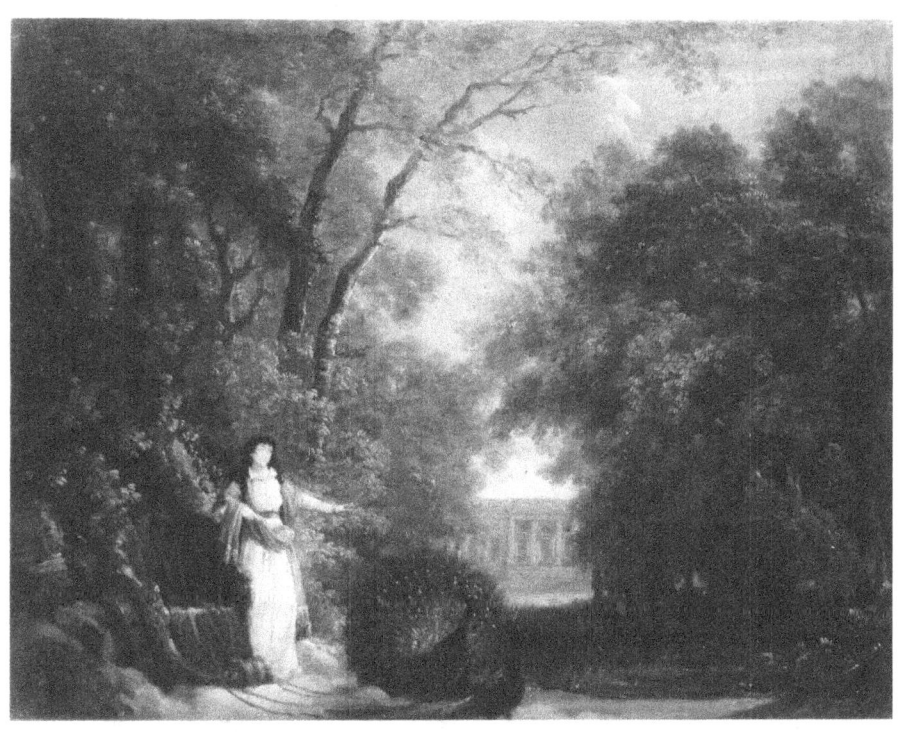

Maria Czartoryska in the Park at Puławy, by Jan Piotr Norblin,
c.1800 before cleaning (photo S.Michta, 1985)

true galleries of England. Landscaped gardens and park were of particular interest as Izabela was a skilled gardener. She saw works of art collected on the Grand Tour, studied how collections were catalogued, learnt to hone her eye from connoisseurs, and began a collection of souvenirs for Puławy, her palace south east of Warsaw. In Stratford-upon-Avon she used all her energy and charm to secure the purchase of a chair said to belong to Shakespeare, whose poetry she loved. She wrote many letters to her daughter, Maria, whom she looked after until old age, when the roles were reversed.

I picked up the broad circlet that held the magnifying glasses, pulled it over my head, lowered the visor that holds the lens, and carefully examined the paint surface of the Norblin portrait of Maria, inch by inch, checking its condition. After half an hour, I lifted the painting off the easel and turned it round to examine the back. The wooden stretcher supporting the canvas was in a reasonable state.

Straightening up with a stretch, I opened the doors of a cupboard, lifted out several glass bottles, assembled them on the table and poured small quantities of acetone and white spirit into a measuring jar, into which I dipped the cotton wool swab I had wound round the sharpened end of a hogs-heair brush, and squeezed out the residue. I rolled the swab on the lightest part of paint – Maria's dress. The swiftly-lifted swab was brown, the small patch of paint white, fresh and bright.

I made various tests, in different strengths, for pigments react differently to cleaning and it is vital to achieve a balance between cleaning safely and minimum rubbing. In this case the varnish lifted easily, revealing fresh leaves that seemed to rustle in the breeze. The peacock's feathers were blue again, for time had turned them green. And the chariot no longer seemed bogged down, for I removed brown over-paint covering damage to the canvas, to reveal remnants of cloud. How ironic that in this portrait Maria's chariot is pulled by peacocks, symbol of the goddess Hera, defender of marriage, protector of women. I was struck by the contrast between light and dark, concealment and revelation.

I was delighted to be given carte blanche to work in my own way, with the materials I brought with me. Jan provided paraloid B-72, a durable and non-yellowing acrylic resin soluble in solvents which I used as a medium thinned with xylene. This fascinated the other conservators as they coated paraloid on metal such as armour, to protect it from atmospheric damage, just as varnish protects oil paint. With the pigment I brought, they no longer had to rely on oil paint which they used to retouch, after removing the excess oil. This was less than ideal as oil paint darkens when dry and only then could they varnish. When I told them I could varnish a picture within a day, they were astonished.

The youngest restorer, Krystyna Wanicka, spoke excellent English and acted as my interpreter. Highly intelligent, she was full of energy and enthusiasm. Anna Stolzman worked in the science department, and over the weeks we also became friends.

When the picture was clean, Maria's features became clearer. Her sad, dark eyes suggested an inward gaze, even as her hand points towards her home. Her palace took four years to build, and her marriage was over before it was finished. When I discovered this, I felt an affinity with her despite her riches and high position. I too had moved into a new home after its refurbishment, only to separate from my husband six months later.

Maria was only sixteen when she was married to Duke Louis of Wurttemberg. Louis was made Commander of the Grand Duchy of Lithuania's army. But he refused to fight against Russian troops while feigning illness throughout the Polish-Russian war of 1792. When his perfidy became public, he was dismissed from his post but never prosecuted. For a woman as patriotic as Maria, the shock was devastating. She divorced him. In reaction, he took their one-year-old son Adam to St Petersburg where he became playfellow to his cousin, later Tsar Nicholas I of Russia.

After the military defeat and the second partition of Poland, between Russia, Prussia and Austria, Princess Izabela, Maria's mother, could see no other means of national survival than through armed insurrection. With her husband, Adam Kazimierz, she supported Kosciuszko's uprising in 1794. In retaliation, Catherine of Russia ordered her troops to devastate Puławy and sequestrate all the family's lands. This confiscation was only lifted when Maria's two brothers, Adam Jerzy and Konstanty, were sent to the court in St Petersburg, in the guise of hostages.

Two years later, after the third partition deleted Poland from the map of Europe, Izabela and her family returned to the ruined Puławy. They began rebuilding, first the house, then the beautiful park which was designed by James Savage, whom they brought over from London. (Savage later created a garden for Count Zamoyski's Blue Palace, adjacent to the Royal Castle in Warsaw. The 200-year-old garden was returned to the Zamoyski family in 2012.) Izabela was determined to erect a national museum dedicated to preserving the memory of Poland's past. She had seen rotundas in English parks, inspired by the half-ruined temple at Tivoli, dating from the first century B.C.

The Polish architect, Christian Piotr Aigner, worked on several commissions for the Princess. During his studies in Rome, he had visited Tivoli, and it was probably he who suggested the model for the Puławy museum. A temple at Tivoli was dedicated to the Tiburtine Sibyl, an oracle guarding the books in which the prophecies concerning the Roman state were contained. The connection with the Sibyl, combining classical antiquity so dear to the Enlightenment with elements of Romantic mysticism, probably clinched the matter. The Temple of Sybil was opened to the public in 1801. The museum's artefacts of Polish sovereignty, many given by Izabela's friends, were an added spur to patriotism in a nation gobbled up by its neighbours.

Carved over the portal was the inscription *Przeszlosc Przyszlosci*. Izabela's concept of *The past to the Future* was fulfilled by artists later in the century; their images of events still inspire a people subsisting under another Russian power. The Gothic House was built for Izabela's collection of foreign works of art including the Leonardo, Raphael and Rembrandt masterpieces. The two museums welcomed the public until the 1830 November Uprising. Maria's son, Adam von Wurttemberg fought against them. On retreat from Warsaw, Adam ordered cannon balls to be fired into the Puławy palace: one for his mother and one for his grandmother.

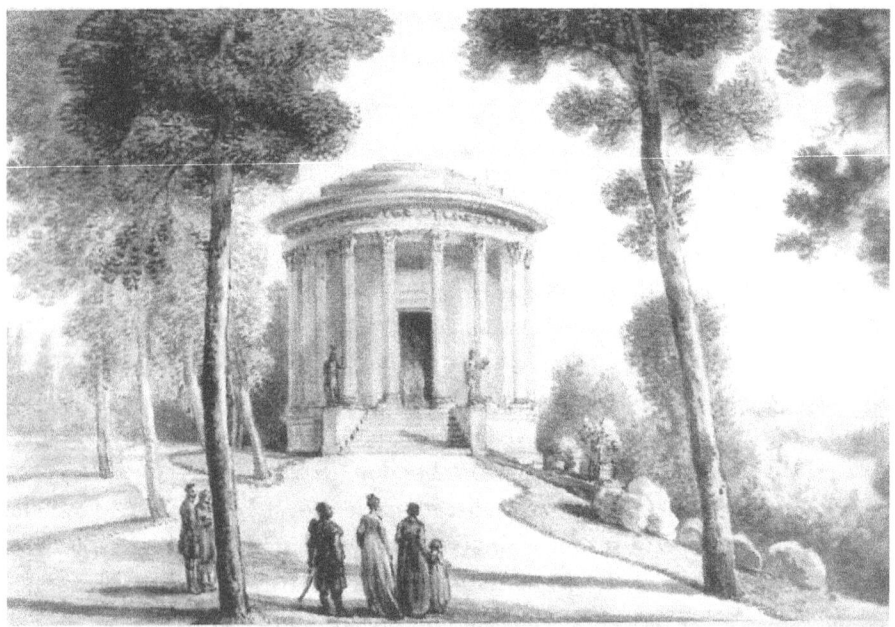

Temple of Sibyl, **Drawing by Jan Piotr Norblin, 1802**

Looking at Maria as I worked on her portrait, I learned that the French artist Norblin had been invited to Puławy by Izabela Czartoryska as court artist and tutor to her young children. He stayed in Poland for thirty years and even took part in the 1794 uprising. He must have known Maria well, and felt her agony.

At the Czartoryski Museum which was now open, Janusz showed me round the collection. I realised how fortunate I was to handle Leonardo's portrait last year. *Lady with an Ermine* had been placed in a bullet-proof glass cage, on a silk-lined wall in a room of her own, trapped, like the Polish people who came to appreciate her. She would not be seen in the West until after communism ended. Her only companion was an empty gilt frame that hung on the adjacent wall.

'This is the frame of the lost *Portrait* by Raphael,' said Janusz, 'probably a self portrait. One day the picture may return.' This painting, along with the Leonardo and the Rembrandt – all in Izabela's original collection – had been looted by the Nazis and decorated Governor Hans Frank's residence at Wawel, until they were sent briefly to Berlin and Dresden to become part of Hitler's own collection at Linz. In January 1945 Frank brought the paintings back from Germany to Wawel. When the Germans evacuated later that month ahead of the Soviet offensive, Frank took the paintings with him. The Raphael has not been seen since.

'There is a copy of the Raphael at Knole Park in Kent,' said Janusz. 'Do you think you could look at it and let me know its date and quality?' I felt honoured to be given this commission, and hoped I would be able to carry it out.

Later, over a strong cup of coffee in his office, I told Janusz about the little Norblin portrait I was restoring at Wawel.

'Helen,' he said, with the enthusiasm I had come to recognise, 'we're arranging an exhibition in the Temple of Sybil at Puławy at the moment, to mark the 150th anniversary of the death of Princess Izabela Czartoryska in 1835. There'll be portraits of Izabela, including the full length one painted in London by Maria Cosway in 1790, memorabilia of the uprisings, such as sabres used by officers, and a banner carried in the 1830 uprising. And Izabela's death mask. I'd love to include this portrait of Maria. Do you think you can finish it in time?'

'I'm sure I will,' I reassured him. I was happy to help this kindly man who had done so much for me. 'Because I'm not using oil paint, I'll be able to varnish it as soon as I've finished retouching. I've already cleaned it, filled the holes, and applied the first coat of varnish.' Our grins widened as, from different viewpoints, we considered what this meant.

'Come to Wawel and look at it.'

*

I looked around me. My fellow conservators were coping stoically with their own problems. Far away from my natural habitat, but with the familiar smell of solvents, I felt at home with the people around me.

The picture conservation studio was a large room with a parquet floor and two long windows which provided the only natural light. Cleaning could be done under the artificial strip lighting, but easels were moved to the windows when it came to matching colour. Anna Kostecka was cleaning a portrait of Tsar Alexander which I was told had been lost during the war, found in someone's cellar two years earlier and returned to Wawel. Most of the heavy old retouching had been removed.

Restoration is more than an analysis of a painting, a study of the materials that give it substance, and the methods that give it shape. A good restorer reaches into his or her own depths working on a picture, seeking some communication at a deeper level with the artist's heart and mind, just as portrait painters seek the soul of their sitter.

I heated the spatula and laid a few dark areas of flaking paint with beeswax. When it cooled, I wiped off the residual wax with white spirit and left the picture to settle, before filling the holes where the paint had long been lost, mainly in the over-painted area by the chariot. When the filling was dry, I brushed on a coat of varnish for this enlivens the colour, and acts as a barrier between original paint and my retouching.

*

Krystyna procured us tickets for a concert in the Senator's Hall. The Spanish classical guitarist, Narciso Ypes, who transcribed many unknown 17th and 18th century composers in his illustrious career, would play music by Domenico Scarlatti and J.S. Bach. While we waited, I absorbed the rich variety of textures in this 16th century room, lit by low-watt candle bulbs in twelve-branched brass chandeliers and ten-branched ormolu standard lamps. The coffered larch ceiling was mirrored in the marble floor, the Cordovan tooled leather attached to the walls glistened, stone lintels enclosed the double doors, and the tapestries enriched the whole.

The grey-haired guitarist arrived. Everyone clapped loudly. He lifted his instrument and played a canticle to the Holy Mother by an early 12th century

Spaniard, El Sabio. I wondered if the sound penetrated to St Mary's. It certainly reached deep into me, delving into dark places. Only as the last note faded and the applause had died away, was I able to come back into the room.

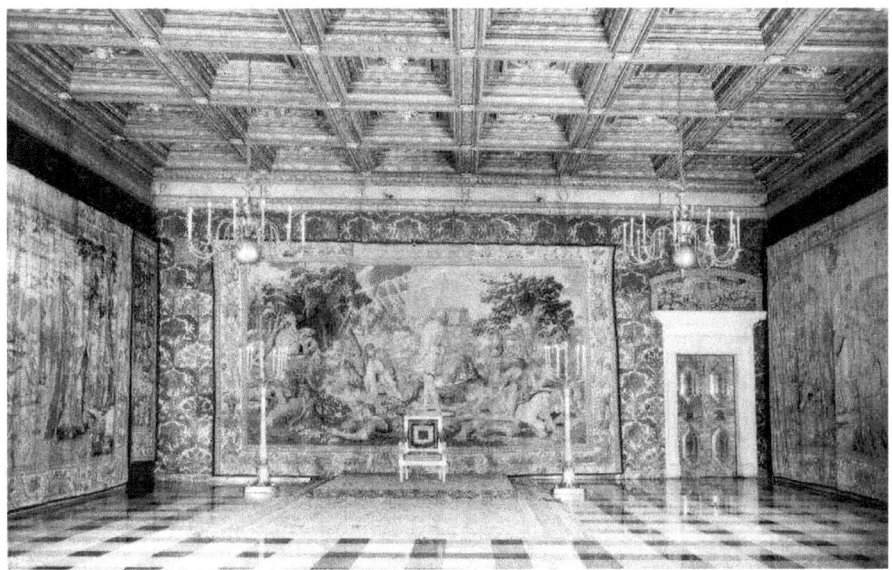

The Ballroom, or Senator's Hall at Wawel Castle, with The Flood Tapestry. (photo S. Michta 1985)

I observed the huge drama of *The Flood,* unfolding on the end wall, and shivered. The rain sheeting down had covered much of the earth and struggling humans huddled together on tiny hillocks or climbed trees, spears of lightning highlighting their terror. Children clung to their mother, a dog looked up at a heron, a man clutched at his drowning horse, screaming at us to save him, while another, standing beside a helpless lion, blasphemed against Heaven. Behind them, the ark bobbed along on the water, sealed by God's grace and good craftsmanship.

The Flood was one of eight monumental hangings from the *Story of Noah* series. The cartoons were designed by Michiel Coxcie, an eminent Flemish painter, known as "the Raphael of the North", since he was strongly influenced by the Italian Renaissance. In the 16th century Brussels was the main centre of tapestry weaving. King Sigismund II Augustus commissioned a large number of tapestries woven with wool, silk, gold and silver, in various shapes and sizes to fit the rooms of Wawel Castle. They were completed and hung in 1553, in time to add splendour to the marriage of the King to Catherine of Austria. Stanislaus Orzechowski counselled his contemporaries to look carefully at the tapestries "...

that you should thereby become acquainted not only with the work of a great artist but also with the personality of the noble monarch, which is best expressed in his love for just such things".

Krystyna and I walked round the room, marvelling at the energy and exquisite detail as the drama unfolded. King Sigismund, being childless, bequeathed the tapestries to the nation – a rare gesture in those days. Two hundred years later, after Poland was finally carved up in 1795, Catherine the Great had the tapestries removed to Russia, and they were only returned by Lenin in 1921. I wondered what connection their return had to the peace treaty at Riga after the Polish victory in the Battle of Warsaw, when Lenin's desire to conquer a shattered, post-war Europe was thwarted. In 1939 the tapestries were shipped to Canada, via Scotland for safe keeping and only returned in the early 1960s. After 400 years of conflict and upheaval, only 24 of the 160 tapestries made to measure for the castle, were lost.

Later we wandered round the Renaissance castle, built in the first half of the 16th century by Italian architects. State rooms were furnished with Italian tables and wedding chests, fine paintings and illustrative friezes below cornices conceived by masters such as Albrecht Durer's brother, Hans. And everywhere, tapestries – armorial and monogram designs, symbols of power and rule, hung in official audience chambers and carried the arms of the Commonwealth of Poland and Lithuania over windows and above doors. The flora and fauna of the *Verdures* series, showing animals in a landscape, the first in the history of tapestry weaving, were also woven in natural silks interlaced with gold and silver thread by Peter van Aalst and other masters.

Krystyna took me out to the loggia where we looked out into the courtyard, and up at a deep blue sky embroidered by stars. It reminded me of the gold and silver thread enriching the natural silks and wools in the tapestries.

*

I was silenced by the beauty of the castle when I entered the courtyard for the first time. I could only stop and stare at the arcaded galleries adorning the three dwelling wings and the south, curtain wall. The former castle was recreated into a splendid Renaissance palace for King Sigismund the Old and his son King Sigismund II Augustus by two great Tuscan architects: Francesco Florentino, who began work in 1502, and Bartolomeo Berrecci who completed it thirty four years later. Here was Italy with a northern twist.

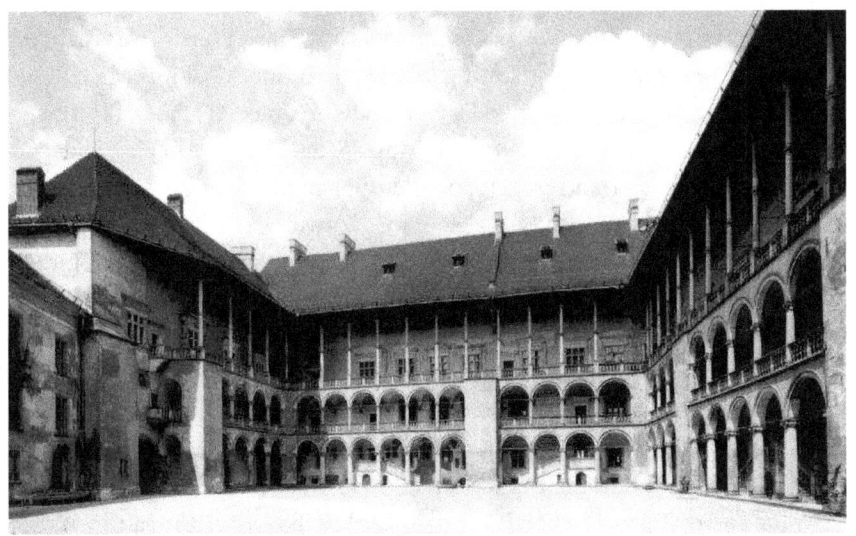

The courtyard at Wawel Castle, (photo S. Michta 1985)

Double-height pillars on the second floor raise the roof, pitched steeply to allow snow to slide off, and to bring light into the second floor state rooms. They stood out against the pale plastered walls, embellished with paintings of busts of emperors and empresses in medallions, on which the restorers worked. The palace soon became a paragon of stately residence in Central and Eastern Europe and served widely as a model throughout the region. Wawel retained its glory for little more than a century. The palace was wrecked by fires, stripped bare by Swedes and Prussians, and turned into barracks by the Austrians. Though restored, the courtyard has survived.

*

One morning I was given a tour round Wawel, by Krystyna Malcharek, who worked in the education department of the castle. Her English was excellent. It's a real privilege seeing places or things privately. You can soak up the atmosphere and aesthetics without the distractions of crowds and noise. It was amazing how much has survived over the past 450 years despite the turbulent history of this country. Unlike Warsaw, Krakow was not bombed during the Second World War. Hans Frank, the cruel German Governor who lived at Wawel, had no time to dynamite the city before he made a rapid retreat after the German surrender.

The Romantic dream of turning Wawel into a Polish pantheon first gained substance at the beginning of the 19th century, when many Polish artists expressed their ideas of restoration with paintings, sculpture or models. Piotr Michalowski, an expressionist painter influenced by Gericault, dreamed of a hall of Hetmans in the renovated walls of the castle at Krakow. He would have been glad to decorate it with life-size equestrian portraits of warriors and leaders, with scenes of old battles. His dreams were partly realised, for Wawel was packed with just such paintings. The idea was strengthened by Jan Matejko who, in 1882, offered his painting *The Prussian Homage* for one of the rooms in the about-to-be restored Royal Castle. The deep-rooted love that Poles have for Wawel was summed up by the poet, playwright, artist and designer Stanislaus Wyspianski around 1900 when restoration began in earnest. "Everything is Polish here, every stone and pebble, and everyone who enters here becomes a part of Poland." I thought of his stained glass windows in the Franciscan church.

By the end of the war, when Poland was, at last, liberated, the castle was ready to receive cherished historical artefacts from all over the world. The collection rapidly expanded with the help of long-term loans, gifts and purchases which harmonised with the royal character and tradition of the interiors. Tourists and schoolchildren now come in their droves.

*

Retouching a painting is more relaxing than cleaning. Errors can be removed. Perhaps helping pictures regain their health helped my inner healing. I settled the little Norblin painting on an easel, and prepared the table beside me. The little phials of pigment never failed to lift my spirits as I appreciated their beauty, variety and history. Titanium and zinc white replaced the poisonous lead white towards the end of the 18th century. Drawn directly from the earth, ochres and umbers were coloured by iron, yellow, brown or red – millennia in the making. After 1828, the synthetic pigment ultramarine rapidly replaced the expensive lapis lazuli, a semi-precious stone carried over the sea from Afghanistan, and used to paint the blue of the Madonna's cloak for centuries. Modern science has given us twenty-odd pigments, equivalent in hue to those of the old masters, but apparently more lasting. I treasure my few phials of Indian yellow purchased from Robeson & Co in the late 1960s. When they stopped producing it, the colour from a different supplier lacked the depth of tone and intensity. Until the early 20th century Indian yellow was manufactured from the urine of cattle fed only on mango leaves and water. Or so it is claimed.

When the pigments were laid out, I placed number 2, 3 and 5 sable brushes (fine to thicker) in a pot, and dripped some xylene and paraloid into two metal bottle lids. One by one, I tapped small quantities of a range of pigments on to my palette, added paraloid and used my index finger to grind the pigment smooth on the rough glass palette, thinning with xylene. Mixing a few chosen colours, I began retouching the damaged area of the chariot, which would need a solid coat before layers of transparent glaze built up the depth and tone.

*

After lunch in the Wawel canteen, Krystyna, Anna, and I walked down the Street of the Canons, past the ancient former homes of Wawel clergy, to the 19th century Literary Club. Inside were comfy chairs, antique tables and old porcelain in a glass-fronted cabinet. We ordered coffee, cake and wine which was cheaper than coffee. In the garden, three little girls wearing white bonnets and yellow sweaters, jumped around in tall grass filled with yellow dandelions and sunflowers, under the shade of lime trees.

'You seem very relaxed, Helen, despite your situation in London,' Krystyna said in her gentle voice. I pondered this observation for a moment, sipped some wine, and said,

'I am surprised how peaceful I feel here. I think it's partly the intellectual stimulation, and partly the slow pace of life. I can get on with what I love doing, away from the pressures.' My companions smiled sympathetically.

'Life is full of surprises,' I continued. 'I could never have imagined working behind the Iron Curtain. Yet, it was coming here last year that gave me the courage to change my life. Seeing how you all live here gives me a sense of proportion.'

The three of us wandered up to the Rynek, where a stage had been set for a splendid entertainment laid on for children. On the stage backcloth of delicate patterns in cream lace, hung the great eagle of Poland. Twelve men and twelve women from the theatre in Chorzow, dressed in their local folk costumes, danced and sang, acted stories and performed acrobatics – all with great professionalism and humour. The square was full; children were spellbound. We sat at a little wrought iron table, ate delicious lody – ice cream – and watched the world go by: a crocodile of school girls, paratroopers, militia…The sun shone on the old stone and brick, the golden coronet on the taller spire of St Mary's glinted, and Krakow basked in the evening sun.

*

When I had made good progress on retouching the Norblin, Krystyna took me to the Academy of Fine Arts where eighty pupils spend five years training in every area of conservation from lining a picture to photographing it. They practised on canvasses discarded by art students after they have torn holes in them. These students study up to ten hours a day, six days a week. There was plenty to do here since works of art as well as buildings and people suffered the obnoxious effects of sulphurous fumes, pouring out of the factories in Nowa Huta, which means New Steel Mill. This colossal centre of heavy industry was created in 1949 on land repossessed by the Socialist government from three former villages.

One of the most famous examples of deliberate social engineering, Nowa Huta was designed to 'correct' the class imbalance of middle-class, high-brow Krakow. By the early 1970s the Vladimir Lenin Steelworks had grown to be the largest in Poland and was producing seven million tons a year. The largest tobacco factory in the country and a colossal cement factory were also increasing pollution.

*

After three weeks, the retouching was finished. My colleagues liked my handling of the damage round the chariot with curvaceous clouds lifting it out of the mire. I left it a day before varnishing the little picture. I swept the brush diagonally over the surface as Professor Ruhemann had taught me, then up and down, covering every millimeter and brushing until the coating was even, semi-matt and getting tacky. I find varnishing a stressful job. The threat of having to wipe off badly applied varnish and removing painstaking glazes focuses the attention. I leant the portrait in raking light and sighed with relief when I saw the finish I wanted.

As this was my last day working here, I visited the other studios. In the metal and china department, John and his wife Sasha worked on early silver sconces, a 17th century Turkish shield studded with turquoise, and some early Meissen porcelain. In the fabric room five women spend months, even years, repairing one of the priceless tapestries, stitching with fine silk thread. Among the framers I met Josef Dutkiewicz, one of twelve architects employed in Wawel. His father was a professor of history of art at the Academy and a conservator. He had died falling off scaffolding while restoring frescoes in a church. It was an accident that would not have been allowed to happen in Britain.

I was summoned by Professor Szablowski, the Director of the Museum. We chatted for fifteen minutes in German, and he said my colleagues wished I could stay longer; that it was a pity foreigners did not appreciate Krakow more. He was a delightful man in his Eighties, with a head of thick white hair, who engineered the return of the tapestries from Canada in the 1960s. It took all his charm, because the Canadians were not keen to return them to a Communist state. As I rose to leave he opened a large illustrated book, *Collections of the Royal Castle of Wawel*, on the table in front of him and wrote, in a beautifully neat hand, a message of thanks to Mrs Conservator Helen de Borchgrave, signing and dating it with a flourish.

'This is the last copy in English. I give it to you as a sign of my gratitude.' He said he would have it posted back to London. This was kind, for I later discovered that new books were taxed at 100% of their price when taken out of the country. Back in the studio, I relayed my conversation and when I mentioned the book I had been given, Krystyna said, 'He gave a copy to Princess Alexandra of Kent when she visited Wawel.'

I was sad to say goodbye to my new friends. They gave me seventy slides of Wawel, including the tapestries. Krystyna gave me a crucifix, Jan pressed a medallion of the Black Madonna into my hand as he thanked me for my help. I was conscious these few weeks in Poland had given me a different view of life and its priorities.

That evening Krystyna and I took a taxi to Anna Kostecka's studio, for the restorers supplemented their meagre salaries on private restoration commissions. The state allocated studios to artists on the eleventh floor of huge concrete blocks. Anna had laid on a splendid party for me with her husband, their son Gregorz, who was training to be a conservator, Mary, Anna Stolzman and Krystyna. We drank Romanian sekt, ate canapés, moved on to coffee, cake, and then red wine and chatted until midnight.

There were pictures on the wall, paint, turpentine and brushes on tables, piles of canvasses stacked against walls. The studio ambiance was conducive to talking. After the inevitable discussion about art here and in England, the differences between Poles and Germans cropped up. We came to the conclusion that whereas Germans are efficient, but prone to conform, the Poles share the little they have, and rebel against injustice. I silently hoped my German blood also contained some Polish somewhere in my ancestry.

'I've never experienced such generosity as I've found in Poland,' I said, remembering how, on my visit to friends in Gdansk last year, food rations had been saved for weeks to feed me royally. Krystyna told me her sister moved to

Canada and she was thinking of joining her. I was not surprised. There was little to offer an intelligent young professional in this captive country. Anna was staying. She was thirty perhaps, her beautiful face enhanced by thick Titian hair. As well as working in the conservation scientific department, she designed and made tapestries in her studio not far from the castle. I looked out of the window, to a superb view of Wawel in the distance. How fine it looked, rising on the limestone hill with the Vistula curling round its base. What a contrast to these blocks of concrete boxes, built haphazardly, it seemed. In the spaces in between, allotments had sprung up – man's escape from the´enforced environment, turning back to nature to feed themselves.

*

Janusz collected the painting I had restored from Wawel, the day before the exhibition opened at Puławy. He was pleased with the result and relieved it was finished in time. Preparing an exhibition in a venue far away was stressful. When I popped in to say goodbye, on my last day in Krakow, he gave me the Czartoryski album – a beautifully illustrated tome printed in 1978. The illustrations, many in colour, reminded me of some of the treasures I had seen. Inside the book was a black and white postcard of the Raphael portrait, taken by the Nazis and never recovered. Looking at this pre-war image later, and contemplating the huge loss to the Collection, spurred me on to contact the Sackville-West family at Knole on my return home.

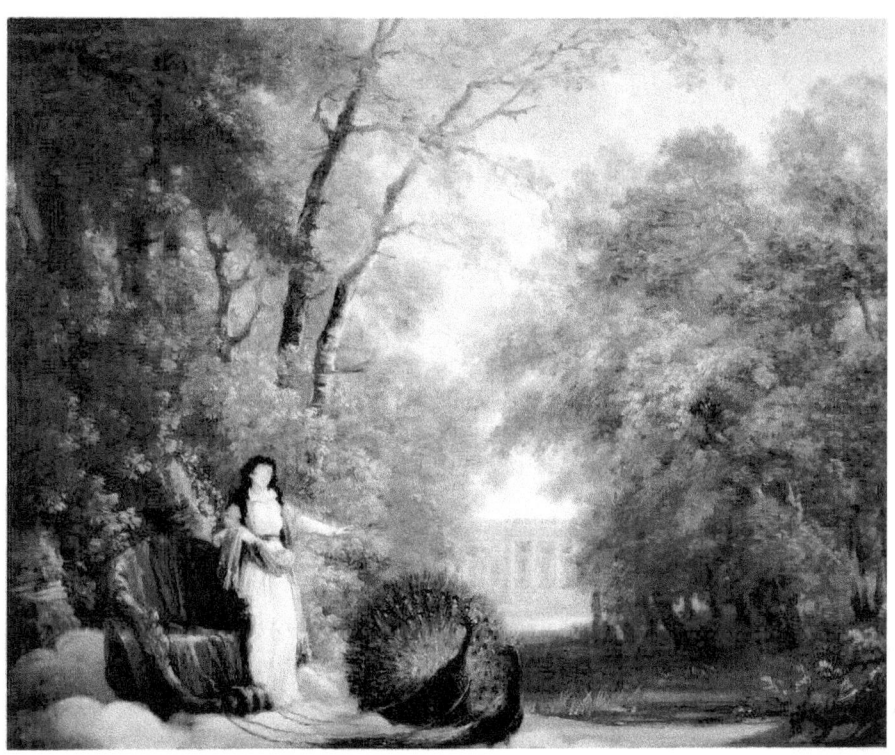

Maria Czartoryska in the Park at Puławy, by Jan Piotr Norblin, c.1800 after
restoration (photo S.Michta, 1985)

9

Art and Artists

THE ROSTWOROWSKIS INVITED me to lunch soon after my arrival. It was good to see them together. Boguś's mother had helped me buy a train ticket in the travel agency last year, and invited me to the family home for lunch. Boguś had kept in touch and I met Chris, his childhood sweetheart, at their wedding at the Little Oratory in Knightsbridge. In his homily during the service, Monsignor Tadeusz Kukla used an image of a beautiful garden:

'God gives the key of love to enter this garden: blessing and consecrating love in the sanctity of marriage. Happiness comes by your own work in developing genuine love and sharing it; accepting who you are – origins and roots – and realising how tense situations widen problems and test your love. Mature love is a long and complicated process of development. Trust each other.'

In early March I received letters from Bogus and Chris, who had experienced their first winter in Krakow together. "...how glad we are about your coming in April" wrote Boguś. "Six weeks should give you a feel of the place and ample time for an emotional airing. And I hope it will provide you with the spiritual strength to face difficulties back home." Their home looked cosier with a wife's touch, and an atmosphere of deep happiness prevailed.

Happiness is rooted at birth and nourished by love. For love, Chris had left London to live in a polluted city in a Communist country. Boguś reminded me of Tigger in his ebullience. I recognised myself in his enthusiasm. Chris was small with a pretty face framed with thick black hair. She taught English in London and now her intellectual skills were put to work at the Language Centre for Academic Staff at the Jagiellonian University, her salary supplemented with

116

some private teaching at home. Living in this polluted city under Communism was a far cry from liberal London.

'It feels like being inside a decaying tooth,' Chris said as we looked out on the blackened courtyard and flaking wall.

'Why is the house called the Popiel Palace?' I asked.

'By the early 18th century, Krakow was on its knees, occupied by Swedes and suffering a horrible bout of the bubonic plague. Eventually several aristocratic families bought up dilapidated merchants' houses and converted them into sumptuous residences, particularly in the Rynek and in this street.' Bogus told me that his great-great-great-grandfather Konstanty Popiel, a friend of Tadeusz Kosciuszko, bought the house. When his son Pawel inherited it, after fighting in the 1830 uprising, the house became a meeting place for intellectuals and politicians. Bogus's grandfather married Pawel's great granddaughter Roza in 1910.

'We house barristers' chambers now,' Bogus reminded me as we finished eating and left the table. He showed me his family collection of paintings which ranged from a 15th century Tuscan *Madonna and Child* with gold background, to 19th century portraits.

'I fished pictures out of the coal cellar, where they'd been kept safe during the Nazi then Soviet occupation, and had them systematically restored by the best people,' he said.

'How did you pay for it?'

'I earned foreign currency for a couple of months every year on the Swedish Riviera during the 1970s. I washed dishes then moved on to cooking. You know how far a dollar goes here.' Bogus pointed to a pair of landscapes of Rhineland scenes, exquisitely painted by a 17th century Dutch artist, who worked in London after the Great Fire.

'These panel paintings were restored some years ago, but as you see they've gone yellow.'

'Who's been smoking?' I teased, aware that neither of them did. 'Actually, I've brought some CRP with me.' They looked puzzled.

'Cleaning, restoring and protecting cream. I'll bring my little pot round one day and surface clean them.' Bogus was delighted. Then he said, 'Would you like to trawl the new galleries? They've sprung up like mushrooms in the last few years since Solidarity.'

We started at the Galeria Inny Swiat, two streets way, which was opened a couple of years ago by two art critics. Among a variety of ceramics, graphics and some carved and painted pine chests, there were some disturbing paintings by Zdzislaw Beksinski. His Gothic oil paintings of interior visions were popular with French and German collectors. I found them dark and frightening. The back of a skull with hammer and sickle carved into the bone was painted with precision. Skeletons hugged each other in an apocalyptic landscape.

Maciej Szybist, one of the gallery owners, told me that 'Beksinski trained as an architect but turned to painting. His first exhibition in Warsaw in 1964 was a sell-out, and now his work is bought by a dealer in Paris and a film is being made about him. I'm fortunate to have a couple of his paintings to show. He is a very nice man, but reclusive. He listens to classical music as he paints.'

Boguś took me to a DESA (state) gallery where his fourteen miniature – carved and polished shapes of Carrara marble placed in glass boxes – were hung by brass rods from the ceiling, and confided, 'I worked in secret for three years on these and surprised everyone. The Polish sculptor Tadeusz Koper, a friend of my mother who lives in Carrara, inspired me.'

I was particularly struck by a small painting by Kepinski called Dot, (illustrated on the back cover) painted in 1984. Somehow I felt my own vulnerability being reflected back at me but with a hope for change.

Later Boguś took me to meet the restorer who was working on his paintings in the Lubomirski palace, where she had three rooms on the top floor. She used the beautiful 19th century billiards table as a work bench.

*

When I finished cleaning the two Dutch panel paintings for Boguś, he took me to lunch with his cousins Karol and Maryna at Rybna, their lovely old manor house forty minutes from Krakow. A layer of socialist dirt hung over the place for there was no money for repairs and no paint. In fact Karol, like Boguś, had worked abroad for foreign currency – painting houses in Battersea. Although the Russian Army had occupied his house after the war, the parquet floor survived. The Biedermeyer furniture, piano and 17th and 18th century paintings spent the war safely in Krakow.

After a lunch of minced veal, potato, salad and cake, washed down with Karol's homemade blackcurrant and gooseberry wine, he took us round his little estate. The seven hectares were put to good use – there were bushes which produced juice, sixty 'mongrel' sheep, his wood workshop and his brother's iron workshop. Karol also had two beautiful horses which I longed to ride.

*

Walking helped me to relax. The fear of losing my own home vanished as the wide variety of façades provided a fascinating distraction. Each street, each house in the old town was different. During the 16th century wealthy owners refurbished them in the new Renaissance style. Portals were richly decorated, window frames carved in stone and arcaded attics added. The coat of arms of a former inhabitant carved in stone or stucco, curved from the blind attic at the height of the building which hid the steep roof, or leaned out below a pediment above a first-floor window. I smiled at sculpted women's heads peering down to stare at open mouthed old men, whose moustaches stretched sideways into garlands of leaves. Small cherubs staggered under the weight of a basket full of fruit upon their shoulders. Grand porticos crowned with coronets spoke silently of a ruling class now extinguished. All facades were masked by soot. Missing chunks of plaster revealed old brick.

Looking up was better than looking down at chipped and broken paving stones, the gaps filled with dirty grit. The city escaped bombing during the war; now the enemy was neglect. The shabby, depressed atmosphere matched my mood, but the sense of dogged endurance was an example to follow. Living here was a serious business. On the positive side, there were no advertisements, no loud music or tourists getting drunk on cheap vodka. Shops were fuller than last year, but prices were higher. There were also many secondhand bookshops. I liked gazing in their windows which were stacked with prints and maps, books and catalogues in a variety of colours and shapes in several languages.

Inside I looked for art books in English, conscious I had room in my suitcase since the supplies I brought with me filled up nearly half the space. Entering a shop took me into a different world. Here were a variety of beautifully printed pre-war books with colourful illustrations. In contrast, most post-war books were printed on cheap, thin paper, looking as deprived as the people who managed to acquire a copy. I bought a 1970s book on Krakow, filled with black and white photographs. Nothing much had changed except the depth of grime. In fact, over the weeks I sent fifteen books home. The walk to the main post office outside the medieval city to post them became a regular event. Boxes of old postcards were also a delight and I bought a couple of dozen spanning the century.

One day, as I turned a corner, I watched as a gypsy, settled on a velvet-covered seat between two fellow musicians, preparing to play. This wizened, crippled old man lifted his bow and swept it on to the strings of his ancient violin. His eyes closed. He seemed to breathe a different air as he transported himself and those gathered round him into an exotic world of music and dancing, of tents and movement, of wild mystery beyond ordinary lives. As the notes faded away, I needed to sit down. I threw some coins into the battered hat and walked to Planty, the park that encloses the medieval town.

The low iron railings, broken up with pleasing frequency by iron-framed wooden benches, were still painted racing green. So were the tall lantern street lamps and the iron rubbish containers set at hand-height on iron stands and wearing what looked like protective hats. I often lingered in Planty with a bagel bought from one of the old ladies who sat all day behind their cobalt-coloured carts. I wondered what life was like for these old pensioners as one handed me a bagel with a smile and I pressed a few grotchen into her wrinkled hand.

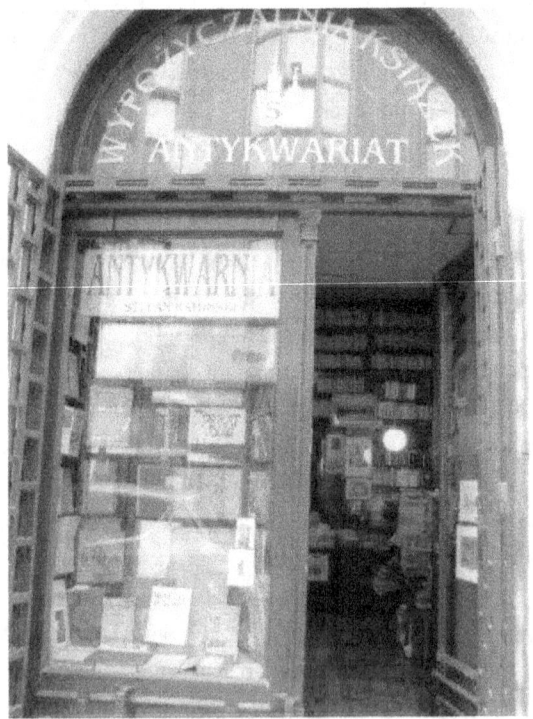

Bookshop in Krakow

Planty was a tranquil haven for all ages. Blue sky peeping through the leaves, green trees and daisy-filled grass were a soothing contrast to dirty streets. Children laughed and played, lovers nestled close, old people pondered. Lilac blossom, pansies, and lilies-of-the-valley sweetened the air, candles blazed on chestnut trees. One could forget that the pollution in this city was dangerously high and get lost in the rural beauty of it all.

As I sat there, amongst the verdant new buds, I began to feel that everything I did – read, write or paint – had been predestined and followed a cohesive pattern. As if I, who lived in a free country, was bound up in my past and staying in Poland was somehow liberating me. My awareness of inner space – the universe within – was unfolding. The serenity I had barely touched at twenty, and had allowed to be snatched away from me through fear, anxiety and pain, was awakening here. Had I enough faith and inner security to wait for my story to unfold, I wondered. Could I watch the leaves on my tree turn yellow, wither, and fall, without fear?

※

In the modern concrete building of the National Museum, set outside the medieval city opposite the equally ugly Cracovia Hotel, I had a look at some post-war art. A painting of the Pope called *The Pole* drew me. In this small oil painting, a strong man, naked to the waist, one hand clenched, the other resting on it, frowned. The suggestion of a papal cap confirmed it was Karol Wojtyla. This was a portrait of a man who waited, conscious of the past, determined to change the present. Academic, sportsman, actor, poet and man of God, he was stripped of everything except his faith. His studies were interrupted after the German occupation of Krakow. The university had been closed, 105 professors and 33 lecturers taken to concentration camps, and students like Wojtyla sent to work in the limestone quarries, while continuing their studies in secret. After the war he watched his country suffer under Communist rule. But he never lost hope, as Sobocki revealed in the blue sky that fills his breast despite the surrounding darkness. The clenched fist harnessed by prayer symbolised the incredible strength and acumen that was to be instrumental in helping to demolish the Iron Curtain only a few years hence.

Nearby I paused in front of a painting by Jacek Waltos called *Seeking the Tomb Today*. I found the image of a kneeling woman with one shoe missing, strangely haunting. All around her swirled a background of camouflage. A big window hung above her, filled with wheat and poppies, cornflowers and daisies, reflecting a promise of life. I wanted to know more about these two artists. Fortunately Stas Michta, the official photographer of Wawel, was able to arrange a meeting. I was introduced to this small energetic man soon after my arrival when the Director gave him permission to take any photographs I required for articles back home.

Since many studios were demolished during the war, the top floors of concrete tower blocks were adapted for artists instead. The entrance to Leszek Sobocki's studio, in a series of long, concrete blocks three kilometres from the centre of Krakow, was not salubrious – dirty yellow walls, a pungent smell of urinals and damp, paint-spattered iron railings beside endless concrete steps, and an unfriendly light. The lift did not work. On the first floor, a poster proclaimed "Water is life." As I climbed eleven floors, clutching a bottle of Hungarian red wine, I intermittently lowered my nose into the thick bunch of flowers I had also brought.

The welcome I received from these two middle-aged strangers, Leszek Sobocki and Jacek Waltos, was a complete contrast to the building. Warm and deeply courteous, they were tidily dressed, good-looking with tidy hair and clear, honest eyes. Sobocki was shorter than his friend and thicker in build. He sported a beard and moustache. After they settled me down on an antique chair, they brought tea in pre-war porcelain cups, bread and butter covered with ham and cut into pieces and cakes you associate more readily with elegant drawing rooms. While the wine was opened and the flowers placed in water, I looked around the room where Sobocki painted. It was long and narrow with windows along one side, facing a forest of concrete blocks. Grey sky outside, grey walls inside.

Pointing to the view as he lit his pipe, Sobocki said, 'Blockovisko!'

A brilliantly concise word he had coined for the eyesores that blocked the view.

'The artist's union gave me this studio in 1979. I usually drive here, but sometimes I walk.'

Large paintings were stacked in piles along another wall. I wondered how the larger ones fitted in the lift. These two artists, mellowed by time and shaped by their search for truth, explained something of their aims.

'In 1966 four of us formed *Wprost*, which means direct or outright. It was born out of a sense of frustration. While other artists experimented with current trends from the West, we wanted to evoke the traditions of Polish art – to portray the personal and social problems which were absent from art,' said Waltos, articulating with long delicate hands that reminded me of a subject in a blue-blooded van Dyck portrait. In 1967 *Wprost* won the prestigious Norwid prize which included Sobocki's lino cut *Eat Bread*. A red loaf lay in a black supermarket basket – stark and simple. He showed me several of these lino cuts, each hand-printed by himself. Since that series *Transfiguration* he captured significant events in a series of graphics ranging from the Pope's first visit, to *Solidarity, Exodus to the West,* to Father Popieluszko's murder. In the *Solidarity* series, Sobocki played with the logo designed by Jerzy Janiszewski to capture the feeling of hope for a new, democratic Poland, for a people weighed down by suffering.

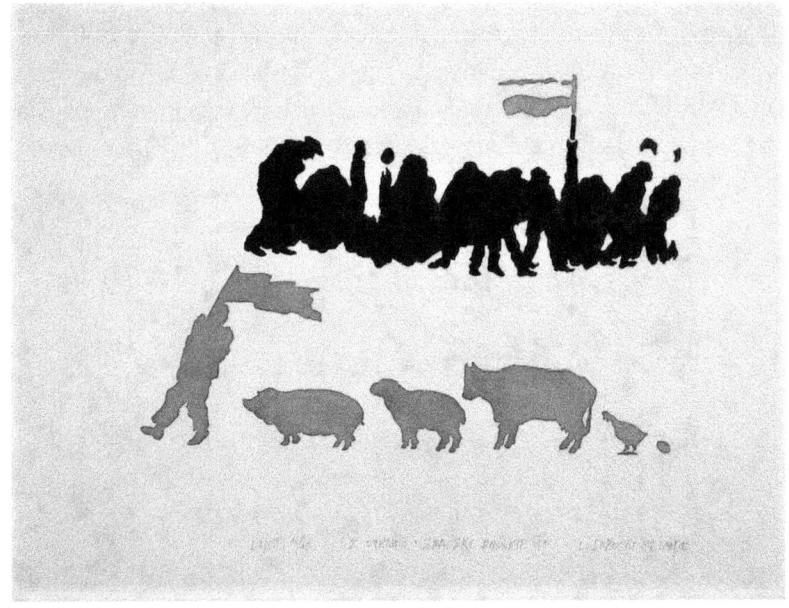

Lino cut from the cycle: *Polish Stamp*, 1981 by L. Sobocki

They told me that in fourteen years, *Wprost* held eighteen exhibitions all over Poland, and one in Sweden. Though their work was very different, in constantly changing methods and mediums, they were united in their common desire to communicate in a direct and drastic way. They disbanded in 1986.

Jacek Waltos became Professor of Painting at Poznan and then Krakow's Academy of Art. He said, 'Life changed when Solidarity freed us. We left the Artists' Union. I had already begun teaching in 1972, Leszek designed advertisements. Now little art galleries have opened up where we can show and sell our work.'

'I saw some of your pictures in the exhibition *Towards the Person* in the cloister of the Dominican Church.'

'Yes, the church is the most strategic place nowadays to make artistic statements.' As he said this I sensed a sadness that the State galleries were no longer open for them.

'I paint what I must,' said Sobocki. 'When I look back, I see the progression of the way clearly. Like Matejko's pupil Malczewski, I use my self-portrait to symbolise a theme. It's cheaper than paying a model,' he quipped.

As an example he lifted *Stifling* from the wall and placed it on an easel. A man, a portrait of the artist wearing a jester's cap, was pulling a tight red jump suit away from his throat. I recognised Matejko's jester *Stanczyk* in modern dress. The same Polish Romanticism applied. Matejko's jester sits in hopeless dejection after the failure of the 1863 insurrection; now they are stifled after martial law.

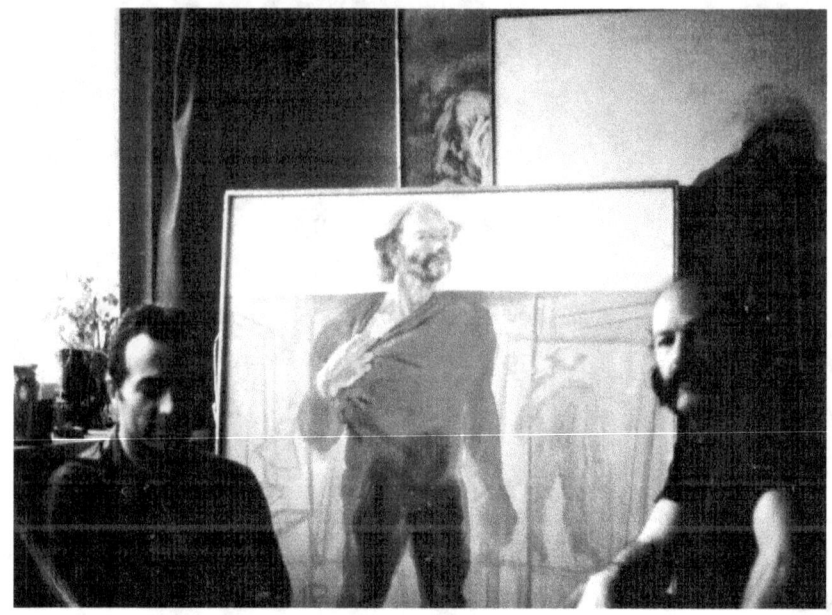

Waltos and Sobocki with *Stifling* 1984

A blown-up photograph of a blond, naked young boy and his sister standing in a garden, facing the camera with serious faces, caught my attention. I asked Sobocki who the children were. He said, 'It's my sister and me in the garden at home. Do you see my father on the left? He's come out of the house to see what we're up to. He's still wearing his stripy pyjamas. It was the summer of 1939. I was five and my sister was four.' He pulled out an oil painting, the same size as the photograph. The little boy stood alone on a sun-filled yellow hillock, holding up a little Polish red and white flag. It was unbearably poignant.

The light has gone out behind him. Bushes are mauve, a leafless tree supplicates. His father appears to the left in stripy pyjamas, standing in the blackness. An aeroplane flies overhead.

'Do you know Mehoffer's painting of the naked boy playing in a flower-filled garden with a colourful dragonfly overhead?' I remembered the century-old evocation of gilded youth well enough to appreciate Sobocki's subversion of this painting from joy to sorrow.

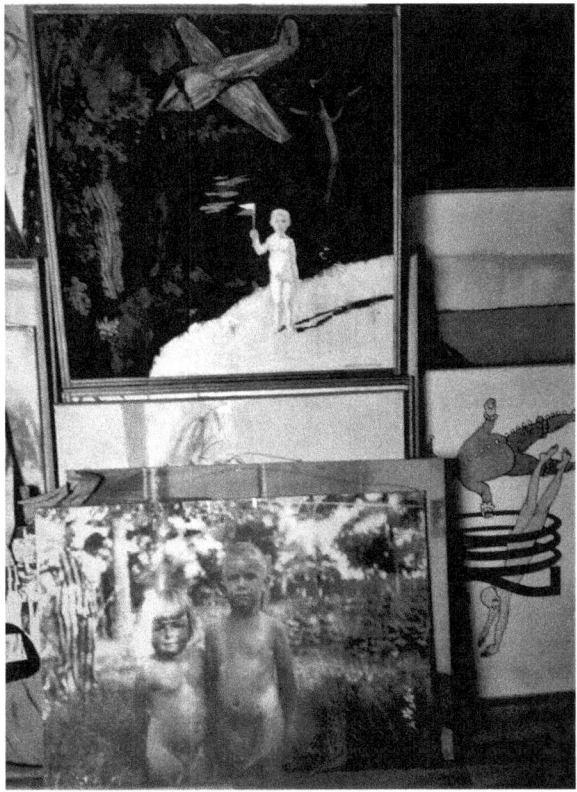

Magic Summer by Leszek Sobocki

'I call this diptych *Magic Summer*. It was the end of childhood for us. My father, an electronic engineer, was taken to a concentration camp and died three years later. We never saw him again. I was eight when I lost my father and my home. Bavarian foresters took our flat.'

'What happened to you?'

Quietly he related how they moved with a friend of his mother's to Tarnow, then, when the Russians arrived, to Berlin.

'It was 1944. My mother's friend had a good job and we stayed there for eight months. Every afternoon at 3pm the American bombers came. Every night at 11pm it was the turn of the British. We hid in the cellar, barely able to breathe from the smoke and brick dust. I preferred to be in my bed, where I could see the stars through the cracks in the ceiling.'

Leszek walked to the other end of the studio and returned with a small framed copy of the *Black Madonna*. This ancient icon draws pilgrims to the monastery at Jasna Gora, where, as at Lourdes, miracles of healing happen. I had seen the veneration the copy in St Mary's evoked.

'When the Germans became threatening, my mother would walk around like an Orthodox priest, holding this representation of the icon. There was a distinctly 'felt' presence, and it kept us safe.'

He carefully laid the icon down, and continued his story.

'In January 1945 we travelled to Katowice and lived in a flat the Germans had abandoned. In the chaos our luggage was lost. The Russians arrived. They were barbaric. They took my mother upstairs...' He looked at me, the pain of remembering filling his eyes. He drew on his pipe, and poured more wine into our glasses.

'I started painting when I was fourteen.' I learned that Adam Hoffman, a brilliant artist and teacher, taught him graphics and drawing at the Katowice Academy of Art before he moved to the Krakow Academy where he was taught painting.

'I also painted protest pictures in the streets, on walls and windows...'

After three hours I got up to leave. Sobocki carefully wrapped up one of his graphics within another sheet of handmade paper and gave it to me. It was an extravagantly generous and typically Polish gesture, for I well knew that artists' materials were in desperately short supply. Waltos found me a taxi and gave me a tightly clasped handshake before seeing me safely away.

*

A few days later I took tea with Jacek Waltos and his mother at their flat in Ulica Zamenhofa, a cul-de-sac barred by the railway, just outside Planty. The houses wore their age with tired dignity. I rang the Waltos's bell, and when the door opened with a click, entered to find the usual entrance with metal pigeonholes for mail. I walked up the first flight of stairs, where the chocolate brown walls and wooden railings darkened the already sombre staircase. Jacek was waiting for me by his open door. After greetings were exchanged he led me through a room where paintings, drawings and etchings covered every inch of wall space, into a second room where his mother waited to receive me. After introducing us and settling me down in a comfortable chair, Jacek disappeared into the kitchen.

Despite her infirmities, blindness and eighty-eight years, Elma Waltos greeted me with the grace of a gentle woman. Small and grey-haired with thick glasses, she took my hand and held it tight. How much was expressed in that clasp. Then she bade me sit down beside her and in a soft voice asked me about myself.

'I am intrigued by that painting of Jacek's in the National Museum, *Searching for a Tomb Today,*' I said. 'It exudes such restrained desperation.' I did not tell her that its very helplessness touched me deeply.

'Ah, do you know the story?'

'No.'

'My elder sister Florence was a member of the Underground army along with her husband and two sons in their twenties. In 1943 they helped rescue a group of soldiers imprisoned by the Nazis.' There was a pause before she continued.

The group was caught, imprisoned in Krakow, and at some stage taken to the woods outside the village of Warzyce and shot. The Nazis held mass executions in that area. Orphans, Jews, soldiers in the Home Army, dissidents, anyone they didn't want alive was killed there. My sister was shot alongside three Ruthenians. My nephews disappeared.'

She was silent for a while, then continued as if the tragedy happened yesterday,

'We still don't know where they lie. They have no gravestone.'

"Are you the woman kneeling in the painting?'

'Yes. Always hoping, always praying the grave will be found. It never has been.'

I thought of Mary Magdalene's distress, when she rushed to the tomb of Jesus after his execution, and the body was no longer there.

Jacek arrived, set a tray on a table and poured coffee into old porcelain cups. He cut a slice of apple cake, laid it on a porcelain plate with a dessert fork and passed it to me with a napkin. We settled down to enjoy the delicacies.

'That painting was the second in a series called *Searching,*"he said.

'A painting from an earlier series called *Overgrown* showed the gateway to Auschwitz, you know, with *Arbeit Macht Frei* inscribed in iron on the top.

'I haven't been to Auschwitz yet.'

'Well, I painted the gate overgrown with bushes. Growth is a process. I was dealing with trauma.'

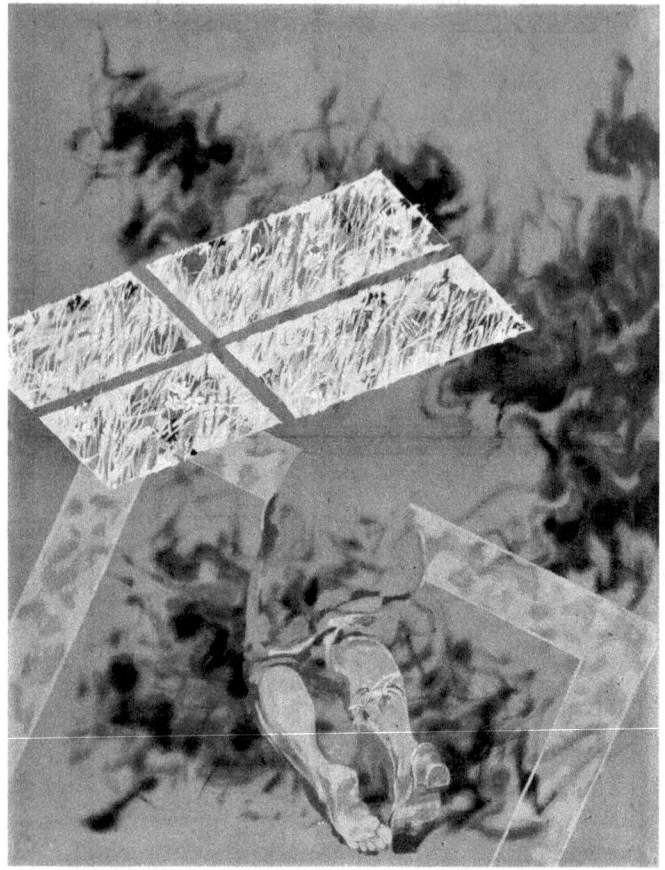

Searching for a Tomb Today IV by **Jacek Waltos**, 1973

'Is that why you painted your grieving mother in green?'

'Yes.'

'And why does she have one shoe on and one shoe off?'

'This refers back to an earlier series, when I used a man stripping off his clothes and shoes as he walks into the sea as a metaphor for despair...for an emotional state of great anxiety.'

'Jacek, why did you paint wheat and flowers through a window at the top half of the painting?'

'This is a projection of reflected light, contrasting with the camouflage which I lightly painted over the rest of the painting.'

'Clarity and subterfuge?' He nodded.

Jacek led me through to his studio/bedroom/sculpture storeroom and showed me a bronze from his series of the Greek tragedy *Phedra,* according to the 17th century French playwright Jean Racine. The cast was one of twelve plaster figures displayed in the Krakow National Museum.

'I explore the problems of human relations in my work,' Jacek explained, 'I try to express the human drama and eschatological dimension that place humans face to face with love and death.' We were silent. I knew only too well what Jacek was trying to explain in his faltering English.

Since the quality of casting in Poland was poor, I volunteered to carry two at a time of these works to London and have them cast by Remo Fiorini.

'Top British sculptors have trusted Remo to cast their work over the past sixty years,' I explained to Jacek. 'Soon after the war Henry Moore sent him pieces and he was followed by Caro, Chadwick, Epstein, Frink…the list goes on.' Jacek was interested.

'Remo's father was born in Rome and served his apprenticeship in the famous Nelli Foundry there. Remo suffered – he was a child during the Depression. He will understand your work.'

'Thank you, Helen, that's a generous offer. Perhaps when all are cast, you might find a dealer interested in them in London.' As I bid farewell to this mother and her son, whose work spoke clearly of the pain of parting, of the flaws in human relationships that bring tragedy, loneliness and loss, I realised how much I still had to learn.

*

I loitered in the Gallery Inny Swiat and bought an etching by Waltos from the same series as his painting in the National Museum. Called *Looking for Grave Space,* the same window had a blank white face. Instead of camouflage, a second woman, unclothed, knelt in supplication beside a crucifix, and patterns of leaves and branches floated in a bottomless space. Maciej Szybist carefully wrapped it with a protecting board before I uttered another 'goodbye'.

I bought some flowers for Maria in the Rynek and staggered back on the tram. Aware this was the last time I would pass this way, I paid attention to the people, the noise and the buildings. The tram trundled noisily through the suburbs, stopping and starting for passengers to quietly get on or off, clutching babies, bags and baskets. The sun tried gallantly to penetrate the clouds, occasionally succeeding to enlighten us with the promise that endurance produces hope.

'Why didn't you take a taxi?' asked Maria when she saw me laden down.

'Because I wanted to remember the tram journey,' I replied.

Maria and I shared our last supper together with a bottle of Beaujolais. She had made borsch, that beetroot soup so beloved by Poles, to which she added sour cream and chopped chives. We felt peaceful sitting at the dining table in what doubled as my bedroom.

'Humanity has become too earthed,' mused Maria as we sipped our soup. 'People tend to look no higher than shop windows, seldom raising their eyes to the sky, to the cosmos.'

'Yet the churches are full of praying women,' I responded.

'Women seem to have more faith than men, perhaps since the birth of Christ. Mary, his mother, developed spiritual perception through her humility and suffering and passed this on through her example.' Maria asked me to stay put while she took the soup bowls into her tiny kitchen and returned with steak, rice and salad.

'Your last supper must be a good one,' she said with a smile as my eyes widened.

Over chocolates and coffee we planned to meet on her next visit to England. She poured out more wine, leaving a glassful in the bottle saying, 'This will help with the tears after you have gone.'

PART III

1986

10

Chernobyl

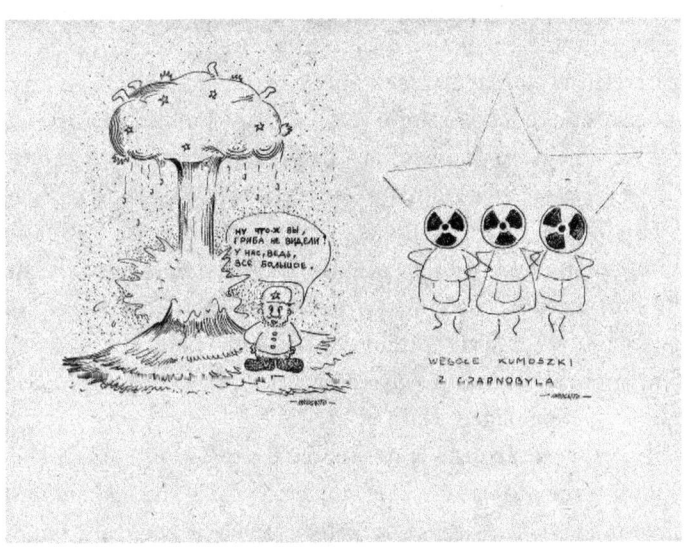

"Well, haven't you ever seen a mushroom? In our country everything is that big" **and**
***The Merry Wives of Chernobyl* (cartoon by one of the Wawel restorers)**

'TO BALANCE THE plane please sit in the front seats', the cabin steward told the few passengers as we climbed aboard the plane in Warsaw. I had already noticed the tyres were as bald as a hairless head. Rising anxiety was crushed as the propellers were turned on and continued to deafen us throughout the forty-minute flight to Krakow. The date was 26th April, 1986.

As we left Krakow airport a kind man, seeing me struggling, carried my heavy suitcase to the bus and paid for my ticket, since I had no small notes. In my haste to change US dollars into zlotys when I arrived earlier in Warsaw, I had accepted 1000 zloty notes in the Kantor, (where one dollar bought 820 zloty in contrast to the official rate of 198). When we reached the Holiday Inn bus stop, outside the old city, the stranger again picked up my case and helped me through the crush of humanity until a porter at the hotel came out and relieved him of his burden. The porter gave me two zlotys to telephone Maria, who had offered to collect me. I bought a bottle of Rioja in the Pewex shop and changed my large note for smaller denominations – a wedge of well-used ones losing value even as I held them – and gave the porter five zlotys.

I settled down on a sofa to wait for Maria. There was plenty to see since this hotel was a favoured spot in Krakow for upmarket prostitutes and black marketers, who mingled around me in a forest of black leather – long legs, short skimpy dresses, faces masked by make-up and seductive smiles, meeting Mafia-type men wearing shiny suits and sunglasses – all in a haze of cigarette smoke.

Maria hurried in, looking rather uncomfortable in this alien environment. Her worried face creased into a smile when she saw me and she stretched out her arms to embrace me. Andrzej, her son-in-law, kissed my hand and took charge of my luggage as we walked out into the street and into Maria's brand new Fiat Uno. The Trabant had finally been replaced. After last year's experience, Maria had invited me to stay until I found suitable accommodation. As we drove through the suburbs to her flat, memories flooded back. How I loved those walks past gardens white with scented lilies-of-the-valley, and the tram rides to the city observing other passengers. When Maria told me bus fares had doubled, I wondered how they managed.

In Maria's flat we drank the wine with cold supper and reminisced about her visit to London some months before. During her stay she had come with me to Clare Priory for a few days. It was the only time I saw her really happy. She had loved the ancient buildings, steeped in history and prayer, the beautiful garden in which to relax and breathe clear air, and wise friars who listened with a loving ear. One morning after Mass, I introduced her to Baroness Ryder of Warsaw, whom I had met a couple of years earlier with Lady Salisbury at Hatfield. This diminutive English woman had worked in the SOE Polish division during the war, and now lived with her husband, Group Captain Leonard Cheshire, in the next-door village of Cavendish. She invited us to visit her at her house which was the headquarters of the Sue Ryder Foundation – one of the original homes that cared for the sick and the disabled. Forty-one permanent residents, ranging from paraplegics to motor-neurone disease sufferers, were cared for here; one of twenty-one homes scattered around Britain. After a cup of tea, Lady Ryder led us to the chapel, where she said she spent twenty minutes every morning before dawn. As she lit a candle this tiny woman, who had achieved so much for her beloved Poles, invited us to pray together. As we left, she gave us words of advice which she, no doubt, lived by:

'Think deeply, speak gently, love much, laugh often, work hard, give freely, pay promptly, pray earnestly, and be kind.'

*

19⁰C heralded spring. I basked in the sun and inhaled the scent of lilies-of-the valley as I waited at the tram stop. The tram I boarded was old, noisy and rusting to pieces, but nevertheless trundled stoically to the centre. I entered the Dominican church during Sunday Mass and squeezed into a pew at the back. The contrast between the sunshine outside and the muted tones inside was stark, like the atmosphere.

After the service, I joined the stream of young people whom this teaching order attracted, and paused on the pavement to look around me before wandering up Grodzka Street towards the Rynek. Krakow looked even more run down than last year and this was epitomised by Countess Potocka, shrunken and old, carrying her rubbish to the bin beside the Sukiennice as I arrived there. The Communist State stole her family estates and filled her palaces with sitting tenants, yet she remained a dignified relic of pre-war freedom. I sat down at a café and ate lody – Polish ice cream is delicious. It was hot, quiet, and peaceful. Everyone looked tired.

*

Maria's family devoured my bananas. After they left, Maria and I waited for the girl who may rent me a flat. She wanted a hundred dollars a week – an extortionate amount – and refused the fifty offered. So I spent another night with Maria, waiting to see what the morrow would bring. I could not impose on her kindness again this year as she looked too tired and fraught and in need of her space. We decided to take an evening walk round the nearby army barracks, an area softened by burgeoning blossom. At the gates a soldier kissed his girlfriend goodbye. This seemed to be the only area of life where discipline was laxer than in England. I woke in the night to find that my throat felt oddly gritty and swallowing was painful. I wondered if I had picked up a germ on the plane.

In the morning I noticed my arms and legs were covered in a rash. Maria left long ago, so I took the tram into town alone. In Planty the chestnut and cherry trees were burgeoning and the grass was green. I walked up the hill to Wawel, filled with quiet joy at the thought of working again with those kind and talented fellow restorers. When I arrived at the studio, I was welcomed with real enthusiasm. The practical gifts I brought them – coloured tights for the women, art catalogues for the men – were gratefully received. No work today. Anna Stolzman was a scientist who worked on the technical side in the conservation studio and she graciously accepted the *National Gallery Technical Bulletins* I had again brought with me.

Anna and I had lunch together and talked about her time in London when she had stayed with me. She had found herself a job during the day to earn some foreign currency, and worked such long hours I hardly saw her. She had not mentioned that she was pregnant. Now her baby Caroline was two months old.

'Anna, I'm looking for somewhere to live. Do you know of anywhere I can rent?' I asked her.

'Would you like my studio? It's not far from here. Come and have a look at it after work.' I gave her a hug. We agreed to meet there and Krystyna offered to escort me.

When we arrived at 34 Ulica Sebastiana, on the edge of Kazimierz, the Jewish district, Anna showed me round and gave me a key. Later I returned to Maria's flat and collected my things. Although Maria said she was sad I was leaving, I sensed her relief.

The studio had a painted wood floor and white walls. There was a loom, and two large chests overflowing with multi-coloured balls of twine, an easel, three cupboards and a sofa that doubled, Polish fashion, as a bed. Two of Anna's tapestries hung on the walls.

'You are the artist,' said Anna, pointing to the one above the bed, where dark green and brown leaves were connected by ropes, 'you can change the shape.'

Under the lightly curtained windows that stretched across one wall was a large rectangular work table. An old tiled stove heated the room. The kitchen area with fridge, kettle and electric ring, and the bathroom, were partitioned off with textured walls that reminded me of the ruffled icing on my Christmas cake. The leaky tin bath was propped up on blocks set on a rubber mat. Anna warned me to be careful not to splash as only the floorboards separated water from the flat below. The loo worked – and there was paper! When I had a bath soon after I moved in, there was just enough hot water to reach the end of the tub by an inch and a half. Afterwards I mopped up the leaks.

Living in Krakow was like living at a large railway station. Soot poured through the window, turning everything black, including my newly hand-washed clothes. (No washing machine here). The fridge shuddering off and on, a sudden short rainstorm, and the itching, played havoc with sleep. I felt increasingly lonely and depressed. What was I doing here?

*

Red flags had been hung on buildings and trams in readiness for May Day. Despite their sinister significance, they added colour to the drabness, and counterbalanced the serried ranks of vivid tulips in Planty. The Rostworowskis had kindly offered their home as my base, and soon after I arrived for supper one evening, Boguś booked a call to London for me, to friends of mine, who were planning to drive to Krakow. It took two hours to get through, which Bogus said was fast. When we were connected, my old friend promised to phone the boys' schools to say all was well with me, find out the result of a meeting between the solicitors, and check all looked quiet at home. I in turn, offered to book them a room at the Francuszki for Sunday and Monday nights. But the tourist season had arrived and I drew a blank at three hotels. Boguś and I finally found a room at the Pod Roza in Ulica Florianska, which turned out to be the nicest hotel of all.

*

After finding a hotel for my friends, Bogus and I had just returned to his house when a friend arrived from Kiev. His red eyes streamed and his chest heaved. He said,

'There has been a terrible disaster at the Chernobyl Nuclear Power Plant. An explosion and fire have released huge quantities of radioactive particles into the atmosphere, a hundred kilometres from Kiev.'

'When did this happen?' Bogus asked as he handed his friend a glass of wine.

'Last Saturday, the 26th April,' he replied, taking a large gulp. 'The effects have spread to Europe. Because of the pollution in Krakow, cancer is likely to be 20% more prevalent here than anywhere else in Poland, even though at 4pm today the radioactive level was normal at 10.2. Sixteen is the danger point. In Stockholm the level is 19 and 25 in Finland. And the fire is still burning'.

As I walked back to Anna's studio, I found myself wondering what could be done when the air and the earth was polluted, deep down to the roots; if pastures and rivers, lakes and forests, animals, birds and fish were contaminated. I thought of the beautiful Wawel tapestries vibrant with health and beauty. I knew I must not think about the possibility of the wind changing and bringing the radioactive contamination here. This invisible danger threatened life, health and freedom, which I had always taken for granted. I pictured Rupert and Simon, friends, family, home, holidays, paintings I had recently restored.

Perhaps Julian of Norwich was right when she said, "all will be well, all manner of things will be well". If she had such hope after the Black Death destroyed three-quarters of the city's inhabitants in the mid-14th century, and aged six, she saw dead bodies "stacked in carts like so much cordwood...[lying] simply where they fell, in the streets", so shall I. Even though with this plague no one really knew what the long-term effects would be. Maria had given me some antihistamine cream which I applied to my arms. They went livid red and still itched. What was this allergy caused by - pollution, radioactivity? I woke up at 3.30am feeling very nervous because, on the first few days after my arrival, lured by the sun, I had been lying in the grass reading. When I eventually climbed out of bed I washed all the clothes I had worn on those days, and my hair, and decided not to expose myself to the sun again. The drier was old; I kept catching my hair in it.

*

In the studio in Wawel, Jan handed me a *Portrait of Napoleon* by Kazimierz Wojniakowski. This young Polish artist was taught portraiture by Marcello Bacciarelli, court painter to King Stanislaus Augustus, in his painting studio at Warsaw Castle, towards the end of the 18th century. Like our King Charles I this Polish monarch's love of art and culture blinded him to the dangers of the opposition.

'When you finish restoring the painting, we can take it back to the Stryszów Manor house where it hangs,' Krystyna said. 'The Manor belongs to Wawel and it's one of very few still in existence. It was used as a barn for storing hay and so forth during the occupation, and has been beautifully restored.'

As I cleaned varnish and scraped off tough old re-touching with a scalpel, the strength and determination of the little Corsican, who rose to rule France, shone from his face. This British enemy was beloved by the Poles for he supported their desire for freedom from Russia. He created the Duchy of Warsaw which gave them some sense of independence.

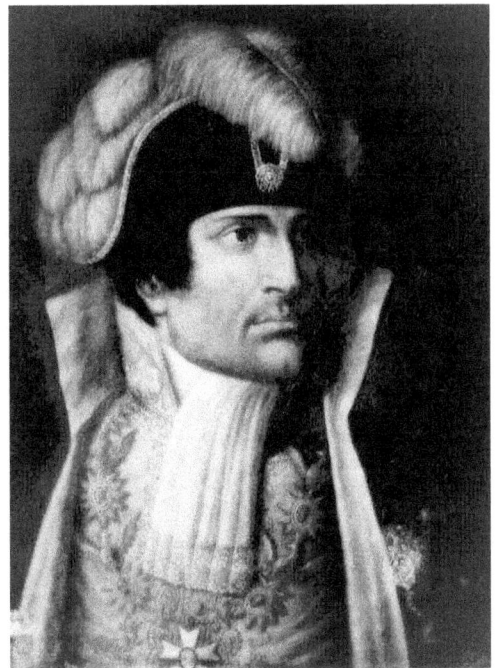

Portrait of Napoleon **by Kazimierz Wojniakowski**

Jan also gave me a 19th century *Rural Scene* by Aleksander Kotsis, who painted portraits and scenes of the countryside, to work on.

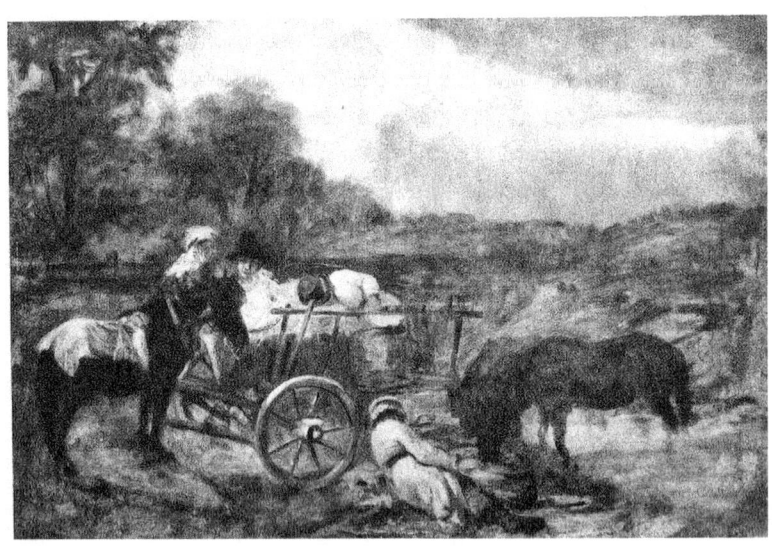

A Rural Scene **by Aleksander Kotsis, 1860's**

First, we had to deal with laying down the paper on which the artist painted, which was lifting from the canvas. We considered various types of adhesives. Out of the array of methods Jan had at his fingertips, he chose to keep to the traditional approach. We applied rabbit glue to the picture, laid on weights, and left the painting to dry. As I absorbed this little scene, untouched by modern technology, something of its quiet reflectiveness soothed me; as if time was in tune with the rhythm of nature, not something to be anxious about.

Later, Jan asked me what I would charge for a 16th century panel he was restoring privately for a Polish-Canadian client. He had cradled the back, running with the grain of the wood, believing this was still the best way to secure cracked and warped panels. We discussed our fees for the x-ray, cradling, restoration, research and chemical analysis and he decided to quote a price somewhere between Polish and London prices.

At 2pm when work for the day was over, I took Krystyna to lunch at an old Hungarian restaurant, which I had discovered on my previous visit. We ate placki, a potato pancake filled with bits of meat and spicy sauce, and drank red wine, before strolling to the Rynek to drink coffee at an outside table of a café. Like many central European cities, the pre-World War I café culture had not died. Five country men in Krakovian folk dress, with peacock feathers in their hats, played and sang charmingly. Two little girls, also in local garb, danced with pigtails flying. They were happy.

Walking home, the floodlit Town Hall tower stood sentinel across the square as I reached the Rynek, where the Sukiennice glowed under a deep blue sky. I paused when a window opened in the tallest tower of St Mary's, and the trumpeter played what seemed like the Last Post, the sonorous sound adding to the general unease. The last flower sellers were packing their stalls. At least their produce gave pleasure without fear of contamination.

Nearby stands the statue of Adam Mickiewicz, the greatest Polish Romantic poet, whose description of a table centrepiece opens my story. He looks out from his lofty plinth towards Siena Street, where the Znak Publishing House is sited. On the steps around the base sit four elegant allegoric groups symbolising Motherland, Science, Courage and Poetry. Destroyed during the war, most of the figures were recovered from a Hamburg scrap metal yard, and the restored monument reappeared in 1955. On Christmas Eve the florists of Krakow decorate the statue of their favourite poet with flowers.

*

I woke in the night to the sound of a child screaming from the flat next door. Voices were raised in anger through the wafer-thin walls. I heard the helpless cry of a woman as the wall shuddered under the thud of a fist. I turned on the light, looked around me, and breathed deeply. How did physical abuse compare with a nuclear disaster? The contrast between private agony and a world catastrophe could not be compared. Or could they? Both violence and radiation were insidious, eating away at inner health.

The Poles have talked for years about living in apocalyptic times, and this was terrifying, tangible evidence. Priorities were heightened while petty problems remained petty; life, health and freedom were precious. An invisible danger was more frightening. The people had still not been told by the authorities about the Chernobyl disaster, and carried on in partial ignorance, tempered by rumour. It resonated. Chernobyl is the Ukrainian name for wormwood, a bitter herb that grew in abundance at the nuclear site. I was reminded of the verse from the *Book of Revelations,*

"A great star fell from heaven, blazing like a torch, and it fell on a third of the rivers and on the fountains of water. The name of the star is Wormwood. A third of the waters became wormwood, and many men died of the water, because it was made bitter." *(Book of Revelations 8:10, 11)*

*

At Wawel, Maria returned my old green Gucci shoes, beautifully re-soled. I gave her the money and a hug, and spend the morning working on the Kotsis. Fortunately, while browsing in a bookshop, I had found a book on the artist and inside there was a black and white photograph of this picture, which showed what the farmer's hat looked like before it was damaged by previous over-cleaning. This was invaluable when it came to replacing what was lost. I found it restful here in this studio, for even though it was exacting work, there was no pressure, and the presence of Mary, Anna, Krystyna and Jan working away beside me was a happy contrast to working alone at home. John, another conservator, brought in a 17th century Turkish sword of steel inlaid with gold which someone had brought to Wawel to sell. We all examined it, then a long discussion took place over second breakfast, when John presented me with a cartoon he had drawn of the three 'Merry Widows' of Chernobyl and the mushroom cloud.

Krystyna and her boyfriend accompanied me to Jama Michalika's café, situated in Florianska Street near the northern walls. We sank into the comfortable green fin-de-siècle padded banquettes, under windows of eccentric stained glass which included bats and cats, spiders, Pegasus, and Art gushing forth pearls from its breast upon the fleeing Faust. Founded in 1895, this was a favourite haunt of artists, who covered the walls with their work, and watched puppet shows. Puppets on sticks not strings, relics from the Green Balloon cabaret, stood silently in glass-fronted cupboards on the walls wearing exquisite costumes and a presence bigger than their two-foot height in the newly restored café. A pianist played as we tucked into coffee and lody.

'What do your friends think of your visits to Poland?' Krystyna asked.

'The Poles think I'm mad because the place is so depressing, and the English think I'm mad because it must be so uncomfortable. I have a more balanced view now that my rose-tinted glasses have gone.' As we discussed the news of the Chernobyl accident, I didn't mention my anxieties. There was nothing I could do with the fear that the wind might change and the fallout come here. Even though I sensed impending doom, I had to get my work done – pictures, articles, research on Wawel for lectures back home. I hoped Ela would come down from Gdansk next weekend.

Krystyna compared the BBC World Service with Polish Radio, which only gave the official line from Tass. Everything Tass said was unreal – the alternative universe. She joked about Russian radio, saying 'this is the beginning of a fairy tale to put children to sleep'.

On my way back to the studio, I bought calcium tablets at an apotecke which Krystyna had advised were good protection against radioactivity. Looking through the glass door of a church I watched five young postulants sitting in pews as still as stone. Their silent prayer comforted me.

*

My friend was on the phone from London as I arrived at Boguś's house. They were not coming. According to The Times, women and children were being evacuated from the British and French Consulates. People had been advised not to fly to Eastern Europe unless it was strictly necessary. The price of grain and sugar were going through the roof. She promised to phone Rupert's housemaster to reassure the boys that I was all right. She also comforted me, saying,

'The Consulate from Krakow sent a statement saying the radioactive level was barely above normal, and less than having an x-ray. It's six times higher in Warsaw. Some say travel agents are stopping flights to Eastern Europe for fear of being sued for causing cancer in ten years' time.' This conspiracy of silence and misinformation by the Russians, who had spurned foreign help, was frightening.

Over supper with the Rostworowskis we listened to the news on Voice of America, (the US radio version of BBC World Service). The accident, we were told, started during a safety test on the nuclear reactor, a type commonly used throughout the Soviet Union, going disastrously wrong. A combination of unstable conditions and reactor design flaws caused an uncontrolled nuclear chain reaction of steam explosion followed by fire that released airborne radioactive contamination, initially into vast swathes of Belarus and the neighbouring countries. But later that night strong winds pushed radioactive fallout further into Western Europe. Within days, higher levels of background radiation were observed in places like Sweden, France, Romania, Switzerland and parts of Britain

In Britain, after heavy rain in April and May drenched higher ground with alarming quantities of radioactive caesium and iodine, the British government banned the sale of sheep across thousands of farms. By June, almost 9000 British farmers were affected. Livestock had to be scanned by government officials before they were allowed to enter the food chain. The last restrictions on the movement and sale of sheep were only lifted in 2012 – 26 years after meltdown.

*

'If you go back to England now', Maria said gently, when I saw her at Wawel the next day, 'you will despise yourself. The West now knows how immoral the Russian government is, prepared to murder millions of people by keeping quiet about the disaster. Children will drink milk and be affected.' She frowned, 'and there is a dire shortage of powdered milk. Eat no fresh vegetables or eggs, drink no milk, boil your water. The earth is polluted and the Polish export of agricultural goods will be affected, worsening the economy even further. The earth will be dangerous for years, if not decades.'

I found working on the little Kotsis painting a comfort. Life has always been hard for the Poles, yet their belief in a loving God has lifted them above bitterness; has certainly strengthened and sustained those I have come across. They would survive this latest disaster. Whenever I felt frightened I remembered Julian of Norwich's conviction that "all will be well".

Since bottled water was becoming increasingly scarce, I went on the hunt for wine, determined to buy local rather than wasting my dollars at the Pewex. The shop where I had seen wine for sale was shut, so I walked round the corner into a courtyard where I found another selling a variety of Yugoslavian red and white wines. There was no one else here, unlike the main grocer in Rynek

– the Fortnums of Krakow – where a serpentine queue had developed. I felt triumphant: a foreigner beating the queue.

I walked sadly into the Pod Roza Hotel and cancelled my friends' booking. I discovered in the loo that if I paid the old attendant five zlotys, she would give me a ration of soft paper to use in a super clean loo, and soap to wash in the basin. No towel though. I walked to the big post office where I queued for stamps to cover postcards and express letters. Even these were slow. Letters were a better way to communicate in any detail than the telephone.

At the Rostworowskis, Chris had news. Russians had been evacuated up to 30 km from the reactor, even though the clouds were beginning to recede. Kiev was supplied by the water from this region. Even though it shouldn't be, the level of radiation in Krakow was now higher than in Warsaw, perhaps due to the chronic pollution, according to environmental experts who had flown in from the USA. The International Atomic Agency was seeking an agreement for instant information, worldwide, as work continued to decontaminate the reactor. Party members in Poland were informed about the disaster early on, to enable them to protect themselves. The Wednesday and Saturday readings were very high, when the wind came from the east. Radiation no longer pervaded the air; it was in the ground to the depth of a metre. Militia men advised mothers to keep their children inside. According to the BBC, Austria had barred the sale of fresh vegetables, Yugoslavia had withdrawn vegetables and milk, Germany had banned any vegetable grown outside.

I took the Rostworowskis to dinner at Wierzynek, the oldest restaurant in Krakow, named after Mikolaj Wierzynek, a wealthy merchant and councillor of Krakow. He offered to host the wedding reception for Elizabeth, granddaughter of King Kazimierz the Great, to the Emperor Charles in 1364. The feasting continued for twenty days. We ate a lavish meal: celery soup, wild boar steak with spinach and mushrooms, ice cream and good Yugoslavian wine. All killed and picked before the explosion, the waiter assured us. Good food and wine kept up the spirits.

*

At the U.S. Consulate I managed to see the Consul, Charles L. Glatz Jr., a helpful young man. He sat me down and reassured me that the second reactor was not going to blow up. It was unlikely that an Alpha cloud would come to Krakow. He also reassured me that the radiation was barely above normal and confirmed the ions decreased by 50% every eight days.

He said, 'The Chernobyl disaster was late on Saturday, the 26ᵗʰ April'.

Then, realising my ignorance, he tried to explain in simple language what the science counsellor at the U.S. Embassy in Warsaw, J. Loferski, had noted. Seeing my difficulties –science is a foreign country –he stopped, poured us each a cup of delicious coffee, took a sip and told me that the units were such that if we find ourselves in a radiation environment where the exposure rate is one roentgen per hour, the absorbed dose rate will be about one REM per hour. Background radiation is about 0.130 REM a year. Safe exposure for radiation workers is five REM a year, or 30 times higher than the recommended limit level for the population of the world as a whole. Because of the amount of cobalt, iodine and cerium in the fallout, he said,

'Don't drink any milk because strontium is a 'bone seeker', wash all vegetables carefully, and wash yourself, your hair, clothes and soles of your shoes frequently.'

He invited me to watch the ABC news if I wished, to read the newspapers and magazines in the library, and suggested I register at 65 Grodzka Street. I didn't. I thanked him and left wondering how anxious his family back home must be.

At Wawel, having listening to the BBC with Boguś and Chris, I passed on the news to the other restorers. The fire at the reactor was out and the ground had not melted. Three weeks after the Chernobyl disaster, the Polish newspapers proclaimed it was now all right to drink the milk. They conveniently forgot they had never told us at the start, that it was dangerous.

11

Sightseeing

WHEN GOODS ARRIVED in a shop, queues swiftly formed. The wait was worth the effort, for if you didn't buy something as soon as it became available, you may have had a long wait before it appeared again and at a higher price. The joy of success was illustrated one day while I sat on a bench in Planty. An old man walked slowly by leading a small dachshund; loo-paper rolls stretched the length of the lead, from collar to hand. I remembered stockpiling in London during the strike-ridden years in the 1970s, when the rate of inflation reached over 25% due to rising oil prices and wages; coupled with the anxiety I felt as groceries kept costing more, while my housekeeping money stayed the same.

Passing through Florian's Gate, I stopped at the little altar to say a prayer, before continuing into Florianska street. The gypsy band was playing. The old violinist looked smaller and even more crippled than last year. He played with such passion and virtuosity, that the music reached deep down into the well of my soul as I looked into his dark, sad face, wise with experience.

*

I walked through the city, beyond the rocky escarpment on which Wawel rises, to the tow path beside the Vistula. For as long as people remember, the Vistula has been called the queen of rivers, for it was the sphere of power for the monarchs who once united all these lands under their sovereignty, and built their castles along its banks. The river was the main waterway transport from its source in the Carpathians in south-west of Poland, through the whole land mass to the

Baltic Sea; it also saw conflict and division, when areas through which it flowed were divided up between the partitioning powers.

A boat was about to leave for Bielany. This is where the zoological garden is located, so I went with it. The sun shone as Wawel receded, and disappeared as the river curved away. The boat passed Salvatore where cousins of Boguś lived, then trees slid by and the countryside began. Oxford with its green, unspoiled banks came to mind. After forty minutes the boat nudged up to its landing place and the passengers alighted.

The path disappearing up the hill initially seemed perpendicular but grew friendlier to the legs as I continued through a silver birch and beech wood. With their outstretched branches and rustling leaves, the trees seemed to lift me up to the white towers of the Camaldolese Monastery looming above them. This hermit order was introduced to Poland in 1603, by Mikolai Wolski, Grand Marshal of the Crown. Away from the hubbub of daily life, these wooded hills provided the peace where the monks, who still subject themselves to the severe rules of their order, live simple, secluded days, close to God. Each monk has his own individual hermitage, joining others only for Mass and prayers in the church. Polish kings visited the monastery during times of danger. Jan III Sobieski prayed here before setting off to relieve Vienna from the Ottoman siege in 1683.

The forty two acres below the monastery have been home to the Krakow zoological garden since the 1920s. I smiled as I remembered being told that in 1406 a pair of lions were sent from Florence to Krakow, to join the royal menagerie on the Wawel Hill. This flourished until the end of the 16th century when, to position it closer to the centre of the Commonwealth, King Sigismund III Vasa, moved the Court and Parliament to Warsaw Castle. The elephants looked more comfortable among the greenery than those in Regent's Park. I wandered around, careless as a child about time or schedule, smiling at a herd of pigmy hippopotamus, watching a couple of Przewalski horses dozing in the sunshine, and eventually walked down from the seemingly unpolluted air, back to the boat. Just as the captain cast off, a family of four arrived at the jetty. He went back for them.

*

I woke up hungry. There were problems with liquid in this heat. Tap water, like milk, was polluted. The shops selling mineral water were constantly filled with people and then empty of water. Fruit juice was sometimes available in Pewek.

So it was down to sickly Sok, or Pepsi if you were lucky, and wine. This was the hottest day so far.

After breakfast, I walked to the Sukiennice and climbed up the circular stone staircase with its pretty balustrade to the National Museum on the first floor to look at the Polish paintings. In the heat, *Thunderstorm*, by Jozef Chelmonski was a cooling contrast, while evoking the current unseen threat. Barefoot boys endeavour to escape the worst buffeting of the wind and the rain as the cows they are tending gallop away in terror. Like his contemporaries who lived through the 1863 Insurrection, Chelmonski recreated those dark days in romantic metaphor.

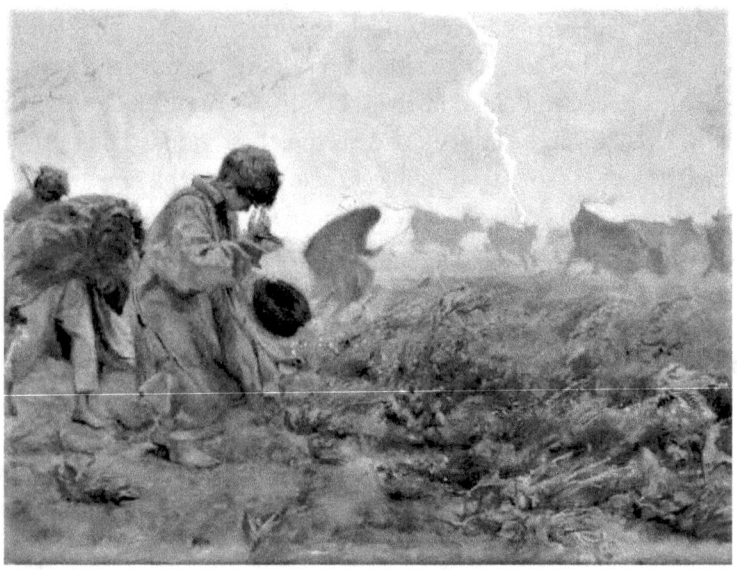

Thunderstorm **by Jozef Chelmonski, 1896**

Like Gierymski and other avant garde young Polish artists, Chelmonski studied in Munich – the epicentre of the art world in the mid-19th century – and then spent ten years in Paris where his spirited views of Polish and Ukrainian villages and wide canvasses of three-in-hands galloping towards the viewer found eager buyers. He returned to Warsaw and settled on his small estate, where he farmed and painted pictures that reflected his love of nature, mainly landscapes with bird or animal motifs that evoked nostalgia.

Several little oils by Kotsis hung in the same large gallery. Kotsis used a dark palette in his portraits and scenes of rural life, often painting on paper which he laid on canvas, like the small picture I was restoring. In *The Evening Prayer of a Farmer* a young man with arms crossed stood immobile, silhouetted against a dusky sky where sunlight was squeezed out between heavy clouds. He has dropped his plough, left his horses to graze in the distance and looks across the valley to a church on a hill.

*

Having seen gobelins (tapestries) and kelims (rugs) exhibited at the Polish Cultural Institute in Portland Place, I was keen to visit the Wanda Workshop, the only place in Krakow where they were made and marketed. Krystyna came as my translator. We were assaulted by the clackety-clack of the huge looms as we entered. The interior was badly in need of re-decorating; paint was a rare commodity in Poland. The director gave us coffee and introduced us to the Manager who had been working there for thirty-three years. As this was the fortieth anniversary of Wanda, there would be a jubilee party later and an exhibition next May. The lady in charge of the tapestries section had been there thirty-five years. This loyalty was reflected on the faces of the workers; they seemed committed to their craft.

In the office where the women brought their work, and were paid monthly according to production, we saw two kelims ordered for clients in Denmark. One of the two designers, Emilia Marchut, had also worked here thirty years. She had just delivered her designs to the committee who decided which should go into production and how many should be made. Emilia led us to a huge room filled with looms with a passage down the middle. Ten women wove gobelins here. One had worked for twenty years on *Playing Cards,* ordered by a French client. This was designed by Helena Golkowska, who, with her husband, founded Wanda. The design, water colour on paper glued to canvas, was rolled like a scroll and hung up with a working drawing beside. Colours matched exactly. Each weaver finished up to one square metre a month. Two small kelims were being worked on next door, but many weavers worked at home. I now realised the immense work and skill that went into creating them.

When I asked if I could buy a kelim, Emilia gave us a book of designs to look at and I chose one by Danuto Michno, whose work I had most admired in London. There were deer, birds and trees. Emilia took me to the storeroom which was an Aladdin's Cave of colour. Shelves lined the walls, filled with natural wools spun and dyed here: mauves deepened to purple, blues to turquoise, oranges turning red then brown. Emilia helped me chose the colours, with the right tonal values and contrasts. It would take a month to make.

*

I met up with Jaznusz, and Dorota his colleague, at the Czartoryski Museum. It was good to see these old friends, and to chat in their cosy, cluttered office over a cup of coffee. They wanted to hear all about my visit to Knole Park in Kent, the home of the Sackville-West family, which I had visited on their behalf. I was there to look at the Sackville-West copy of the lost Czartoryski portrait by Raphael. The historic house was gifted to the National Trust after the war, but the private apartments were leased back to the family. Mr and Mrs Sackville-West were delightful hosts. They lit up the portrait for me to examine and photograph, and then we settled down in their picture-lined sitting room to discuss it over a cup of coffee. Their copy was earlier and of better quality than I had expected, but it had been insensitively restored some thirty years ago and I wished I could have a go at it. They told me the picture was bought by the third Duke of Dorset in Rome in 1770 for £50 – only 28 years before Prince Adam Czartoryski bought the original for his mother's collection. The Knole copy emphasised the quality of the original, with its three-dimensional animation and beauty. I felt useful when I reported back to Janusz. It was a small return for the generosity he had showered on me, and he was very grateful.

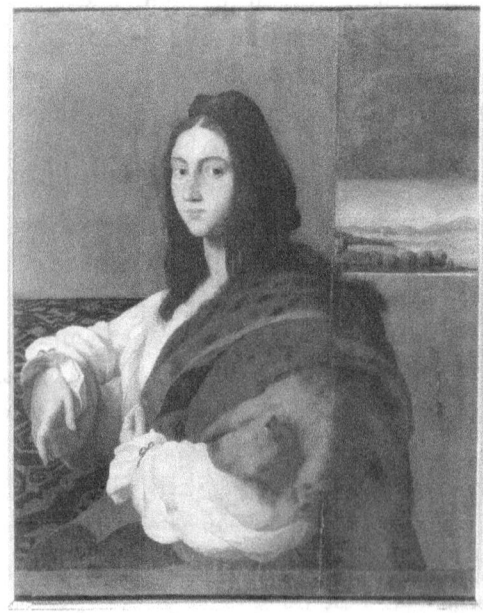

Copy of *Raphael Portrait* at Knole Park

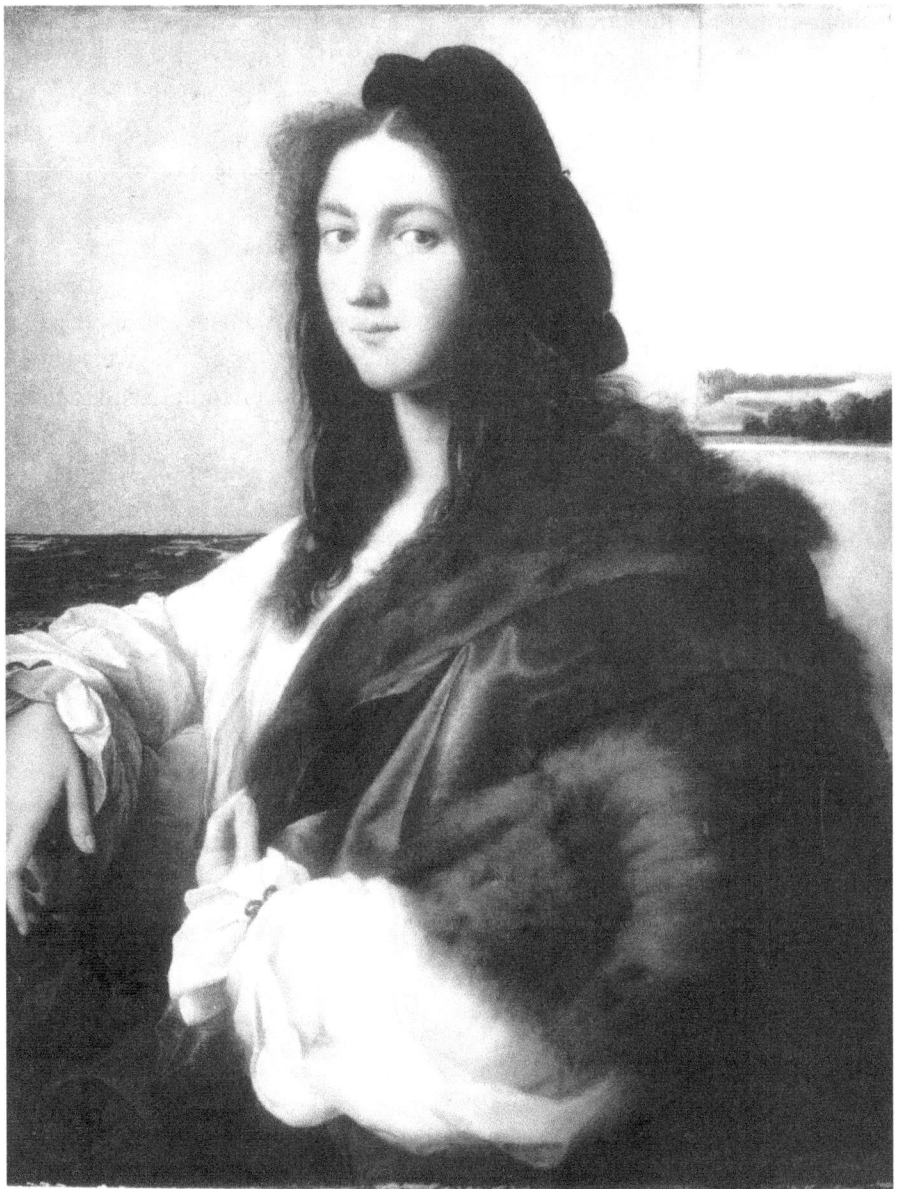

Portrait of a Young Man **by Raphael, 1514**

During the summer of 1937 the art dealer Joseph Duveen sent a representative from his art gallery in Washington to Krakow, to try and persuade Prince Adam Czartoryski to sell the *Portrait of a Young Man* by Raphael and the Leonardo *Lady with an Ermine*. The Prince was asked to name a price, but he refused to part with either painting. In the summer of 1939 with war imminent, the most valuable items in the family collection were removed from the museum in Krakow to the family estate at Sieniawa, and walled up in underground vaults, just as they had been sent for safety by Izabela during the 1830 uprising. Unfortunately the Nazis knew exactly where they were, and the collection was brought back to Krakow and housed in the Jagellonian University library.

Hans Frank, Governor-General during the occupation of Poland, took six paintings including the Leonardo, Raphael and Rembrandt and hung them in his apartments at Wawel. The Raphael was his favourite and he probably carried it with him on visits to his other official residence. As the Soviet Army closed in from the East, Frank retreated to his villa in Fischhausen am Schliersee, in Bavaria, taking his old master paintings with him. At some stage on the journey, in December, 1944, the pictures were held at Schloss Muhrau in Silesia, the home of Herta von Weitersheim-Kramsta. Her daughter, Melitta Sallai, remembers being woken one night and taken downstairs in her night clothes. Her mother shone a flashlight on two paintings: the Raphael, and the Leonardo, saying "something equally beautiful may never be seen again". Frank was arrested by the Americans in May 1945, and subsequently hanged at Nuremberg. Shortly after the end of the war, Prince Adam's son-in-law Count Stefan Zamoyski was in Paris to join the Polish forces. He was approached by a Duveen agent, who repeated the pre-war offer to buy the paintings. He was again refused, for the family did not know where the paintings were. In May 1946 stolen art works were recovered and brought to Wawel Castle which was being used as a depository for reclaimed Nazi loot. Among them was Leonardo's *Lady with an Ermine.* The Raphael has never been found.

*

It rained all night and all day. Ela arrived from Gdansk at 6am and we fried eggs for breakfast, before I left her at 8am to work on the Kotsis, which was going into an exhibition of Polish 19th and 20th century paintings in two months' time. Professor Director Szablowski summoned me. He was delighted with the Reynolds exhibition catalogue I brought and with the piece I had written about Wawel for *Arts Review*. I told him I had just begun lecturing on Wawel Castle to art groups all round England and that I planned next year to bring a party of English people to see the art and architecture of Krakow and Warsaw. The professor promised to invite me as a guest of Wawel any time I needed to be there for restoration or research. The wiring was being renewed next year and the restoration studio would be closed.

Maria introduced me to the keeper of paintings, Stasia Koszak, who showed me the latest acquisitions in the store room: a Frans Frankel panel, a Wozniakowski portrait, and a couple more portraits. When Ela arrived, diminutive Krystyna Malcharek, Head of the Education Dept and expert translator, took us round parts of the Royal living quarters on the first floor that I had not seen before. There were four 17th century carpets, made at the Potocki factory in Brody, and a Bosch triptych in the Alchemia Room, Sigismund I's favourite room, which later Sigismund Vasa used as an alchemic workshop. The silk carpets were stunning. Krystyna Malcharek volunteered to be our guide if I brought groups here. It was good to see the tapestries again, to clarify how and where they hung. Art, craft, botany, religion and history were all woven into these magnificent 16th century masterpieces.

Krystyna took me to meet the Director of the Krakow Historical Museum in Rynek as I needed official permission to take photographs in the Jewish museum in Kazimierz. His beautiful office, heavy with Biedermeier furniture and a Gdansk cupboard overlooked the Sukiennice.

After hastily consuming soup, pasta and carrots in the Wawel canteen, Ela and I walked to Kazimierz in the pouring rain. A permanent exhibition devoted to the history and culture of the Jews was organised in 1980 by the Krakow Historical Museum. The only exhibition of its kind in Poland, it was displayed in the 16th century Old Synagogue, which the museum had rented from the community for a peppercorn rent. Mr Duda, the curator, filled us in on the past six hundred years of history over the course of nearly three hours, as we got steadily colder in our wet clothes.

The synagogue had been left silent and deserted for forty years. Yet despite the newly white-washed walls and vaulted ceilings, a dignified atmosphere prevailed. Artefacts connected with religious rituals, festivals and customs, well used for centuries, lay under glass. Upstairs, paintings in the museum revealed life a century ago when everything was shut on Friday evenings and silence reigned. Passers-by would see candles burning through many windows, flickering in the darkness as Jews walked to the synagogues. Paintings illustrate what was; rabbinical vestments what could still be. In another room Jewish martyrdom during World War II was presented.

Later Janusz and Dorota from the Czartoryski guided us round Kaziermierz. It was terribly poor. All the Star of David signs had been removed from the houses. A lozenge shaped scar on the right side of a door frame was all that remained of a mezuzah: a wooden case affixed to the door post containing a verse from the Torah on parchment. The disintegrating interior of a house in Isaac Street conjured up living conditions during 'the last days' and rough wooden beams just managed to prop up a weary staircase. As we walked through the silent courtyards with iron balustraded balconies, I thought of Isaac Bashevis Singer. The Jewish writer grew up in Warsaw, and although he moved to America in 1935, he continued to write in Yiddish. He claimed that although the Jews of Poland had died "something – call it spirit or whatever – is still somewhere in the universe. This is a mystical kind of feeling, but I feel there is truth in it." (From an interview with *Encounter* in February, 1979). Now it was mournfully quiet – a ghost town. Old women sat on balconies or peered out of windows of buildings that should have been condemned years ago.

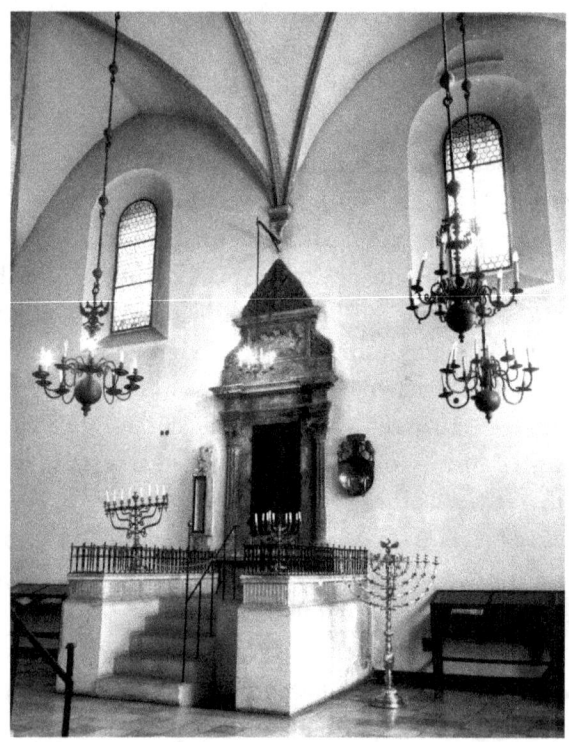

Prayer Hall in Old Synagogue Museum (photo by S.Michta)

In the market square, there was little for sale – potatoes, root vegetables, eggs, a few scrawny chickens. Meat was of course rationed. Old women sat by their drab stalls drinking milk and chewing crusts of bread. All around, creased, suffering faces told their own tale. A stench of decay reached my nose; I felt sick at heart.

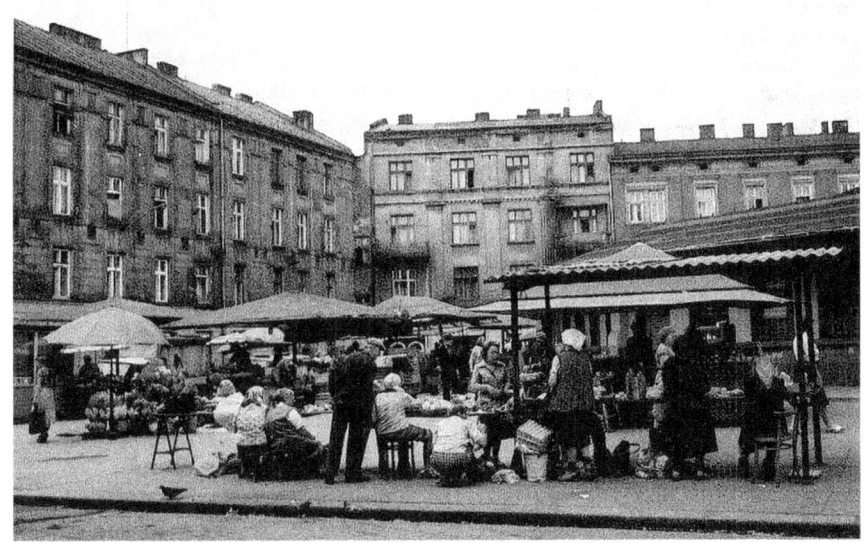

Market Square in Kazimierz (photo S.Michta)

*

At the Remu synagogue in Kazimierz next morning, Ela and I watched the Shabbat service. There were about twenty men present and a woman whom, we later discovered, was visiting from Israel. The last two cantors died last year, and there was no one left who knew the ritual. One man led the prayers. The wavering voices were interspersed with whispered mutterings behind the prayer shawls over what to pray next. The synagogue was built in 1553 for his family by Israel Isserles, father of the famous Moshe. It was still a family place – the family of remnants, those few left over from pre-war days.

After the service, we trooped outside into the hall, where a table was laid for Shabbat breakfast. Plates of rolls, cake and tinned meat had been placed neatly on the oblong table in the outer hall. About fifteen people turn up for this weekly service. They were a motley group: a rough labourer, a petty merchant with trilby, a bearded intellectual with woolly hat, older gentlemen with well-cut suits, others wearing Shabbat shawls and skull caps, with an average age of seventy. The atmosphere was respectful but relaxed, and they chatted to each other as if to confirm who did what when. They prayed on alternate Saturdays, either here at the Remu or at the 19th century Temple synagogue – the only two that belonged to the community. If they stopped using one it would be closed by the authorities. These old men seemed out of place and time, like endangered species

155

that had somehow survived. They accepted their lot with resignation, a shrug of the shoulders, or a lop-sided, wise smile.

'Every year there are fewer of us,' an old survivor of Auschwitz sighed. 'There is no future here for Jews. Kazimierz is a dead district now. But still our memories live. Every stone is a reminder.' Remu synagogue and its cemetery were, like Wawel, listed in the top grade of buildings of historical and architectural importance.

'The Jews may go, but Kazimierz will stay,' I was told firmly by eighty-three-year-old Romuald Spira, a direct descendant of the famous Krakow cabalist Natan Nat Spira, who died in 1633. Romuald stayed in Krakow after the war because of his Polish wife. Other synagogues had taken on new roles in Gentile life – as State craft workshops like Cepelia, cultural centres, even a co-operative factory making slippers, we were told by Czeslaw Jakubowicz, president of the Congregation of Moses Believers in Krakow, who showed us round the jaded ghetto later. As this gentle, modest man pointed out the various buildings, he seemed to see them as they were before the war, when Krakow was a beautiful little architectural gem set among green hills: unpolluted, filled with intellectuals and artists. He still seemed to hear the noise, the bustle, the laughter among the courtyards and balustraded balconies, the marketplace and ladies' bath house. A quarter of the Krakow population was Jewish then and Kazimierz had 304 prayer houses, schools, theatres, and cabarets. The marketplace resembled an Oriental bazaar full of people and noise. On Friday evenings everything was shut and silent.

A change in government policy, strengthened by a meeting between Pope John Paul II and the Chief Rabbi of Rome, had generated new interest in Jewish culture in Poland. Intellectuals in Krakow were determined to preserve the bonds and traditions of Kazimierz, where Jews were granted the freedom of worship, trade and travel by Bolesław the Pious in 1264 and flourished under King Kazimierz the Great in the 14th. It was the greatest and last Jewish community in Poland, and unlike Warsaw and Lublin, was not razed to the ground. Of the 500 mainly assimilated Jews living in Krakow, the intellectuals still predominated. Among them was the artist Jonasz Stern, who miraculously escaped death by firing squad in 1943. He is famous for his collage compositions in which feathers, fish skeletons and animal bones describe death, destruction and disintegration. Stern founded the famous Krakow Group of abstract painting after the war when Social Realism was the order of the day. Later, Krystyna, Stas and I walked to Kazimierz. On this cloudless May evening as Stas photographed Remu cemetery the sun began to set, shining light on to the grave stones, sharpening the contrast in the carvings.

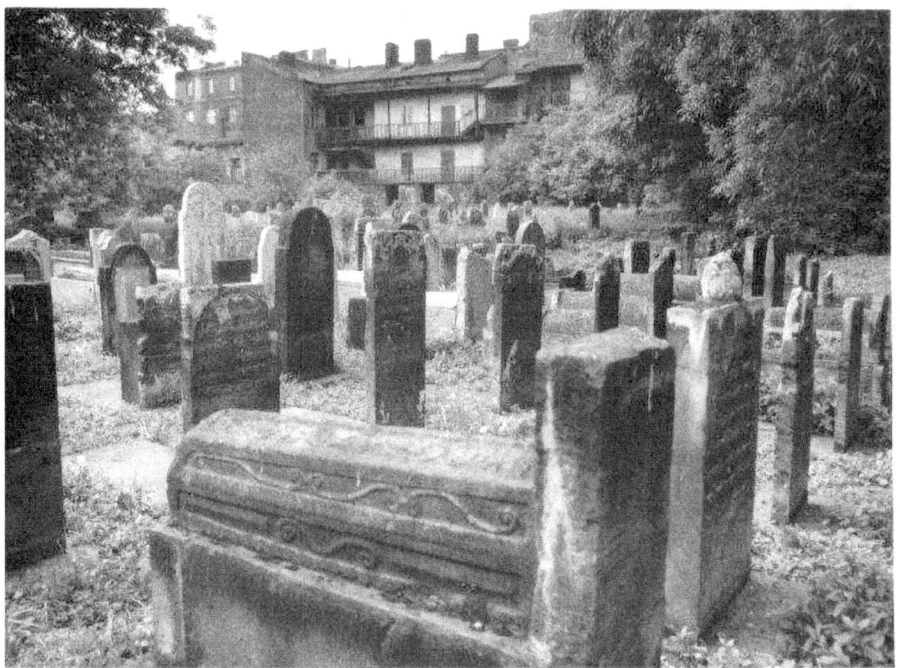

Remu Cemetery with tenement houses in Ul. Miodowa (photo by S. Michta)

*

Ela and I strolled through Rynek towards Florianska Street for the private view of an exhibition of Henryk Waniek's paintings in the small private gallery Inny Swiat. I wanted to meet Henryk, having seen two of his paintings a month before at the Polish Cultural Institute in London, where I reviewed an exhibition called 'The Emotional and the Rational'. His paintings had stood out. They were mystical – a mixture of cabalistic and Manichean philosophy in a theatrical setting, sometimes surreal. Henryk, I discovered was a writer and philosopher as well as an artist, and his mind wandered far and wide as we talked. I gave him a copy of my review and he invited me to visit his studio in Warsaw, which I did the next time I was there.

Henryk took part in Professor Bogucki's 1983 exhibition 'Sign of the Cross' and described it to us as 'Open Sky under Everybody'; the second exhibition 'Apocalypse' as 'Darkness in Darkness'. Back in the studio Ela translated the catalogue before we fell asleep.

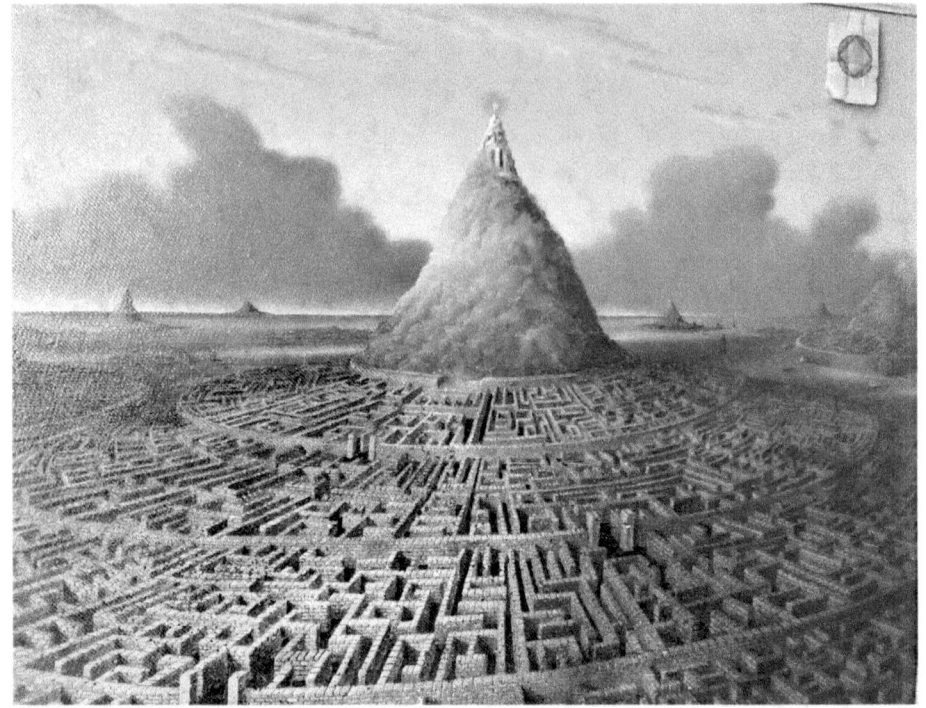

Labyrinth by Henryk Waniek

*

The young restorer Grzegorz was the son of Anna Kostecka, who worked in the Wawel studio, and gave a party for me last year. He arrived with his girl friend and drove Krystyna, Ela and I to Pieskowa Skala. This was one of twenty-five castellan castles on the ancient Eagle's Nest route from Krakow to Czestochowa, of which only three remain. The journey took us through dandelion-dotted meadows, woodlands and strangely clumped limestone rocks reminiscent of some 16th century Flemish landscape.

The six hundred-year-old castle was a mini version of Wawel and there was still a sense of it being a gentleman's home, thanks to the Krupinskis who had looked after it for eighteen years. Jadwiga Krupinska showed us round. She looked like a typical stately home-owner with her pearls and twin-set. We leaned out of the loggia to look at the Italian Renaissance garden, wandered round the library which housed thousands of books in beautifully made new cases, examined precious manuscripts which Jadwiga pulled out of drawers, including four volumes of *Phytanthoz Iconography of Plants*, printed in Augsburg in 1738 with 1025 pictures hand-painted in the manner of Audubon.

The museum was laid out on two floors in a reconstructed part of the castle and represented all branches of the arts from early Gothic to Biedermeier. We wandered from room to room admiring beautiful Polish carved Madonnas, a Tournai tapestry, an English Jacobean bed and Italian furniture. Upstairs, French, Dutch and Mannerist furniture and paintings were superseded by an Empire bed and Biedermeier drawing room furniture for the middle classes. Our final treat was a glimpse in the Sarmatian Room, which reflected the time of Polish magnate mania after King Jan Sobieski's victory over the Turks at the Battle of Vienna in 1683. The nobility liked to believe they were descended from the ancient Persian Sarmatians, the legendary invaders of Slavic lands in antiquity.

Lunch in the restaurant was memorable. Even before we sipped the Russian champagne a party atmosphere prevailed. Boiled trout freshly fished from the river followed borsch, then lemon mousse and cake. Replete, we were ready to walk in the Ojcowski National Park; a short car ride from the castle. We peered into Ladislaus the Short's cave. According to legend, the king was protected in the 14th century from the invading Czechs by a spider spinning a web over the entrance. We admired two massive limestone rocks with a gap between them, before driving back to Krakow. Ela and I were in time for Mass in St Mary's, before a Bach cantata accompanied the closing of the great doors carved by Veit Stoss. She took a train back to Gdansk after supper, after a happy weekend together.

*

The sun shone on old men playing chess in Planty. Life moved slowly here. There was time to talk, time to be. When I got back to no 34, the stairs were thick with scraped off paint. Builders had been working since early morning uncovering the original ceiling under the yellow wash. Stencilled flowers and borders were peeping out from the walls. How charming this house must have been before the war. Over the weeks I sent over fifty postcards to family and friends and posted twenty second hand art books to myself, as they were too heavy to pack.

*

At Wawel it was too dark to retouch, so I was taken round the gilding and framing department. Models of Renaissance painted Italian, black Dutch 17th century, and

French gilt Empire hung on the walls. Stasia and John had renovated a painted wooden chandelier with swans arching their necks out to hold candle sprockets, and an Austrian standing lamp, both of the Empire period. They applied ten layers of whitening and fish glue mixture before gilding to achieve a thick, solid base.

As it was a horrid day and the museums were shut, I decided to buy my train ticket to Warsaw. I queued for half an hour. It would have taken longer, but Jacek Waltos was also waiting and as he got to the desk first, he bought my ticket. I've always had guardian angels in the Orbis office where only Polish is spoken – last year Krystyna helped me, and in 1984, Teresa Rostworowska.

I dressed up for the first time as the Rostworowskis had invited me to a dinner party. On the way I stopped to buy three roses for Chris in the Rynek as the bugler played. Around me everyone stopped to listen. Time melted into past and present, becoming one. The haunting sound drew me into a different, inner world.

It was good to relax with a whisky and soda in the vaulted salon with fine paintings on the walls and antique furniture, lit by candlelight from an 18th century Berlin seven-branched candelabra. The party was made up of USA Cultural Attaché John Brown and his wife Connie, Bill Brand, an American translator and teacher and his Polish wife Kasha, who loved books by C.S. Lewis and Tolkien. Chris fed us coq au vin washed down with Italian wine they brought back last year, apple pie and ice cream. It was a feast of all the senses. Bogus walked me home at midnight.

One weekend Bogus drove us to Lanckorona, to his country cottage made of wood which had not been modernised since the war, though he had added a wing. The roof sloped sharply to enable snow to slide off quickly. A window in my room looked out on Kalwaria. This pilgrimage site, the second most important in Poland after Częstochowa, was established in 1600 as a substitute for Jerusalem which was lost to Muslim Turks and no longer accessible. Thousands came every Good Friday to watch the Passion play which unfolded across the ten kilometre site where chapels of various shapes and sizes lay scattered over the slopes of Zar Mountain. After a morning sitting in the garden reading last week's *Sunday Times* from cover to cover, we walked to some of these Stations of the Cross. Pope John Paul II was born nearby in Wadowice, near this UNESCO World Heritage Site, and considered it a place of special grace.

We left the clean air for Krakow after supper. There was little traffic on the road back surely one of the perks of petrol rationing. Smog hung like a pall of death over the city as we drew close. On the way back I watched trails of black smoke spiral up into the sky.

'It's burning tyres,' explained Chris, 'some pagan rite. My sister commented on the paganism in the country when she first came out here.'

*

Stas drove Krystyna and me to the Wieliczka Salt Mines in his little Fiat. He told us the police had questioned him while he was taking more pictures for me in Kazimierz. The road went east, past a big chemical factory, past allotments with their sprinkling of wooden huts, past the children's hospital built with US dollars a decade ago, past apple orchards, cows grazing in meadows, and peasants tilling the soil. Sturdy chestnut horses hauled long narrow wooden carts filled with coal as trucks pounded the cracked and pitted tarmac of the E22. Wieliczka began where Krakow ended.

Our guide was a geologist, also called Krystyna. She led us down 394 wooden steps to the first level (built in 1638).This is the only salt mine in the world that has been consistently worked since the Middle Ages. Despite being placed on UNESCO's World Cultural Heritage site in 1978, there were still problems with keeping the place stable. We walked down another 400 steps. The shafts were propped up with pine. When the local supply ran short, the Carpathian mountain people brought wood via the Vistula in return for salt. Galleries, incline drifts, exploration chambers, lakes and shafts extended for 178 miles on nine levels to a depth of 1,073 feet. The tourist route took us along gloomy tunnels, through endless wooden doors, into huge galleries or small grottos, down more steps until we seemed to be in the bowels of the earth, impregnated with salt. It was very cold. Tolkien's dwarfs seemed to inhabit the place, digging away unseen by the upper world, producing the magnificent chapels as tangible evidence of faith.

Deep in the mine, the Kinga chapel had been hollowed out of the salt, at the end of the 19th century. It had taken twenty years to create. Masses were still held here. On the main altar, the figure of the 13th century Queen Kinga of Poland, who, according to legend, discovered the salt mine, was encrusted with crystals from the Crystal Grotto, which also supplied the crystal for the chandeliers. According to old laws, all valuable minerals underground belonged to the king, and a large part of their income came from the salt dug by hand until gunpowder was introduced in the 18th century. Oblivious to the miner's toil, socialites rowed boats in the romantic but murky lakes. Ferry rides, fireworks and music from the salt works orchestra were all abandoned when seven Austrian soldiers drowned.

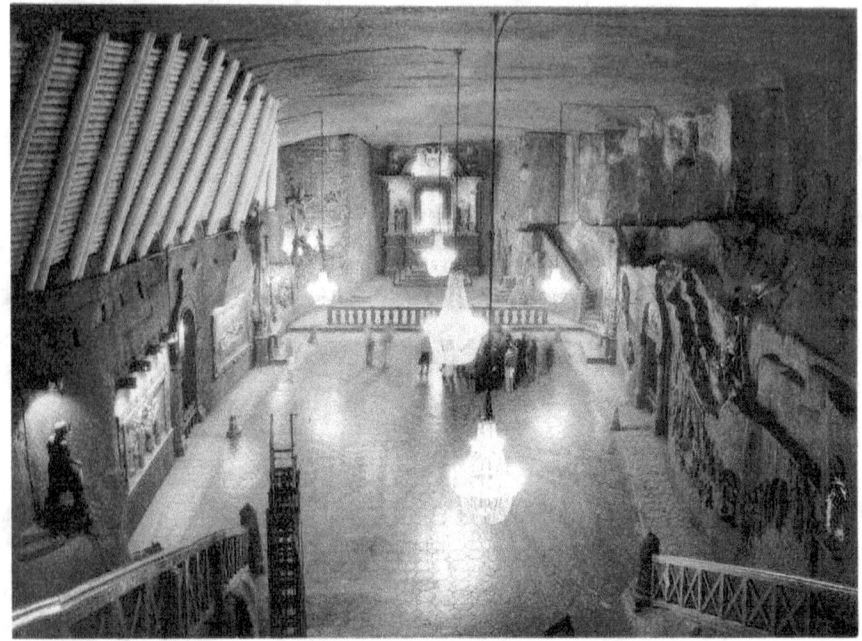

The Blessed Kinga Chapel, 330 ft below ground (photo by S.Michta)

We took the elevator up, speeding past patches of light at different levels. It was a strange feeling leaving the bowels of the earth and returning to light and heat – an almost mystical journey.

*

The restoration of the two paintings was completed. My time here was drawing to a close. As a result of the anxieties over the nuclear fallout, and feelings of loneliness, my friendships had deepened. Professor Szablowski came to the studio to compliment me and invited me back. The restorers clapped their approval. John opened the bottle of Romanian sekt I brought and carefully poured the precious liquid into odd-sized china cups more used to containing tea. This was also Krystyna's last day. She was off to Canada to visit her sister for three months. We felt sad to be leaving Wawel. The gold cupola of the Sigismund Chapel shone good will as we walked past the cathedral, past Kosckiuscko on his horse, down the slope into the town.

Later, I squeezed suitcases and Waniek's painting, carefully wrapped, into Chris's little Fiat and we folded ourselves into the remaining space for the short drive to the train station. Checking in at the airport in Warsaw my luggage was eight kilos overweight. A gallant Frenchman who was standing behind me was travelling light, so took my second bag through. Sir John Gielgud was at the head of the Customs queue, looking debonair and distinguished in linen jacket, spotted cravat, and a huge gold signet ring on his finger. I wondered if it bore the crest of his Polish ancestor Count Jan Gielgud, who fled with his family to England when his estates were confiscated after the 1830 Uprising.

Over the years, I had befriended many Poles whose ancestors had been forced to flee the country, as well as those, mainly artists, who had stayed in London after the war. Despite difficulties, they had flourished. Since my first visit, when Janusz created the exhibition at the Czartoryski for me, I had started another career: writing articles and reviews, initially about Polish art. Before long I would be leading art tours to Poland and beyond, which expanded my professional horizon beyond my restoration studio.

My sons had met some of my Polish friends in London, and had picked up something of life in Poland from my letters and descriptions. This was reflected in a card Rupert sent for my birthday that autumn. His turn of phrase was uncannily similar to those used by my Polish friends, who were also anxious about not speaking freely, coupled with legal jargon.

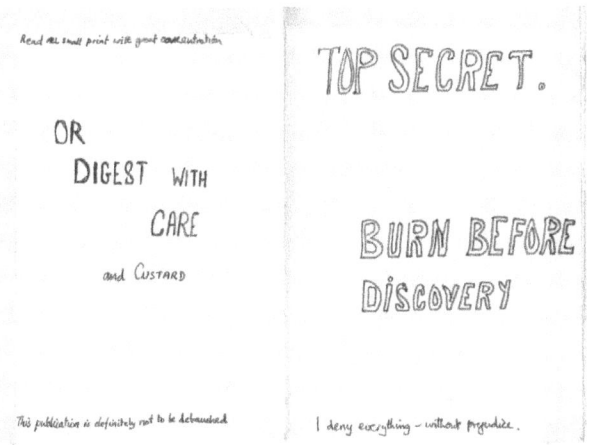

"TOP SECRET. BURN BEFORE DISCOVERY. I deny everything – without prejudice." On the back page he wrote, also in red ink, "Read all small print with great concentration. OR DIGEST WITH CARE and CUSTARD. This publication is definitely not to be debauched."

I hoped, in time, to take the boys on a grand tour round Poland to meet the people and places that had come to mean so much to me.

My heart drew me to that unknown country in March 1984; an impulsive decision that changed my life. Coming from a wealthy, democratic Western country, I found greater riches among the poverty-stricken Poles I met, where time was not counted as money. Solidarity through friendship was important, and I felt at home among highly intelligent people, who shared my values of faith, art, and literature. In the closed world they inhabited, they had to learn survival skills and resilience; skills they taught me, that enabled me to cope through this long-contested divorce. I learnt to juxtaposition the professional demands on my time while my sons were at boarding school: restoring pictures, going to exhibitions, writing up reviews and getting the finished piece to an editor, while preparing for another court hearing. Away from my own environment, I was able to develop talents I did not know I possessed.

I packed a whole smoked eel in my suitcase. Back in London, Rupert was off to a dinner party, and had been asked to bring a first course.

'Take this smoked eel from Krakow, your friends will enjoy it,' I said, pleased that he and his friends would enjoy such a delicacy, and mindful of the tangerine he had found me on my first return from Poland.

PART IV
1987

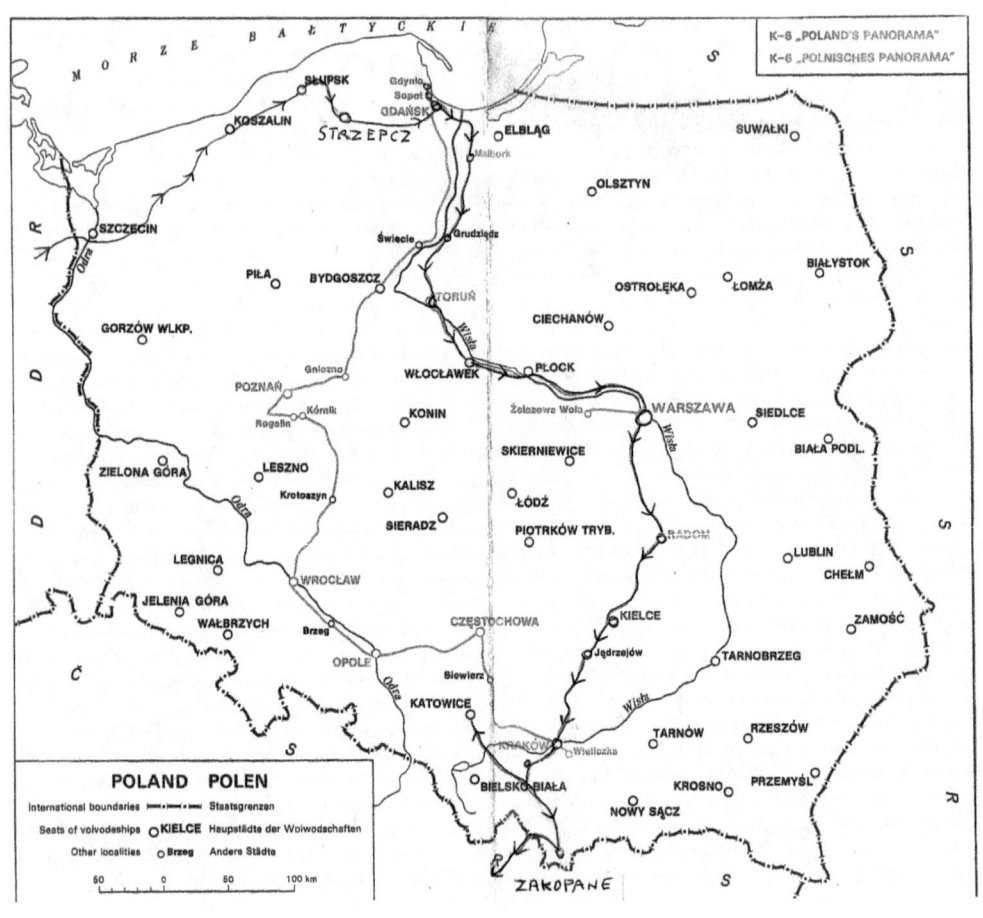

Map of our drive through Poland

12

Driving to Poland

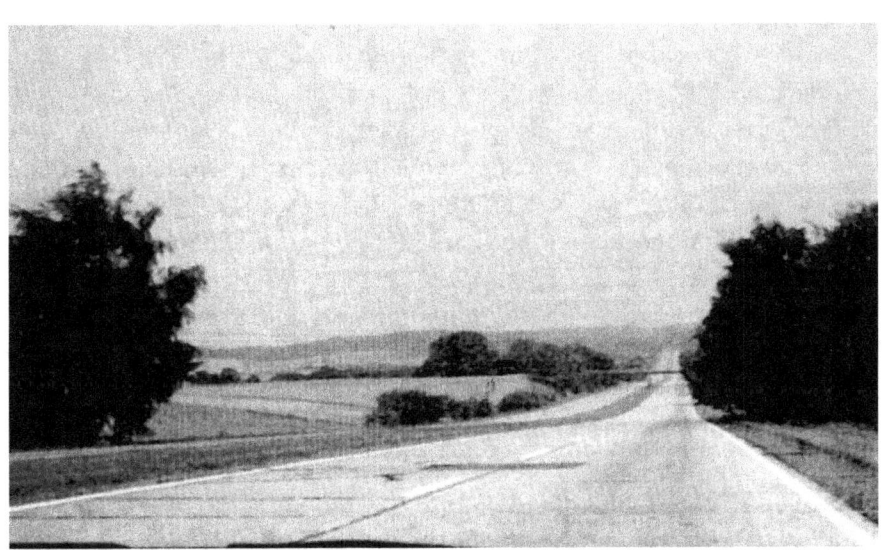

Hitler's road East

T HE SALLY FERRY official walked down the line of cars and tapped on my window. Rain spattered in as I opened it.

'Are your Mrs de Borchgrave?' she asked

'Yes, I am,' I replied.

'You left your Polish petrol coupons at the garage in Ramsgate.' When she saw the look of horror on my face, she continued,

'Don't worry. They're sending them here by taxi and it shouldn't take long. You won't miss the ferry.'

Rupert, Simon and I looked at each other with dismay. This would be my sons' first experience of life behind the Iron Curtain. We had spent time under-lining petrol stations along our route in red. As they were few and far between, they were marked on the Polish road map. Although fuel is rationed, foreign visitors can buy as much as they like, paying by coupons purchased with hard currency. We carried an extra five litre can for the surplus. The ferry official looked at my young teenagers, 15 and 12, and said,

'Off on an adventure are you?'

'Yes,' said Simon. 'We're staying with friends and travelling round Poland. Isn't it exciting?' The girl smiled doubtfully, looked at me with amazement and said,

'When the taxi arrives I'll point the driver in your direction. You'll need those coupons.'

After two weeks of hot weather, the first day of the holidays began with pouring rain. My windscreen rubber had decided only that morning to leak drops of water on to my feet. Coupled with leaving the coupons behind, it was not an auspicious start. My stomach churned with anxiety as I smiled at Rupert who was sitting in the front seat beside me.

'Our guardian angel is looking after us,' I said, turning to Simon in the back as the taxi arrived. We had only dropped nine cars down the queue. With the coupons safely stowed, we were soon on the ferry and rushed upstairs so fast we left our cheese sandwiches behind in the car. We could eat them later. We bought fish and chips and fizzy drinks (always a treat), sat down at a corner table and looked out at the stern of the ship. As the ferry churned through the waves and driving rain, we all felt a bit deflated. We had a long way to drive.

At Dunkirk the ferry ramp was stuck and we waited in the car for half an hour. When we finally reached the French customs, the officer examined my passport carefully.

'Are you a picture restorer?'

'Yes'.

'Where are you going?'

'To Poland'.

'Please open the boot'. Did he think I was smuggling pictures?

We opened the boot, and presented a load of Andrex loo paper and Tampax, cotton wool, deodorant, a large tin of coffee, oranges, olive and vegetable oil, boxes of toffees, bottles of wine, a metre-long Hungarian salami, J-cloths, avocados, our duty-free cognac and chocolate and our suitcases. He took one look, then with stunned surprise shut the boot and waved us on.

We drove 530 miles – Ostende, Antwerp, Eindhoven, Hanover, Brunswick. Steady nerves were needed on the autobahn where BMWs and Mercedes swept past us at horrendous speed. The rain continued relentlessly, as did the drip on to my foot. We told each other silly jokes and kept our spirits high, even when we failed to find the motel recommended by a fellow traveller to Poland. We found another at 10.30pm. A woman in a dressing gown opened the door and gave us a room with three beds and a shower. We walked wearily up the hill for indifferent soup and bockwurst at the petrol station café and rolled into our beds at midnight.

We washed down boiled eggs and toast with strong coffee at breakfast and made sandwiches with the bread, salami and cheese we could not eat, filled up with petrol and reached the border in 20 minutes. It took time to get through due to the cost of the transit visa and car tax through East Germany – an effective way of raising hard currency. I had not counted on these costs and was short of small notes. Supplementing German marks with US dollars and a £5 note, we were 10p short. An old florin was refused, but fortunately we found a decimal 10p. We laughed at this absurdity and thought of Monty Python. (They had watched the film *Life of Brian* in the Cleese's home, while I painted in her studio alongside my old friend Barbara, who was John's second wife.)

It was still raining.

'The speed limit on the autobahn in the DDR is 100km. If you exceed it you will be fined,' a guard warned me.

We soon ignored this advice when other cars, including the militia, overtook us and I gradually speeded up to 130km. On the ring road north of Berlin the countryside opened up, unchanged since the war. We passed forests, woodland, wide plains rich with cornfields stretching to the horizon. There was no graffiti, advertisements or petrol stations, just an unspoilt double track of mainly well-surfaced motorway, like ours of 30 years ago. The sleek Western cars were replaced by a few Ladas and Trabants. For long stretches we had the road to ourselves; the road Hitler built. As I drove, the boys excitedly pointed out a herd of deer in full flight, workers in the fields, horses quietly pulling laden carts. The journey to the Polish border took four hours. There was time to reflect on the paradox of this open road. Here, Nazi tanks had thundered over the concrete to invade, occupy, kill and torture. Now the road was quiet: integrated into its surroundings, posing no obvious threat.

The property market had started rising since Helen Ward agreed a financial settlement with my husband's solicitor. I received less than a third of the value of the home we had to leave, and had to take out a mortgage, guaranteed by my father. All the houses I liked were above my budget, but a month before the deadline, I found a Victorian terraced house, with similar features to our present home, near Wandsworth Common. The boys and I had moved home during the Easter holidays. With the help of a friend we had packed up our belongings over two days, and moved into a house that had been left clean and tidy for us to unpack. The three of us enjoyed preparing our new home together. Rupert and Simon worked with enthusiasm and dedication, hanging pictures, putting books into bookshelves, and preparing the cellar for a ping-pong table. Our furniture fitted in well, the curtains from our previous three houses covered the windows, and our old fridge-freezer, taken out of storage, looked immaculate and still worked well in the kitchen. In the garden there was a tree with mistletoe. After pulling up overgrown greenery we found a garden gnome and a rock garden. At last, the boys and I could relax and enjoy our surroundings, without the anxiety of wondering if we would have to move. The unspoken sense of relief was palpable.

Bowling along on this open road, the holiday was beginning to feel like the joyful celebration it was intended to be.

After some time our straight road took us to the border checkpoint. The boys observed in silence as we passed mile after mile of barbed wire and watch towers, acres of no-man's land, queues and red tape. At Szczecin we ate our sandwiches while we waited. The Polish custom officials took an hour to let us through. Even before the motorway petered out we passed our first horse and cart on the road. Midweek, there were more of these than cars on the beech and elm-lined roads. We took the E28 north via Goleniow, Nowogard where we filled the tank with a 20-litre coupon, Koszalin, Slupsk and several other small towns and villages where life was still focussed on the central square. I drove fast, keen to reach Lucia before dark.

We peeled off the main road at Lembork as the sun cast golden glazes on the trees, drove through a couple of villages and looked out for the farmyard opposite the third pond as instructed. The farmer pointed the way down a deep rutted dirt track past the only dwellings there until near the lake we found a little wooden house with a zinc roof that swept down either side. We rang the bell. It was 8pm. We had left home at 8am the previous morning. It was good to arrive... Lucia opened the door and gave us each a big hug. I had not seen her since my first visit to Gdansk then Krakow in 1984. She had persuaded me to bring the boys to Poland for a holiday, and invited us to stay in her summer house about

40 minutes' drive north of Gdansk, near the village of Strzepcz, in the Kashubian district, famous for its embroidery and beautiful countryside dotted with lakes. There seemed nothing odd about driving nearly 1,000 miles to find a house without a telephone in the back of beyond.

I watched as the boys stared in fascination on entering the little house. Apart from the walls and brick fireplace, everything was made of wood – stairs, floor, benches, double-glazed window frames and shutters. My little room on the ground floor was snug with wall-to-wall cupboards to stow my gear. The boys made themselves at home upstairs in a room with two single beds and magnificent views over the lake. The house, designed by Lucia's husband Andrzej, was paid for with foreign currency earned abroad. Poles were allowed to own holiday homes as long as that is all they were. No central heating could be installed so once the cold weather comes, houses are closed up. We settled down round the fire and consumed pork and potatoes, salad from the garden and a bottle of wine, before falling asleep.

After breakfast we were shown round the garden. Blackcurrants were bottled for the winter, strawberries and vegetables enjoyed now. Orvis, the black and white cat, followed us, but put out a barbed paw if anyone tried to pick him up. He only ate fish, but was not inclined to follow Simon down to the water when he went fishing. Rupert met Marek, a neighbour's son, who had a surfboard and a boat.

Later we drove to Strzepcz (even the locals found it hard to pronounce, but we managed Shtrepch), which was a typical Polish village straight out of a fairy tale. Geese waddled down the road and horses dozed between their shafts. There was a post office with the village telephone, a mechanic's yard where I left the car, and unexpectedly, a well-stocked children's clothes shop where I took the opportunity to buy Simon two pairs of 100% cotton pyjamas, four pairs of pants and socks – all made in China – sandals and green wellies. The mechanic explained that my windscreen rubber had perished and needed special glue. Fortunately, he had some and had stopped the leak. In the store we bought bread, a kilo of cheese and another of butter, three bottles of vodka, blackcurrant juice, soft drinks, ten packets of sweets and some cucumbers pickling in a big barrel.

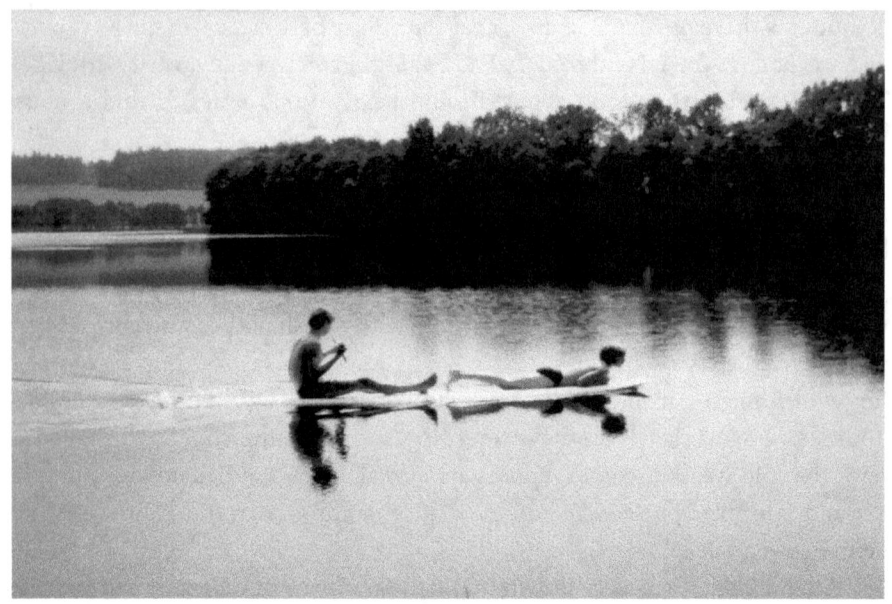

Lazy days on the Lake

Meat was still rationed, but despite being three extra mouths to feed, we ate royally. In the afternoon the four of us walked round the lake, decorated with yellow water lilies, through meadows richly coloured with wild geraniums, marguerites and countless other flowers, to a nearby farm to buy milk, thick cream, eggs and three chickens killed specially for us. The farm boys sat round the kitchen table preparing strawberries for jam – and eating some. Everything was sparse but clean. Lucia supplied me with a large pickle jar which we took to the bee-keeper to fill with honey. This would last us for ages back home.

Ela and Grzegorz arrived from Gdansk for the night. Ela was still teaching English at the Medical Academy, a job she kept until she retired. Thick-set Grzegorz was an architect, happier drawing by hand than using computer images. We celebrated around a bonfire eating the roasted chickens which had so much more flavour than the ones at home, and strawberries freshly picked. As the sky darkened, stars appeared, and wild geese called to each other.

*

The local church, which held 500 people, was full for Mass the next morning. It served six villages, and people walked up to six kilometres to worship there. Lucia told us that during the Solidarity era land had been bought up and churches built. The next morning we went looking for the old blacksmith, who lived in the nearby village of Linia. I was hoping he would make a gate for our garden. We found him attending a funeral in the beautifully frescoed church. Lucia lent him her mackintosh for the procession to the graveyard as it began raining.

Later, we waited for the blacksmith, who was well into his eighties, outside the little wooden forge which lay beside his house on a green, where his father and grandfather had also lived and worked. Old iron ploughs lay around in the grass. Nothing much had changed except for the introduction of electricity. When he arrived, he looked at my drawings and was happy to make the gate, so I gave him the measurements, and we agreed a fee. He went into his house to collect Lucia's mackintosh, and two cats came out to greet us. The delightful old man told us they were called Gorbachev and Reagan, after two leaders he admired. He recounted his wartime experiences: how he had hidden from the Nazis during the war. Their invasion had been terrifying, but the Communist rulers were worse.

'They don't allow you to think,' he said.

I was reading Simone de Beauvoir's *The Mandarins*, while the boys were messing about in the lake with their new friends. Just as the characters in the book attempted to discern what role, if any, intellectuals would have in influencing the political landscape of the world after the war, I wondered what role intellectuals would have in Poland if the power of the Soviet Empire collapsed. I was brought back from my musings when the blacksmith appeared. He had been to two towns looking for square bars of iron, but only found round ones. Was that all right? I felt humbled by his desire to do the best job he could for us. Here was another member of Solidarity.

*

Basia, who, like Ela, taught English at the Medical Academy, arrived with her husband Daniel on a beautiful cloudless morning. Unlike Ela, they were reserved by nature. The boys were very young when Basia stayed with us that summer of 1976, but they remembered her with affection. We lazed in the garden, swam in the lake, and when Ela and Grzegorz arrived from Gdansk, we tucked into pork in breadcrumbs and more fruit from the garden.

'What're the schools like here, Basia?'

'Not like yours in England, Rupert. Children are educated in a strict Communist dogma.'

'Oh, does that mean brainwashing?'

Ela said, 'Our rulers see it as developing proper attitudes of citizenship in the Polish People's Republic, to prepare workers to build our Socialist state. This includes learning Russian.'

'The Ministry of National Education decides the curriculum, textbooks, admission standards, examinations, etcetera,' said Basia, 'but as English teachers in the Medical Academy we're relatively free from all that. We just have to be careful what we say. You never know who may be listening. During the Solidarity era students and teachers demanded a complete restructuring of the system but promises were never delivered.'

'The brainwashing doesn't seem to have been very successful if it sprouted Solidarity,' said Rupert. We all smiled.

'We'll take you to the Lenin Shipyard gates tomorrow and you can see the power of the human spirit, helped by the Church. The Pope, you know, is an inspiration. He speaks from experience, having suffered the tyrannies of an occupying power in his youth.'

*

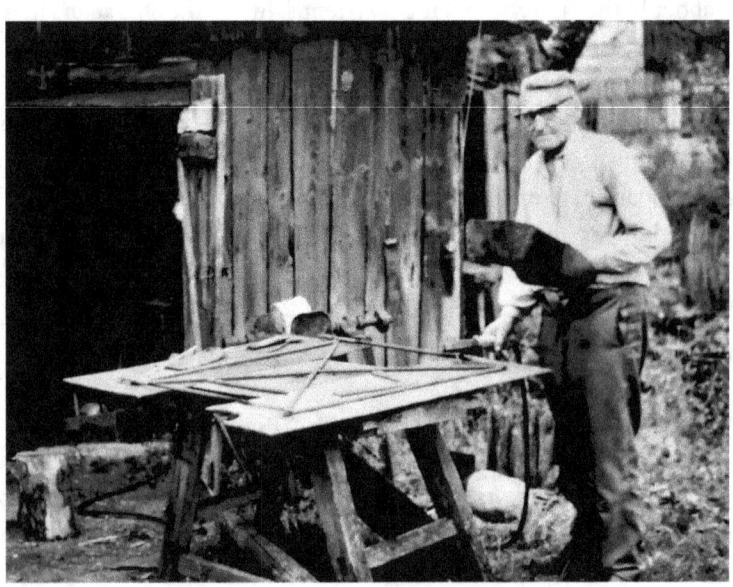

The blacksmith working on our gate

We visited the blacksmith. His electricity had been cut off due to work being carried out on the overhead cables, so he had not finished the gate. Instead he took us into his house. Since his mother died a quarter of a century earlier, he had lived alone. A cupboard stood in his living room, crocheted curtains hung at the window behind brass pelmets. The floor boards were painted light brown, matching the stove tiles set in the wall to keep two rooms warm in winter, and a carved wooden clock chimed. An old table was covered with a cloth exquisitely worked, on which stood a pottery jar filled with freshly-picked wild flowers.

'This was embroidered by my grandfather', he said proudly. He turned to look at pictures of Jesus and Mary on the blue washed walls and said to Lucia (who translated for us),

'When the Red Army marched in, the soldiers smashed everything. They trod on our beloved pictures.'

'Are these new ones?' I asked.

'Years later a monk came to the forge. My father was too poor to buy the two pictures he offered us. They were similar to the ones we lost. I wanted them so badly I bought them with my savings, and my brother framed them. Jesus and Mary are my best friends.' Tears rolled down his cheeks. I looked at my sons and they too seemed profoundly moved by his story. He took us next door into his bedroom which was also plain and uncluttered and likewise spoke of a different era. The walls were pale orange and the floorboards painted.

'The bed was bought second-hand by my father in Lembork in 1913. The single bed turns into a double when the front panel is pulled out,' he told us. It was practical and pretty, though the sheets could have done with a wash. Chintz curtains hung from a brass pole and a bench was placed beside the stove under which his shoes were neatly placed. An old lamp sat on the bedside table. When the old man dies, all this will be lost. How sad. He was unable to find the right iron for our gate and pulled up some of his own railings to use instead.

*

On our way to Gdansk we picked up Grzegorz and walked along the sandy beach at Sopot where swans gathered in a bevy and the sun browned us. Gdansk was packed for the annual Dominican Bazaar which was vast, and attracted people from all over Poland and abroad. We wandered round the antiques section and I bought a blue and white Meissen porcelain salt cellar, on which a jaunty young man, dressed in 18th century fashion, was holding a posy as he contemplated his beloved. Perhaps I was attracted to him for we ate off Meissen onion-pattern plates in my parents' home; or because his rococo elegance reminded me of Izabela Czartoryska. In the National Museum the boys were as transfixed by the Memling triptych, as I was on my first visit.

As we drove back to collect our gate from the blacksmith, Simon and I spotted a shooting star searing across the blue, star-studded sky. Though the gate was finished, the black paint was still tacky. It fitted exactly into the boot of the car. Lucia went into the house and found the old man asleep in his cot. He woke up and was happy to see us. Clutching his trousers he waved us goodbye effusively.

*

It took all our skill to pack up the car the next morning, what with the addition of the gate, two backpacks and a four kilo bottle of honey. Grzegorz was heavy and the car weighed down. I had to drive carefully to avoid banging the exhaust pipe in the potholes. We were loath to leave Lucia.

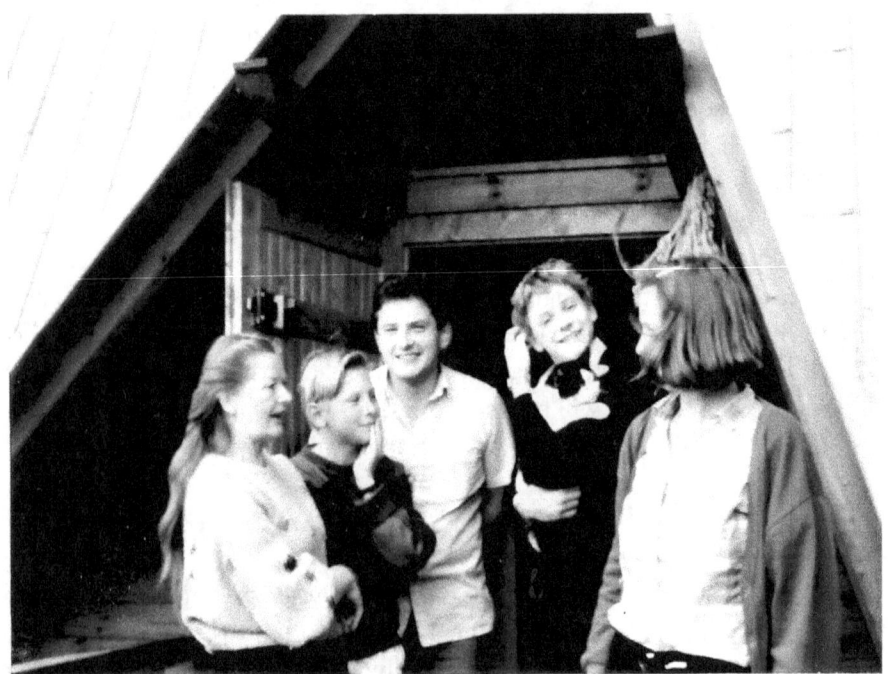

Farewell to Lucia (on the left) as the five of us start on our travels

Brandishing my art critic's card at Malbork, Ela managed to jump a long queue and find a guide, a pretty girl, who showed us round this 13th century stronghold of the Teutonic knights, set in the Vistula Delta. The castle was rebuilt a century ago by the German architect Steinbeck and served as a blueprint for the Castles of the Third Reich, built during Hitler's regime. Its history of cruelty and control seeped from its walls: walls of hatred and fear. In 1945 it became a battleground and half the massive fortress was destroyed, to be rebuilt by the Poles. There was a chilly atmosphere about the place. I felt uncomfortable and was relieved when we left and settled down beside the river to eat our picnic. When we returned to the car, Simon noticed the chrome Ghia plaque from the back of our Ford had been removed. We were puzzled that anyone would go to the trouble to steal something so apparently worthless. There was obviously a market for anything from the West, especially something marking a top of the range Escort.

Seeing cows and horses tethered beside the roadside, unspoilt countryside and avenues of elm trees lining the tarmac, we soon cheered up. As we drove through Torun, birthplace of Copernicus, the boys appreciated the beauty of the medieval buildings, even though they looked worn out by neglect. The Sunday drivers were not as gracious – several cars tried to overtake at the same time, spreading across the road. Traffic cops hid behind trees with their cameras, but were often thwarted by drivers coming the other way, flashing their lights in warning. We did get caught speeding later, and were fined a hefty 2,000 zlotys on the spot: about £2.50 with our black-market money; a fortune for those Poles who broke the rules. The 230-mile drive to Warsaw took over six hours, so we were relieved we did not need to waste time queuing for petrol.

*

We were feeling pretty scruffy and travel-worn by the time we reached Agnieszka's home in Mokotov, a suburb of Warsaw, at 9pm. Curator of Paintings at the National Museum, I had met Agnieszka on my first visit in 1984, and again a year later. This eminent art historian, and Andrzej her writer and theatre-critic husband, greeted us graciously. Iwona, from the Castle, had also been invited. We eagerly devoured the delicious dinner of veal, beans, potato and cake, washed down with white wine in elegant glasses. Meals in Poland were always a celebration: a time to talk, to enjoy each other's company, as well as to eat; far removed from our growing 'eat on the run' culture in London. Later, Iwona drove Ela and Grzegorz to her home. They returned for breakfast and took the boys off to see round the old town while I stayed to rest.

Agnieszka's mother Maria and stepfather invited me to eat lunch with them. Arkady, aged 80, still worked as a publisher. He kept fit playing tennis. We spoke German when we sat down at their antique round table and chairs, (stored during the war in Maria's mother's garden house on the family estate near Lublin). Maria served us mushroom soup, wild boar shot by Arkady in the forest near Lembork, coffee meringue, and we drank the best Pinot Noir from Hungary. Over coffee Maria showed me photographs of her family standing by the pillared portico of their manor house, their horses and their friends. The good life during Poland's freedom between the two world wars came to a sudden end when the Nazis invaded.

'The Nazis and the Reds hated the upper classes,' she said. 'My mother's house was vandalised, our house, here where we are sitting, was shot through with Sten guns, while several of us women hid for three weeks in the cellar. When we were found and forced to leave, we feared being shot in the back by the Germans.'

*

We were invited to dinner by Ambassador Giertych whom I had met several times at the Polish Cultural Institute in London, when I reviewed exhibitions there. The Polish Ambassador to the Court of St James's lived with his wife in a charming flat in the old town near the castle. Also present were a couple named Kazimierz and Barbara, who had recently returned from their posting to London. They were influential members of the Communist party and he was now Political Director of Western Europe, which sounded ominous. Later, Simon described him as tricky, as he said things he thought we wanted to hear – Mrs Thatcher was wonderful, the Poles were idle, unemployment was a good thing – while we ate fish in aspic, tomato soup, veal with peaches, ice cream and fruit rounded off with petit fours and coffee.

When we got back to the car at 10.30pm, we realised with horror that it had been broken into. The radio cover lay on the driver's seat, splintered glass covered the back, smashed from the small window. We opened the boot. Ela and Grzegorz's backpacks, Basia's home-made cherry-brandy, the presents for friends in Krakow – all were gone. We cried with anger and frustration. If only I had safely stored the contents of the boot in Agnieszka's house. We walked back to the Giertych flat with heavy hearts to report our loss. The Ambassador and Kazimierz drove us to the police station. The police were rude and disrespectful, even to high ranking politicos. When our particulars were taken, we drove back to Agnieszka's home.

Ambassador Giertych arrived at nine the next morning with two colleagues and formally presented me with a crystal vase, while the boys were still asleep on the floor and Gapa the cocker spaniel rushed about. Giertych said they would look for new glass for my car window. Several hours passed. Nothing happened.

We went looking in vain. It seemed there was no glass that fitted a Ford Escort in Warsaw. Agnieszka found some perspex which Grzegorz cut to shape and fitted. Since Agnieszka's mother's expected lunch guest did not arrive, we were invited to eat it before departing. I dreaded telling Ela that her backpacks had been stolen.

'What was in them?' I asked.

'Our tents for camping.' She didn't tell me that all their clothes were in the backpacks and they only had what they stood up in. How used the Poles were to suffering in silence. We set out for Krakow. (Agnieszka rang us later for a list of the items stolen, which Ambassador Giertych had been asked for by the police.)

13

The Journey Continues

M EMORIES OF DRIVING in Maria's Trabant two years earlier, and an ocean of upheaval since, entered my mind as I drove up the hill to Wawel and stopped at the guard post. When I gave my name we were waved through, continuing up past the Thieves' Tower into the open area within the castle walls. I parked outside the administration building, where Professor Szablowski had provided a suite of two rooms and a bathroom for us. The sculptor Jacek Waltos loaned Ela and Grzegorz a studio nearby, and when we had unpacked we went out and ate placki at the Hungarian restaurant, followed by lody (ice cream) and coffee in the Sukiennice. There was a fine inlaid French *bombe commode* in my bedroom with ormolu Roman soldiers guarding the corners and huge sun escutcheons embracing the handles. I enjoyed opening the massive drawers to place my clothes in this valuable museum piece, while the boys let off steam next door.

*

We were taken round Collegium Maius by a knowledgeable young student. The oldest academic institution in Poland was founded in Krakow by Kazimierz the Great. He realised the importance of such an institution during his efforts to reform and strengthen the country, which had been reunited in 1306 after a period of feudal disintegration. The king wanted to raise Poland to the maturity and cultural level of other European nations, and a university would educate specialists in the fields of administration, law and diplomacy, help to shape a nation and unite it around its ruler. Within the foundation charter was written: "Let it be a pearl of various sciences so that it could educate men distinguished by the insight of its advice......let it open a refreshing spring so that its richness could quench the thirst of everybody who wishes to learn. Let all inhabitants not only of our kingdom but also of adjacent countries come to this very city of Krakow safely and freely."

After the death of its founder, the university declined, until Jadwiga, the first Queen of Poland, inherited the throne 20 years later, at the tender age of ten. A willing pawn in power politics, she gave up her young Habsburg fiancé to marry the elderly Ladislaus II Jagiello, Grand Duke of Lithuania, after his conversion to Christianity along with his pagan country. Jagiello became king of the Polish-Lithuanian Commonwealth. During his 35-year reign, the 'Commonwealth was for a time the largest in the Christian world. Under his Jagiellon successors, it became a symbol of faith, tolerance and learning.

In her 15 years as Queen and co-ruler, Jadwiga's deep faith and love of her people strengthened both the church and the university. She founded new hospitals, schools and churches, promoted the use of the vernacular in church services and ordered the translation of Scripture into Polish. The ruling couple asked Pope Boniface IX to sanction a faculty of theology in Krakow, which was granted in 1397. Two years later Jadwiga died, four days after her three-week-old daughter. The sale of her jewellery partly financed the restoration of the university, which entered its golden age in the 15th century. It became the cradle of science and culture, with students such as Nicholas Copernicus, who enrolled in 1491.

*

Ups and downs followed as the political climate changed over the centuries. On November 6th, 1939, 180 professors and doctors of the Jagiellonian and other Krakow universities were arrested and sent to Sachsenhausen and Dachau concentration camps. The university was closed down, but within two years reopened 'underground' with students such as Karol Wojtyla, later to become Pope John Paul II. Under the Nazi Occupation, secondary school education was also forbidden to Poles. After the war, though, the university flourished, and the Jagiellon Library has the second largest collection in the country.

The museum is situated in the oldest building, Collegium Maius, and visitors can catch a glimpse of how the students and professors lived and worked there in the late 15th century. Rooms are decorated with ornamental doorways, beamed ceilings, vaulting and frescoed walls. An ornamental wooden staircase spirals round to the upper floor in the refectory, where magnificent tapestries, once part of a Versailles collection, enliven the walls. Behind a gilt grill in one of the rooms, is the treasury. Here, medieval university maces, Rector's insignia, signet rings, seals, and cups are exhibited. The golden Jagiellonian terrestrial globe made in 1510 shows America for the first time. It never ceased to amaze me how much has survived in a country that has been so frequently and brutally invaded. When we reached the end of our tour the young student refused a tip. He asked me to buy him two books in England instead.

*

Boguś and Chris gave us a party. Their salon was gently lit by candelabra with ormolu and brass figures holding three candles each. Wine flowed. I enjoyed introducing my sons to old friends: Maciek from the art gallery Inny Swiat, the American Browns, Boguś's uncle Marek, Director of the Czartoryski, and other members of his family who lived in or around Krakow. There was Indian curry to eat followed by ice cream and raspberries washed down with champagne.

While Rupert read a Sherlock Holmes story to Simon and Chris's daughter Hannah, I took the opportunity to ask Karol's wife Maryna, a psychiatrist, about the effect of broken marriages on children. I was encouraged when she said that sometimes a divorce is a relief for children, who are better off away from the stress of conflict. But I must reassure them that they are not responsible for the break-up. Insulated in this different world, the boys and I were enjoying our adventure together.

The boys loved exploring Krakow. The little medieval town inside Planty, free of traffic, was so different to London. They enjoyed the shops, the restaurants and the social life. In the covered market in the Sukiennice, Rupert bought a little chess set which he still cherishes. We took tea with Jacek Waltos and his psychiatrist friend Jacek Bomba. While the artist made a sketch of Rupert, which he later used in a pastel drawing of his series of the Old Testament Samuel, he discussed his conceptual ideas of the child who heard God's voice. Later, in contrast, we watched folk dancing in the Rynek.

Krystyna Malcharek gave them a tour round Wawel Castle and the cathedral, before we were invited to meet Professor Szablowski. He was delighted with the catalogues I gave him and said I had almost become an inhabitant of Krakow. The boys and I were welcome any time. I thanked him for his official invitation, sent to me in May, to come to Poland during the summer to continue my research for lectures, and to bring my sons with me. This saved me $30 per day for the five weeks we spent in Poland.

'Mummy, you were really oily with him,' Simon commented as we left Wawel. I think he was secretly impressed with my German.

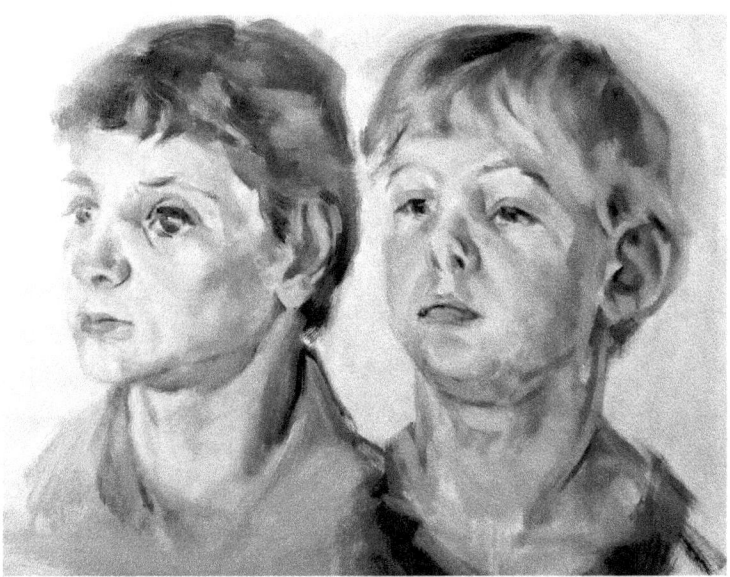

Portrait of Rupert and Simon by Leszek Sobocki, 1987

Janusz Wałek, who captivated them with his stories, showed them the jewels of the Czartoryski Collection. I gave his colleague Dorota some Andrex, which she said she would barter for books. Over two afternoons the boys sat for their double portrait with Leszek Sobocki who had painted my portrait in April. Gazing out at the concrete blocks stifling the view from the eleventh floor of Leszek's studio during those quiet hours, gave me a chance to rest and to reflect on our journey; and try to keep my mind free from worrying about the future. Leszek said he would send the portrait to London by train, when the paint was dry.

I left the boys to roam round Krakow and buy presents to take home, while Ela, acting as interpreter, took me to meet Jerzy Nowosielski. I had not really understood his landscapes when Bogus took me to the DESA gallery a couple of years earlier. A month earlier I had written a review of his paintings exhibited in the Middlesbrough Art Gallery and had learnt to appreciate one of Poland's finest contemporary artists.

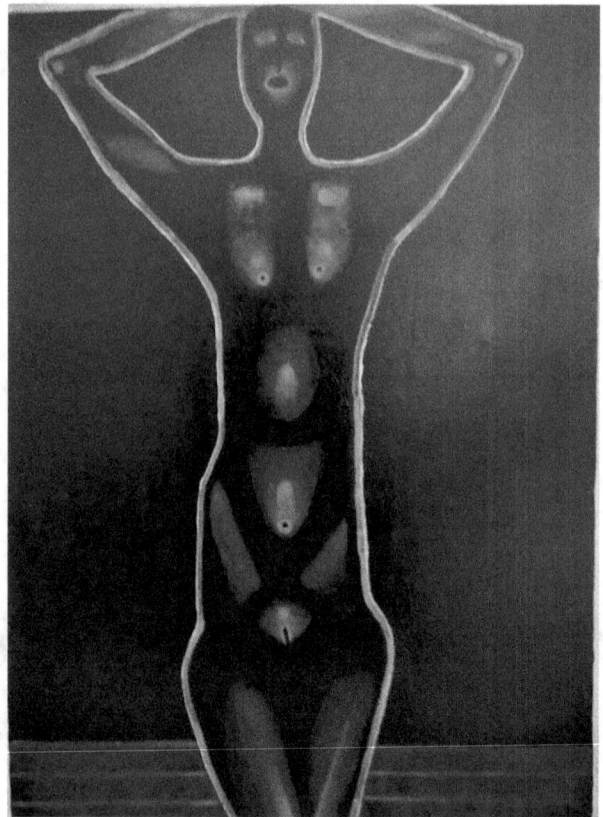

Black Nude by Nowosielski 1973

Nowosielski was a short, dumpy man with curly grey hair and a neat beard. Born in 1923 in Krakow, he became a founding member of the Young Artists Group at the end of the war, represented Polish painting at the Venice Biennale nine years later, and became a professor at the Krakow Academy of Fine Arts. He showed us slides of the interior of the Roman Catholic Church in Wesola, near Warsaw, which he painted. The interior hall was rather small and white with semi-circular windows bordered in red and a strip of black. Over the altar Nowosielski painted a Crucifixion scene and an enormous figure of the Madonna with palms lifted up. The cycle of the Way of the Cross, arranged along the aisle walls was painted in greys and browns. From his background of Catholic mother and Orthodox father he felt united with both Eastern and Western spirituality.

He said, 'I first saw icons in the museum at Lvov when I was 15. This was my first experience of great art. Art is a permanent revolution of human consciousness, therefore I don't need to get political. I feel a foreigner in modern art. I don't know what's happening, yet I'm linked to it.'

He thought Russia and Poland were the places art would emerge from in the future – from that grey reality, and agreed to sell me a picture next year when he had painted more. I did not have enough money now to buy an oil of a black nude standing out against a white background with a sun rising, which he showed us. It expressed his desire to combine elements of the human face and body and elevate the physical to a higher plane of man's spiritual awareness.

Nowosielski studied at the Academy with Professor Adam Hoffman. Some of his early paintings express the sense of fear felt in Stalin's empire, when it was better your face was turned away, so as not to be recognised. Post-war paintings could be exported, but I missed this opportunity to purchase one. Nowosielski was one of six Polish artists exhibited in *Art at the Edge* at MOMA, Oxford in 1988.

We left Krakow, laden to the gunnels, and drove to the Tatra Mountains via Stryszów. I wanted to see the Wozniakowski portrait of Napoleon I had restored. We drove through Lanckorona, with my happy memories of staying with Boguś and Chris.

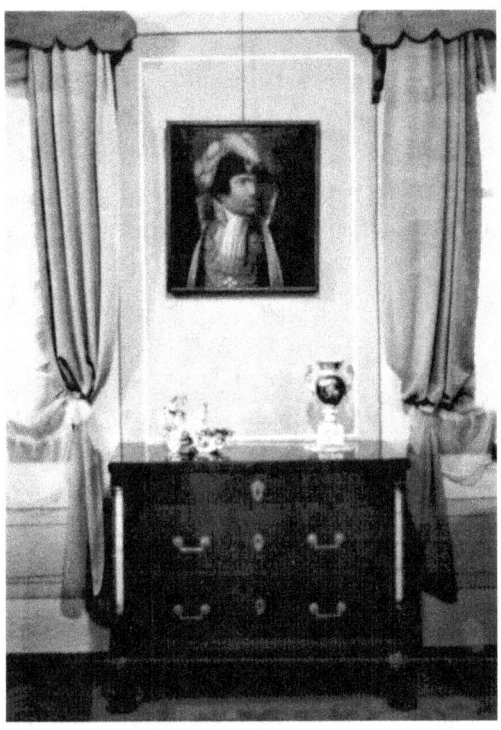

Portrait of Napoleon at Stryszów

We passed a fair in full swing, left the main road and travelled down little windy roads, alive with chickens, cows, bicycles, horses and carts – and potholes. I needed to concentrate. Stryszów, in Lesser Poland, was a typical 18th century Polish manor house, built originally with fortifications in the 16th century and remodelled a century later in the Baroque style. The last owners left in 1939, and after the war the land was farmed by a village collective, with the house used to store corn and fertiliser. The house was saved from demolition, the fate of many other manor houses, in the late '50's by Dr Hanna Pienkowska, who raised the money for its restoration and Grade I listing. Wawel took over custodianship in 1969, and decorated the interior to reflect the manners and culture of the 19th century landed gentry. Three rooms were open. It was a pleasant surprise to see the portrait of Napoleon I restored, the Battle Scene cleaned by Mary and a chandelier restored by John, in situ. Painted walls and ceilings, parquet floors, furniture, pictures and porcelain spoke of a gentler period in history. Despite the cruelty of the partitions and the Napoleonic wars, the old times still retained culture and chivalry, in contrast to the bloodbaths of the 20th century.

We ate lunch at another manor house in the village which opened as a restaurant a month earlier, tucking into rump steak with onions, ice cream and raspberry puree. Simon was so thirsty, he drank four compotes.

The queues for petrol were always long. Fortunately, on occasions my foreign number plate enabled me to queue barge, which saved much precious time. We had to keep an eye on the petrol gauge while figuring out which coupon we could use, and had a tin can for any overflow. After filling the tank, we drove towards Murzasichle, turning left at Lenin's statue, to the last village before the Tatra Mountains. Pani Galica welcomed us to her home. She was short, strong of build, with her hair rolled up in a bun. Laughter lines crinkled the corners of her eyes. Lucia had brought her two children here every summer since Ela was six, for her brother needed the mountain air. In those days there was an outside privy and no bathroom. On a daily basis for years, Pani Galica fed up to 100 guests, who stayed at surrounding farmhouses. Ela especially remembered her delicious pancakes and cakes. This hard work earned Pani Galica enough money to pay for her three intelligent children to attend university in Warsaw and Krakow. Education was free, but accommodation and travel, books and food were expensive. She paid the price by developing heart trouble and an early death. She gave us three rooms in a suite with tables and chairs in a little hall. Straw insulated the wooden beams inside and kelims hung on walls above the beds.

The next morning was cold and wet. As we munched bread and butter with jam and paté eased down with a milky barley drink, we discussed the loo paper problem. Having brought a huge amount we were down to one roll, having given most of it away.

'When I cut my finger, I used a greasy paper napkin and only two pieces of loo roll,' Simon said, and we all smiled at his abstemiousness. Waiting for the clouds to lift, for the air to become pure and crisp, we made sandwiches of salami and fatty bacon before driving to Polana Wlosienica, where we parked the car and took the bus on a winding 10-minute ride up to the next point. We walked to Morskie Oko (Eye of the Sea), the largest lake in the Tatras, and reached the rest house just as the rain started, ate our sandwiches with soup and apple juice, then, fortified, walked beside the lake as the sun appeared. The water was clear enough to see fish swimming. Wild flowers – campanula, aconites, delphiniums – burgeoned around us and crocuses blanketed areas of the ground in purple. We climbed up to the second lake where Simon chatted to the frontier guard and borrowed his binoculars.

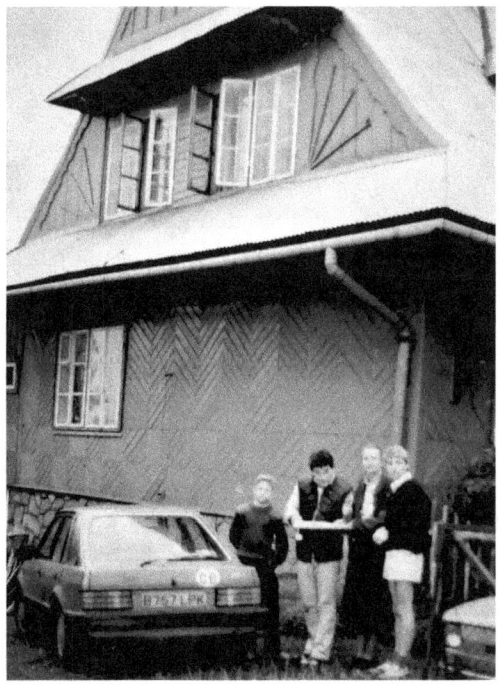

Simon, Grzegorz, Ela and Rupert by the Ford Escort

Back home I parked the Ford Escort out of sight, to save Pani Galica the tourist tax she could ill-afford. After the taxes we had to pay crossing the various borders, and now this, the boys understood more clearly Professor Szablowski's kindness in sending me a formal tax saving invitation. The boys picked red currants and made compote with our hostess, while I had a bath and wrote letters. The next morning we took the same cable car up the mountain that I went up in the snowy winter of 1984. We walked along the path I had previously taken in the horse and sleigh, and descended in a chair lift – a slow, silent passage over houses, fields, farms and green grass.

In Zakopane we shopped and I changed a $100 bill for small change and enquired about the price of a transit visa through Czechoslovakia. The cost was $50 and visas were only available in Warsaw or Katowice. In order to obtain visas we needed to have professional passport photos taken which we did not have. A German car was turned away two hours earlier for failing to comply. We looked at the map. It was too much of a detour going via East Germany. We experienced the frustration of closed borders as we drove back and consoled ourselves with wine before supper. A cow had been slaughtered and we were fed soup, beef and compote. Afterwards we walked to the next village as dusk fell, a village of wooden houses, through the fields, past a cemetery, and back home in time for the boys to help milk the cows that shared a barn with a few pigs, sheep and chickens.

We hunted for a photography shop in Zakopane. None were open. We must wait until Monday. Instead, we took a horse and cart up the valley, through fields where men scythed grass and women gathered it into stooks. We found a photographer in Nowy Targ. She took our passport photographs with a 100-year-old camera that had belonged to her father and grandfather. Feeling relieved, we boarded a raft and spent three hours on the River Biały, shooting the occasional rapid, and revelling in the beauty of the countryside of Poland on our right and Czechoslovakia on our left.

The next morning Ela drove with me to Katowice, a three-hour journey. At the Czech Consulate we found disgruntled Italians, Swiss and Dutchmen who were turned away at the border and had come back for visas. An intimidating dragon at the desk handed us endless forms to fill, several times, in return for $23. We left with relief an hour later, clutching three visas each containing two photographs. The rain continued.

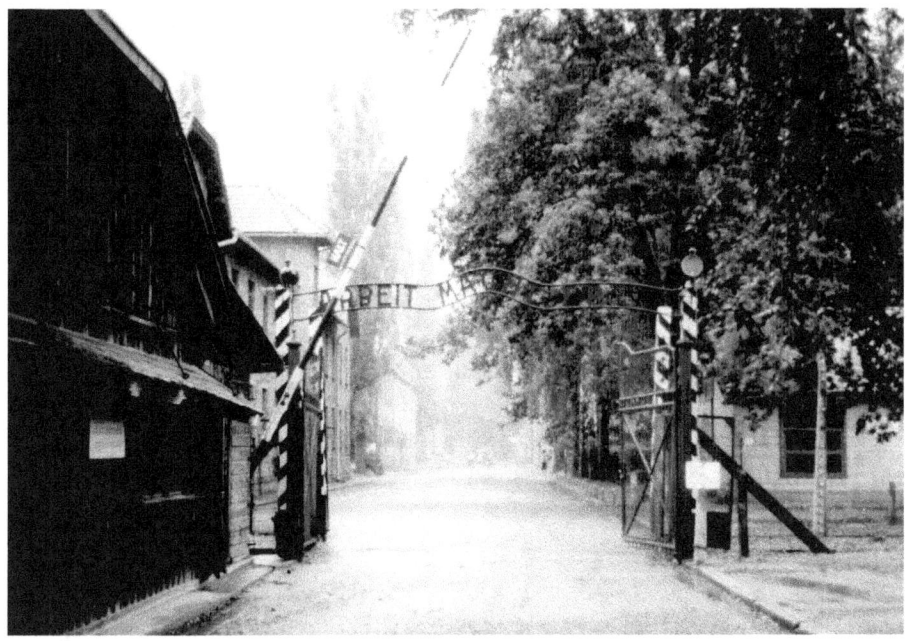

Entrance to Auschwitz, 1987

Our route took us past the remains of the camp at Auschwitz, and I asked Ela if we could stop there. The black iron slogan *Arbeit Macht Frei* still crowned the entrance. The barbed wire, search lights and a machine gun casing were evidence of the terror that had been inflicted here. Each brick building bore traces of their past, when segregated men and women were squeezed in like sardines – six to eight women on a palette in three brick tiers. My mind moved into neutral as we saw glass cases full of suitcases, wooden legs, shoes, clothes, hair....I did not want to exercise my imagination; I did not want to face the evil that took place here. There were many ghoulish groups looking round. I wished those who suffered here – Christian, Jew, dissident, gypsy – could be left in peace. I wondered how Ela felt about visiting the town where she was conceived, but did not ask.

Jacek Waltos was not afraid to imagine. It took courage to evoke the past in pictures, in this case a series of pictures, to keep us from forgetting former atrocities and deep trauma. Jacek was a child during the war. He lost close relatives, some shot by the Gestapo. He painted this dreadful symbol being overgrown by grass and weeds, conscious of our tendency to deny or forget the past. He told me that he wanted his art to condemn the suffering and murder of millions, but also to remind us not to let anger take root and stifle the heart.

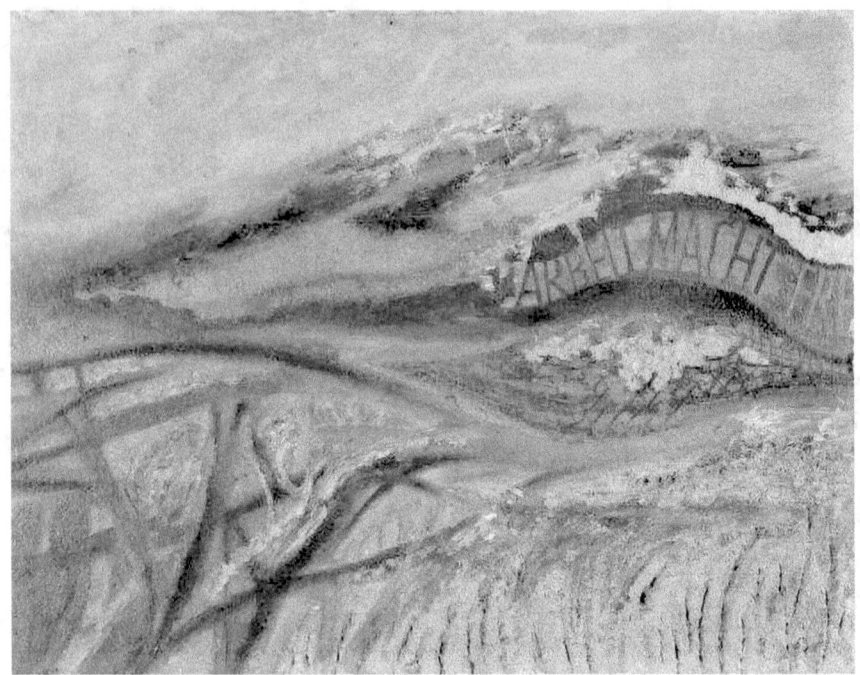

Growing Over by Jacek Waltos, 1965-6 (oil on board)

We used our last coupons, filling the car up to the brim. By the time we got home we had driven 3,500 miles. Before our last supper together we said goodbye to the animals and Pani Galica, and played silly games to stop us feeling sad. After a hearty breakfast it was hard to say goodbye to Ela and Grzegorz, who had been our personal path smoothers for the weeks since we left Strzepcz. I always felt deep sadness when I had to say goodbye to friends in Poland. Who knew when we would meet again?

At the border town of Chyzne, Western cars were segregated and searched, our passports tucked under the windscreen wipers. It took a man and a woman an hour to search through our luggage. Every case had to be put out on a bench and opened. They seemed most interested in our books – Conan-Doyle and Umberto Eco's *Name of the Rose* were examined. They ignored the gate, leather goods, and honey. Ambassador Giertych's ugly crystal vase was dropped, and broke into smithereens, reminding us of our burglary. (I did receive insurance money later for Ela's loss).

It took four and a half hours to cover the 200 miles across Czechoslovakia, passing crusader castles perched on hills. The atmosphere was different to Poland. Here the land was farmed communally and lines of combined harvesters cut the corn. The road was full of trucks. We took a wrong turning off the main road, and in order to get back quickly took a couple of illegal left turns. A police car howled me down. The policeman was kind and let me off with a warning. Later I was stopped for speeding and a fine of 100 crowns demanded. Since I had no crowns and we were late, I persuaded the police to let me go – again.

At the Bratislava border there were three checkpoints and two watch towers. (When we reached home, the new James Bond film *The Living Daylight* had just been released. As we watched Bond being chased by the Czech police and then helping a defecting KGB agent escape from Bratislava through the Trans-Siberian Pipeline, we understood.)

At the first check point passports were examined, the boot and bonnet opened and searched. A mirror was pushed under the car, but all it reflected back was dirt from Polish roads. At the second 'Control' western cars were again segregated, and again we had to take out our cases and open everything. The Czech guards relented slightly when I told them that the Poles had already searched everything thoroughly. Many customs officials milled about. At the third border a single guard, with a sympathetic smile, waved us into Austria. Looking back at the Iron Curtain, a sign of welcome above a dove of peace seemed as big a lie as the sign I saw over the entrance to the concentration camp at Auschwitz.

It felt strange being back in the West. Did we understand or live by the concepts of mercy, justice and truth any more than those struggling under the Communist regime in the East? No wonder the Poles felt buffeted about from all sides. No wonder I identified with them. The elderly parents of German friends of mine awaited us in Salzburg with a big welcome, even though we arrived late. The Baroness fed us well and gave us a good night's sleep. I reflected on how this charming couple had lived through the war and had to fight against us, but that was history. Sightseeing in the city the next day, we were shocked to discover a pretzel cost fifty times more than a bagel in Krakow. When we left, the Baron drove ahead of us to a petrol station near the motorway and filled our tank before waving us off with a smile.

Deep bonds often form during times of crisis, loss and uncertainty, as people seek comfort in human connection. I hoped the kindness and generosity we had received from friends during those five weeks of our journey – the giving of so much from so little – gave my sons a clearer picture of the important things in life. As we drove home from oppression along the road of freedom, I hoped we too could enjoy a fulfilling new beginning, free from conflict and anxiety.

*

Rupert and Simon accompanied me to Krakow and Warsaw the following Christmas when I was leading an art tour. Their support was invaluable. Apart from their knowledge of Krakow, they kept a small stash of coins for us all to pay the cloakroom attendants everywhere we went, and befriended our guests. Away from home at such a family time, the group of twenty quickly gelled. We were awed by the nativity scenes in the churches in Krakow. Real trees and half size figures looked almost real: a focus for prayer at midnight Mass on Christmas Eve, after our dinner at Wierzynek. I had last eaten in this ancient restaurant off the Rynek, with Boguś and Chris after the Chernobyl disaster.

The group was staying at the Pod Roza, where I had booked and then cancelled a room for my friends during that terrifying time. It seemed a lifetime ago. The hotel was not serving lunch on Christmas day, so our erstwhile local guide, Dariusz, brought in a cold feast from outside. No mean feat, since everything was closed on this holy day. (Apart from the food, Dariusz produced all sorts of surprises out of a hat, including tickets to the opera when we reached Warsaw.) Paper hats, crackers, and duty-free alcohol, packed by members of the group, added to the festive spirit.

Christmas 1988 was historic for the Poles: Cardinal Glemp, who had been appointed by Pope John Paul II, and protected Solidarity and other groups, was allowed to give his first Christmas day message on Polish television. This would have been forbidden the year before. Everyone crowded round the black and white television watching in silence as this uncharismatic Cardinal delivered his message. As Dariusz translated what was being said for us, I looked at his face and saw that there were tears in his eyes.

Postscript

AFTER SOLIDARITY WON the June 1989 election, life in Poland changed radically. Basia and Ela still taught English, without the need to watch their words. Bogus retrieved possession of his house, renovated it, transforming half into offices and the ground floor into shops. Agnieszka became deputy Minister of Culture and Art under Bogus's uncle Marek Rostworowski, then Polish Ambassador to Australia and New Zealand. She rose to become Director of the National Museum where I first met her.

As my own situation altered, and I began to establish myself as a single parent, I returned frequently with groups of art lovers and witnessed the changes as the country began to flourish as a democracy. Its history and treasures were again appreciated by a wider audience, and my friends were free to flourish. Warsaw now reflects economic dynamism with smart new buildings rising up to challenge Stalin's monumental Palace of Culture. Krakow's medieval buildings have been restored and the city has once more become one of the most beautiful of Central Europe. Leonardo's *Lady of the Ermine* travelled to London via Berlin like a debutante coming out in society, as part of the European Community.

But old habits die hard. The communist desire to control every aspect of peoples' lives re-surfaced after a quarter century of democratic rule, when the popularist PiS parliamentary party in Poland came to power. The government has been systematically dismantling the democratic checks and balances, and alienating the country from the EU. Poland, to my friends' dismay, has lurched from communism to a far-right agenda. In protest, Agnieszka resigned her post.

Old wounds take time to heal. Many who have suffered greatly still carry heavy loads. In 2016 my friends Jacek Waltos and Leszek Sobocki, invited me to a retrospective exhibition celebrating their work that had, for 40 years, so powerfully protested against communist rule. Grouped together, their violent images powerfully invoked the brutality of the years in which I had made their acquaintance, and first seen their sculpture and paintings.

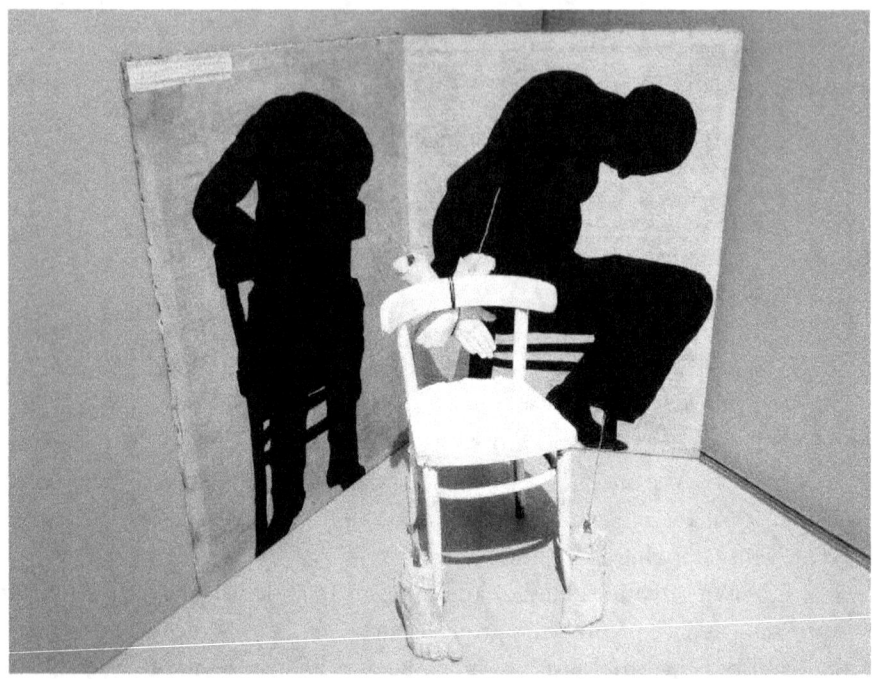

Chair without Properties, 1968. L. Sobocki

Although their work was desolate, it strongly conveyed their belief that a better future was possible. I had been privileged to witness the realisation of their hopes at first hand, and the transformation of their country provided the catalyst for the long process of my own personal restoration.

Restored

The Madonna and Child with John the Baptist

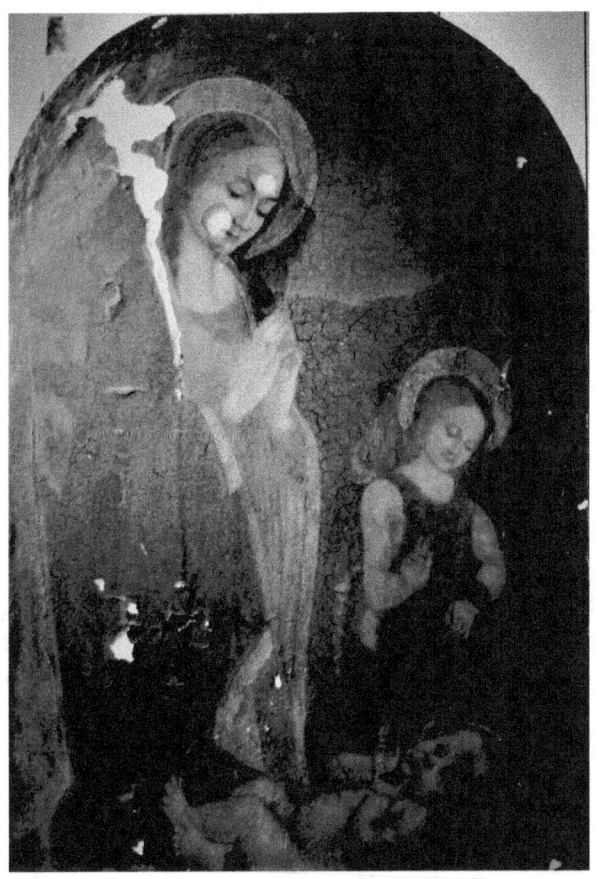

**Condition soon after arrival (with two small cleaning tests
on the Madonna's face)**

O NE DAY, A client whose collection I had been working on for some years, arrived in my studio bearing a large plastic bag. A badly damaged painting was pulled out of bubble-wrapping and we examined it together. My client had come across the picture while clearing out his attics, in preparation for a sale of unwanted clutter. He asked me to put it in a fit state to sell.

The straitened state of this holy picture looked as if it too had suffered the trials and tribulations of life. Chunks of paint as well as a large section behind the Madonna's head were missing. More were flaking badly. Under the degraded varnish lay either an indifferent copy...or a jewel waiting to be revealed. Since the picture was on canvas, perhaps it was a Victorian copy of an early Tuscan tabernacle painting; unless the original wood panel had cracked so badly the picture had been transferred to canvas, perhaps in Italy before being brought to England and sold.

Silently, I acquainted myself with something that was manifestly more than just a painting. Even though partially concealed, the work of art exuded a sense of peace. No worldly woes perturb the mother as she gazes in wonder at her babe. I hesitated a while before disturbing them with solvents. What would I find? When the first test swab revealed pure 15th century tempera paint, my heart leapt with joy. Cleaning more of the face, I wondered how many souls over the centuries, had been soothed by spending time in some little Tuscan church or chapel contemplating this sacred image.

It was too dangerous to disturb the picture further before the paint had been secured. Re-lining canvas and restoring panels is a different discipline, and Jim Wray expertly fulfilled this function. In his Suffolk workshop the fragile painting was transferred from the dried-up 19th century lining onto a temporary canvas to prevent further loss. Now it was safe to clean.

I was relieved to discover when I began the cleaning process, that the 19th century varnish and extensive old re-touching were easily removed – an example of the importance of reversible retouching media. Damage, accrued over the centuries, appeared like hidden hurts. Superfluous old fillings, many of which extended over original paint, were scraped off with a scalpel. The five-hundred-year-old tempera paint and gold leaf, composed and applied by a master craftsman, were impervious to the intervention.

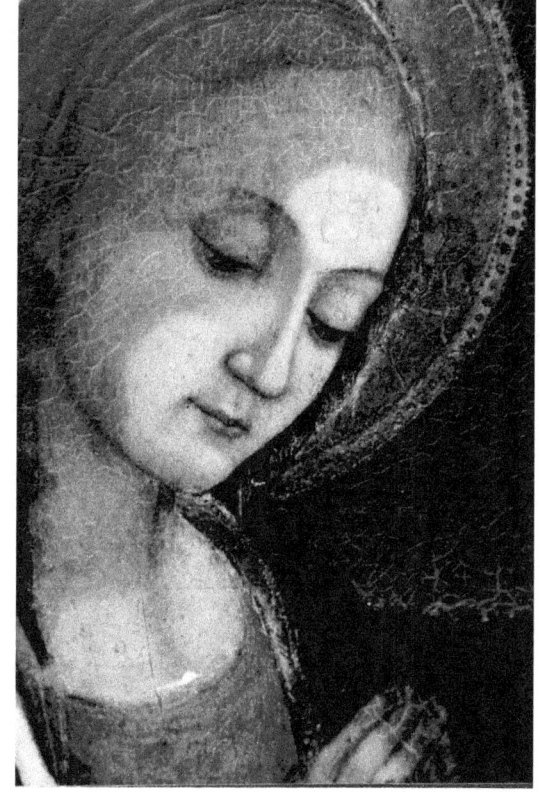

Detail of head showing texture of varnish and original paint

Many details, including the flesh tones, the exquisite gilding and the delicate veil peeping out between the Madonna's hair and head-dress came to light. As the artist painted the path winding up to the hills in the background, I wondered if he was remembering Dante's 14th century *Divine Comedy*. The poet's deeply psychological description of a spiritual journey through hell, purgatory to heaven, inspired the iconography of Christian paintings for centuries.

*

The cleaned painting travelled back to Jim's workshop. He faced the paint surface with protective mulberry paper before removing the temporary canvas support; then transferred the paint and gesso onto a honeycomb panel composed of aluminium with fiberglass skins, laying a polyester barrier between the gesso and support. Unlike wood, synthetic panels attract neither worm nor warp.

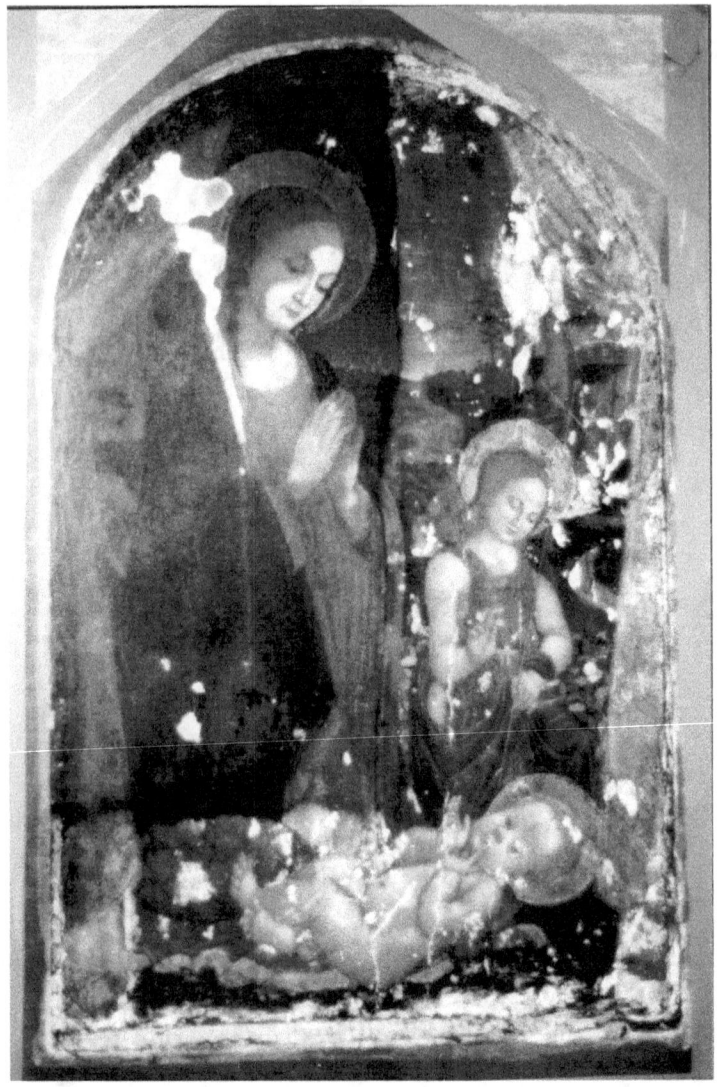

The painting on its temporary canvas support after partial cleaning

The picture now looked more authentic. A coat of varnish was applied, to separate the original paint from my retouching, and left to dry. To restore the areas where the gold was missing, 24 carat gold leaf, which can fly away as easily as breathing, was pressed into gluey red bole. After burnishing the gold – a soothing exercise after the previous challenge, I used tools, bought like the pigment from Zecchi's art shop in Florence, to scratch and stamp on patterns that matched the original. A glaze of earth colours toned the new in with the original gold. When the retouching was completed I gave it time to settle before spraying the picture with varnish, adding cosmolloid wax in the final coat to cut glare.

Over the months, as I brought this painting back, as closely as possible, to the artist's original intention, it became a spiritual aid. As I worked, I wondered what thoughts filled the Madonna – this "highly favoured lady" – as she prayed, or John the Baptist as he blessed his cousin. Whenever the eyes of the vulnerable baby, whose pudgy hands expressed both wisdom and welcome, caught my gaze, I felt it drawing me to a place beyond time. I was reminded of a church service I attended in Italy one Sunday on the Feast of the Assumption. Suddenly, I had a vision of my mother, sitting at home in her favourite chair. She was surrounded by an aura which I came to realize was light, life, and love. She died the next day.

*

The family firm Moscardi had, for centuries, made frames in their shop over-looking the river Arno in Florence. Stepping inside on my first visit I was overwhelmed by the treasure trove of colour and texture, where a variety of beautiful old frames jostled for space. Signor Moscardi examined the photos of the painting I produced. No one knew better than he how to frame a picture. With its rounded top, we decided on a tabernacle-type frame typical of the period, with *Ave Maria Gratia Plena* written in gold on blue paint along the bottom edge. When I collected the finished frame it only just squeezed into my car. This was one measurement I had failed to make.

After nearly three years of work the painting was placed in its frame, secured with brass mounts, returned to its owner and placed above the altar in their chapel. Pictures like this one can often express more than words, since perception is beyond speech. It serves as a vivid metaphor of the beauty of life, full of meaning and grace, where every damaged person can, through faith and forgiveness, be restored to wholeness.

*

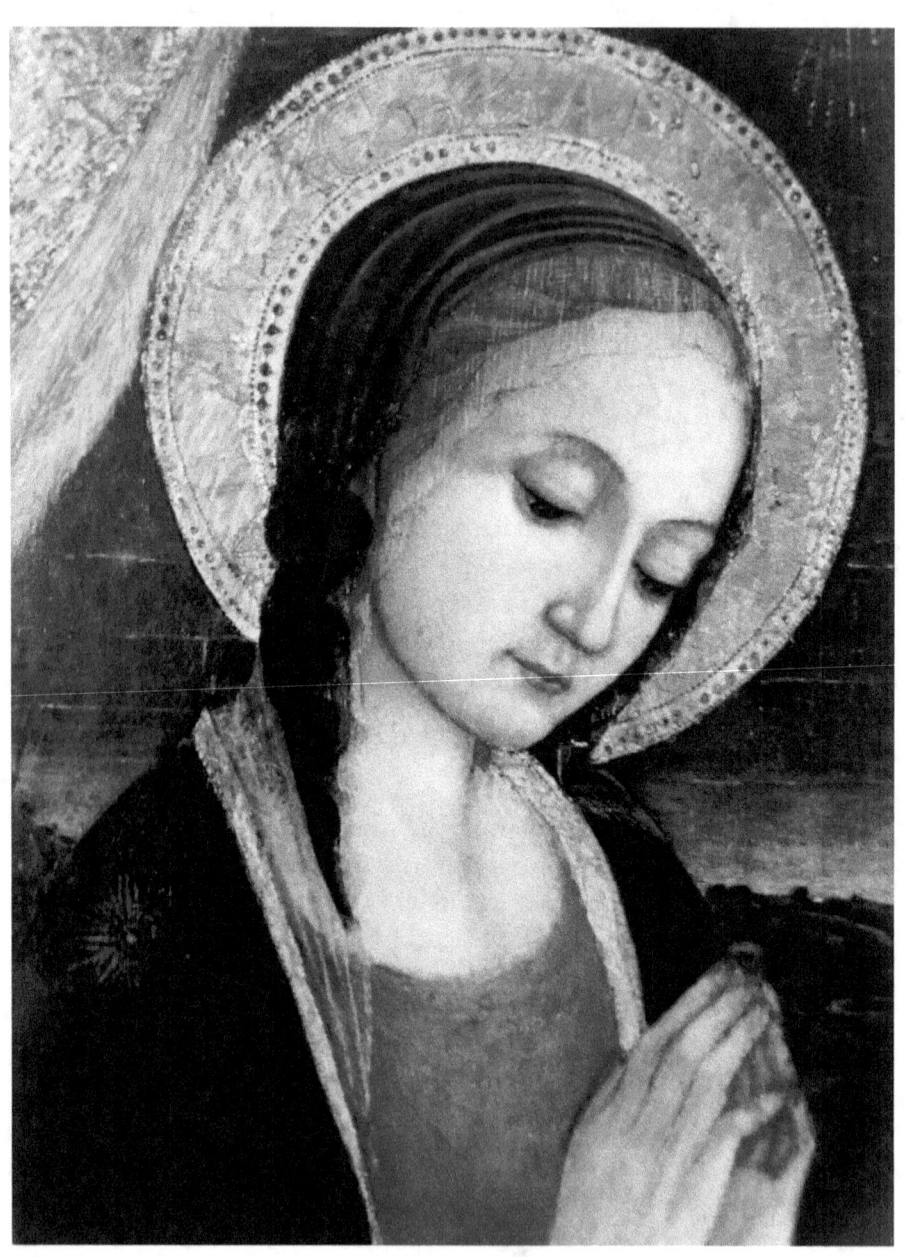

Detail after restoration

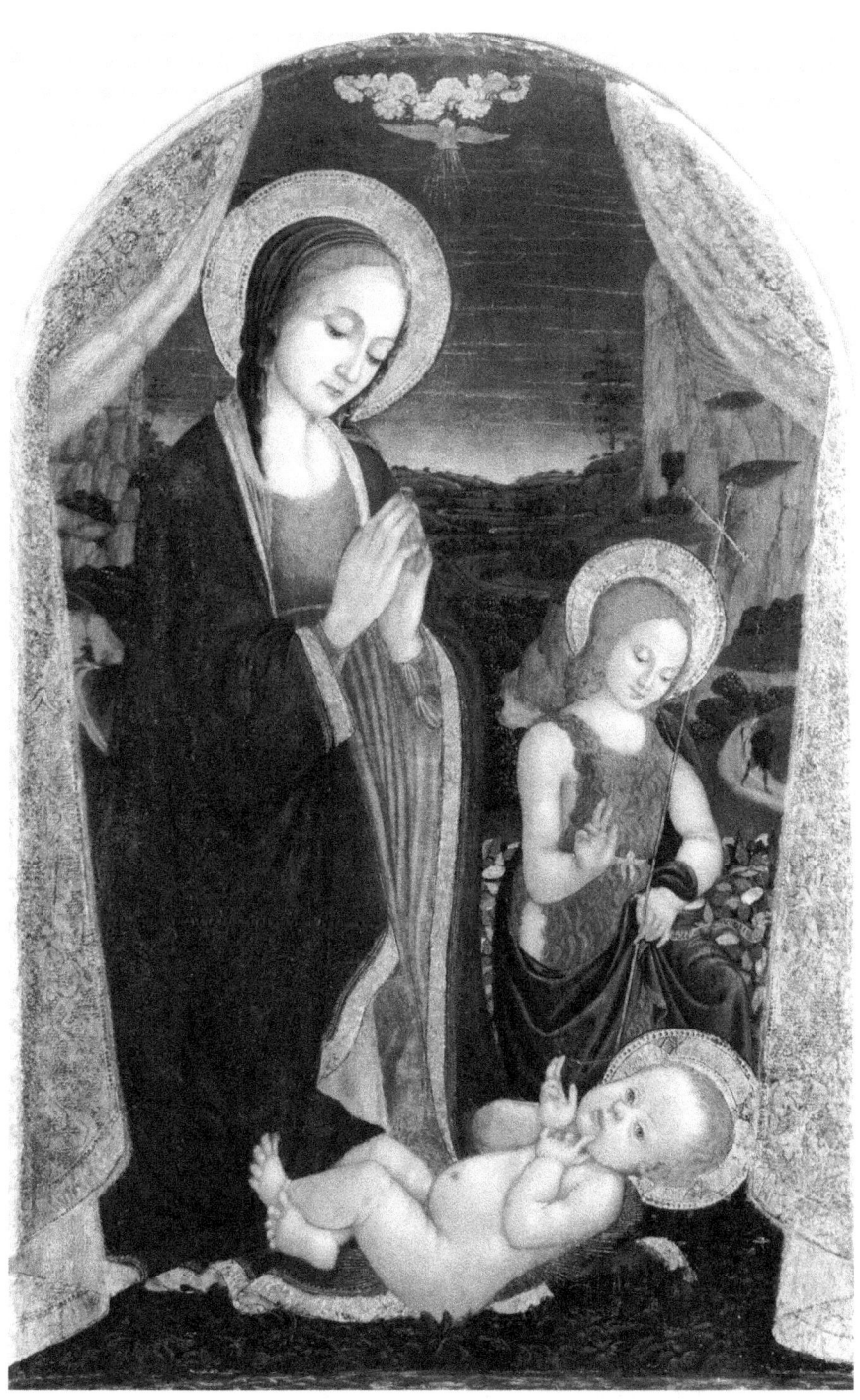

The painting after conservation

List of Polish Sovereigns

Early Feudal Monarchy

Piast Dynasty

960-992   Mieszko I (first historical ruler of Poland)

Kings crowned in Gniezno Cathedral
992-1025   Boleslaus I
1025-1034   Mieszko II
1034-1058   Casimir I
1058-1079   Boleslaus II
1079-1102   Ladislaus I
1102-1102   Zbigniew
1102 -1138 Boleslaus III

The Period of Feudal Disintegration
(Dukes ruling in Krakow)

United Polish Kingdom
Kings first crowned in Krakow in 1320

1295-1296   Przemysł II (King 1295-6)
1300-1305   Wenceslas II
1320-1333   Ladislaus I
1333-1370   Casimir III the Great

Angevin Dynasty

Louis of Hungary
1384-1399 Jadwiga

Jagiellon Dynasty

1386-1434 Ladislaus II
1434-1444 Ladislaus III
1446-1492 Casimir IV
1492-1501 John I Olbracht
1501-1506 Alexander
1506-1548 Sigismund I the Old
1548-1572 Sigismund II Augustus

Electoral Kings

1573-1575 Henry of Valois
1575-1786 Anna Jagiellon
1576-1586 Stephen Bathory (husband of Anna Jagiellon)
1587-1632 Sigismund III Vasa
1596   King moved capital from Krakow to Warsaw
1632-1648 Ladislaus IV Vasa
1648-1668 John II Casimir Vasa
1669-1673 Michael Korybut Wiśniowiecki
1674-1696 John III Sobieski
1697-1706 Augustus II the Strong (Wettin)
1704-1709 Stanislaus I Leszczyński
1709-1733 Augustus II the Strong
1733-1736 Stanislaus Leszczyński
1733-1763 Augustus II the Strong
1764-1795 Stanislaus II Augustus (Poniatowski)

Duchy of Warsaw

1807-1815 Frederick Augustus I

Historical Notes

P OLAND HAS BEEN a nation state for 1000 years. A series of rulers who converted the population to Christianity created a strong Kingdom of Poland and fostered a distinctive Polish culture that was integrated into European culture. In the Middle Ages its agricultural land was the granary of Europe.

Briefly in the early 16th century its Jagiellonian dynasty controlled the largest area in Europe. 100 years later, the Polish Commonwealth (which included Lithuania and the Ukraine) had a population of 10 million (40% Polish) living in an area of 990,000 sq km.

Poland was essentially a democratic state, with a constitution evolved over centuries. But with a parliamentary system open to abuse from the magnates, Poland grew weak and became a sitting duck for her powerful neighbours. The Constitution of 3 May, 1791 was the 2nd written constitution in the world after USA. Within weeks the third partition of Poland removed this once powerful country from the map.

The Poles are a people of paradoxes. Clannish, they created a nation state before the arrival of Christianity; courageous, they never allowed their spirit or national identity to be crushed despite invasion and partition; generous, they know how to share their last crust of bread; proud, they would rather starve than compromise their beliefs, as nearly 45 years of Communism has proved; brilliant and cultured, they have produced such contributors to civilisation as: Copernicus, Chopin, Marie Curie, Paderewski, Milosz and Pope Paul II.

6th - 9th c.	A uniform Slavonic language developed among the five tribes who inhabited the area: Pomeranians in the north; Silesians in the buffer zone in the west; Polanie (people of the fields) in central Poland; Mazovians east of the Vistula river; and Vislanie who built up an early feudal stronghold in Krakow.
960-1385	Piast Dynasty
960-992	Mieszko I (see List of Polish Sovereigns below), was baptised into the Western Latin Rite in April 966 following his marriage to Dobrawa of Bohemia, a fervent Christian. He founded the Polish state on completion of the unification of the West Slavic tribal lands, and won fame in lengthy wars with the Germans. He established a fiscal system, exercised control through a network of castles, invaded Pomerania and founded Gdansk in 980. The boundaries of the State stretched from the Baltic (N) to the Tatra Mountains (S), the rivers Elbe (W) to Bug (E).
993	Mieszko's son Boleslaw I established a Polish church structure, pursued territorial conquests and sought to spread Christianity to parts of eastern Europe. The missionary Adalbertus was murdered by heathen Prussians. His body was brought to Gniezno church which was raised to an archbishopric by the Pope. He was canonised and became Poland's patron saint. Three bishoprics were raised, including Krakow.
1000	During the Congress of Gniezno, Holy Roman Emperor Otto III recognised the Archbishopric of Gniezno, critical for the existence of the sovereign Polish state.
1025	Boleslaw I was crowned in Gniezno cathedral.
1040	Krakow became the capital of Poland and a great trading centre.
1241	Hordes of Genghis Khan attacked Krakow on Easter Day and razed it to the ground. (Only St Andrew's survived.)
1257	Krakow received a town charter modelled on the law of Magdeburg. Rebuilt on a grid pattern system it became "one of the most mature town planning conceptions in medieval Europe"
1079	Boleslaw II became involved in conflict with Bishop Stanislaus of Szczepanow that seriously marred his reign. He had the bishop murdered after being excommunicated by the Polish church over charges of adultery. The King was deposed and expelled by the nobles.

c.1116	Gallus Anonymous wrote a seminal chronicle *Gesta principum Polonorum* an important key source for the early history of Poland.
1264	Boleslaw the Pious granted Jewish liberties in the Statute of Kalisz.
1266	The Teutonic Knights were invited to Poland by Prince Conrad of Masovia to help him subjugate pagan Prussia. (This gave rise to Polish/German conflicts culminating in World War II.)
1308	The Teutonic Knights seized Gdansk and the surrounding area of Pomerelia.
1320	Ladislaus I who re-unified Poland was crowned in Wawel cathedral. (All future kings until Poniatowski were crowned and buried here.)
1333-1370	Last of the Piast dynasty, Kazimierz III the Great "found Poland built in wood and left it built in brick". He secured Krakow, by building 3km of walls with 7 bastions and 8 main gates; codified all laws; tried to protect peasants from their landlords, and reformed the army, the economy and education; founded the University; introduced guilds into towns; paved streets, re-routed the Vistula River in Krakow and built Kazimierz the other side; built a canal linking Krakow to the Wieliczka salt mines; built 65 new fortified towns and 53 castles. He encouraged the exploitation of natural resources: iron, lead, copper, silver, zinc, sulphur, salt; and the export of grain, cattle hides, wood and finished cloth. Casimir laid the foundations for a Golden Age.
1334	King Kazimierz confirmed the privileges granted to Jews in 1264 and allowed them to settle in Poland in large numbers.
1364	The Congress of Krakow where central, eastern, and northern rulers met to plan an anti-Turkish crusade. The future Jagiellonian University was founded.
1386	Kazimierz's grand-daughter, Jadwiga, married Ladislaus Jagiello of Lithuania, who ruled after her early death.
1400	Jagiellon University in Krakow was re-founded on Jadwiga's personal fortune.
1410	Battle of Grunwald. The defeat of the Teutonic army saw the decline of Teutonic power which threatened the freedom and peace of eastern nations.

1466	End of 13 years' war against Teutonic Knights and the freedom of Gdansk from their yoke. Their stronghold Malbork was captured. The Treaty of Torun divided Prussia to create East Prussia that functioned as a fief of Poland under the administration of the Teutonic Knights.
1477	Veit Stoss was invited from Nurenberg to sculpt a High Altar for St Mary's parish church. Krakow merchants flourished.
1493	As the gentry increased in strength, the king's council evolved to become a bicameral sejm (parliament) that no longer only represented the top people in the realm.
1505	The *Nihil novi* act transferred most of the legislative power from the monarch to the sejm.
1502-36	A Renaissance palace was built on Wawel Hill.
1520	The Sigismund bell installed in the Cathedral. It became a major national symbol, rung to announce important events.
1525	The Prussian Homage. The Teutonic Order was secularized. Prince Albert Hohenzollern, former Grand Master of the Teutonic Order, swore oath of allegiance to Sigismund I, King of Poland, in the Rynek (Krakow's main square).Mazovia was finally incorporated into the Polish Crown in 1529.
1506-1572	The reign of Sigismund I and Sigismund II Augustus witnessed a Golden Age of the Renaissance in Poland.
1569	Union of Lublin established the Commonwealth of Poland and Lithuania, including the Ukraine. The Union was run by the nobility through the system of central government and local assemblies, headed by elected kings. This early democratic system was in contrast to the absolute monarchies prevalent in the rest of Europe
1570	First joint Seym (parliament) took place in Warsaw
1573	The Warsaw Confederation guaranteed nationwide religious tolerance.
Late 1500's	The Polish-Lithuanian Union became an influential participant in European affairs, being one of the largest and most populous in contemporary Europe with an area approaching one million square kilometres (o.39 million square miles) and a population of 10 million. Its economy was dominated by the export of agriculture.
1609	Sigismund III Vasa moved the Court to Warsaw.

1650's	Poland suffered decline with constant wars against Sweden, Russia and the Turks. The Swedish 'deluge' laid waste Kraków, Warsaw, Posnan.
1652	The first liberum veto, a parliamentary device which allowed any member of the Sejm to dissolve a current session immediately, was exercised by a deputy. This free vote in the Sejm, meant the system was abused. Magnates became like feudal barons with their own private armies and dependent gentry.
1683	Jan Sobieski (elected King in 1674 after his glorious victory over the Turks at the Battle of Chocim), led the allies to defeat the Turks at the Battle of Vienna, thus preventing Islam entering Western Europe.
1697- 1763	The Saxon kings further weakened the Commonwealth.
1732	Russia, Prussia and Austria entered the secret Treaty of the Three Black Eagles, agreeing to control the future successions in the Commonwealth.
1764	Stanislaus Augustus Poniatowski, cousin of the powerful Czartoryski family, was voted the last king of Poland at the insistence of Catherine the Great of Russia. He ruled the Polish-Lithuanian state until its dissolution in 1795.
1770's	Bernardo Bellotto, nephew of Canaletto, painted various detailed views of Warsaw for the Royal Castle.
1772	The first Partition of Poland between Russia, Prussia and Austria.
3 May 1791	The Constitution was short lived. Russian army entered Poland.
March 1794	National uprising under Kosciuszko (who fought in the American War of Independence).
April 1794	The Battle of Raclawice. Gentry and peasants fought together to give Kosciuszko victory.
Nov 1794	Tsarist General Suvorov quashed the Insurrection by storming Praga, on the right bank district of Warsaw. Civilians were massacred.
1795	Third Partition. The King abdicated and was taken prisoner to St Petersburg. Poland became "a wayside inn for foreign armies".
Jan 1797	General Henryk Dabrowski founded the Polish Legions in Milan.

1797-1803	The Legions fought with France and the Italian States against Austrian, Neapolitan, and Russian troops.
1807	Napoleon rewarded the Poles by granting the Duchy of Warsaw and making Prince Joseph Poniatowski Commander in Chief. He introduced his Code Civil under which citizens became equal in law, serfdom was abolished and Polish became the official language.
1801, 1809	The first Polish museums were founded at Pulawy by Princess Izabela Czartoryska to house momentos of the National heritage, and the family collection of art.
1815	At the Congress of Vienna, Kraków was proclaimed a free and independent city.
1820s	Flowering of culture and the arts in Warsaw. Chopin.
Nov 1830	The November Uprising, initiated by cadets in Warsaw.
Sept 1831	The Russians were victorious. Rebels fled west, the Czartoryski Family held court at Hotel Lambert in Paris, where poets, musicians, artists congregated and expressed the desire for the liberation of Poland through their works.
1846	Galicia, including Kraków, was incorporated into (liberal) Austria. The University reopened, art and culture flourished.
1863	January Uprisings against the Russians, with terrible reprisals. Many sent to Siberia.
1870	After the unification of Germany, Bismark embarked on the Germanisation of Greater Poland, Pomerania and Silesia. The Polish language was barred.
1885-7	26,000 Poles not citizens of the German Reich were evicted from the Prussian partition zone, and German colonists given the peasants' land.
Late 19th.c.	Rapid developments of industry, scientific and technological achievements took place in Poland.
1882	The first Worker's Party founded by Ludwik Warynski.
1905	Demonstrations all over Poland during Russo-Japanese War and the outbreak of the Russian Revolution.
c.1900	The Young Poland cultural movement, centred in Galicia, took advantage of the liberalism of the Austrians and became the source of Poland's finest artistic and literary productions. Maria Sklodowska-Curie, performed her groundbreaking research into radiation in Paris.

1908-14	The Union of Active Struggle and other Polish paramilitary organisations focused on independence, were being formed, mainly in Galicia.
1914	Joseph Pilsudski commanded the Ist Brigade of Legions during WWI. Much of the fighting on the Eastern Front took place in Poland with huge civilian casualties and devastation.
Nov 1918	After internment by the Germans, Pilsudski returned to Poland and played a leading role in organising the Polish State, liberated after 123 years.
1919	First Seym of reborn Poland conferred the title of Head of State on Marshal Pilsudski. Poznan was returned to Poland.
1933	Hitler's rise to power. Celebrations in Kraków of 250th Anniversary of the Relief of Vienna.
1st Sept, 1939	Hitler's army invaded Poland a week after an Anglo-Polish military alliance was signed. France and Great Britain declared war on Germany but during the 'Phoney War' they remained largely inactive. The numerically and technically superior Wehrmacht formations rapidly advanced eastwards and engaged massively in the murder of Polish civilians over the entire occupied territory.
17th Sept, '39	The Soviet invasion of Poland began. The Molotov-Ribbentrop Pact secretly divided up Poland between the two invading powers.
Spring 1940	21,857 Polish prisoners were shot at Katyn Forest as enemies of Soviet authority, to prevent a resurgence of an independent Poland. They included half the Polish officer corps plus landowners, chaplains, professors, teachers, physicians, engineers and journalists.
1941	The implementation of the Final Solution began and the Holocaust in Poland proceeded with force.
1943	Warsaw Ghetto Uprising took place as the ghetto was being liquidated by Nazi SS units, along with others in Poland.
1940-45	The Polish Army in the West took part in the Battle of Narvik and Battle of Britain (1940), Tobruk (1941), Battle of the Atlantic and Monte Casino (1943) Arnhem (1944). 2 million soldiers in all.
July 1944	The Soviet Red Army and Soviet-controlled Polish Peoples' Army entered Polish territory.

1 Aug 1944	The Warsaw Uprising in which most of the city's population took part was instigated by the underground Home Army and approved by the Polish government-in-exile, in the hope the Soviet forces approaching the city would assist in the battle to take the city. But the Soviets never agreed to intervene, and they waited on the other side of the Vistula River during the 63 days of the uprising. Hundreds of thousands of civilians died or were expelled.
2 October	The Poles surrendered. Huge losses sustained, especially among the cream of youth. Warsaw was levelled to the ground by the Nazis. 84% of the city was destroyed, including 90% of cultural and historic monuments.
17th Jan, 1945	The Polish Army fighting alongside the Soviet Red Army entered a devastated Warsaw, 85% destroyed.
1939-45	6 million Poles were killed during the war by the Nazis including 3 million Jews.
Feb.1945	By the time of the Yalta Conference the communists had already established a Provisional Government of the Republic of Poland. At the conference the London-based Government in Exile was not mentioned and the feeble attempts that the provisional government would include democratic elections failed to materialise. Many Poles saw this as a Western Betrayal.
1944-49	Ignoring the Polish Government in exile in London, the Manifesto of the Polish National Liberation Committee called for social and political reform, providing the basis for the political system of the Peoples' Poland. Large estates were broken up and the land given to the peasants.
1948- 1980	Poland under the yoke of Communism.
August 1980	The Shipyard worker's strike in Gdansk led to 16 months of Solidarity.
December 1981	Democracy was quashed by Martial law.
1989	Poland was freed from the Soviet Empire.
1989-2015	Poland flourished again as a free country.
2015	PiS The Law and Justice Party took control.

Bibliography

Ascherson, Neal, *The Struggles for Poland, 1987,* New York: Random House, 1988

Basiura, Ewa & Zarzycki, Krzysztof, *Legends of Old Cracow,* Krakow: Drukarnia Kolejowa, 1994

Chrzanowski, Tadeusz, *The Marian Altar of Wit Stwosz,* Warszawa: Interpress, 1985

Davies, Norman, *Heart of Europe, The Past in Poland's Present,* New York: OUP, 1986

Izabela Czartoryska, *Tour Through England,* Warsw-Torun: Polish Institute of World Art Series & Tako Publishing House, 2015

Dobrowolski, Tadeusz, *Polish Painting from the Enlightenment to Recent Times,* Wroclaw: Ossolinskich, 1981

Hale, John, *The Civilisation of Europe in the Renaissance,* London: Harper Collins, 1993

Hoffman, Klementyna Tanska, *The Journal of Countess Francoise Krasinska,* Victoria, Australia: Onesuch Press, 2012

Lemnis Maria and Vitry Henryk, *Old Polish Traditions in the Kitchen and at the Table,* Warsaw: Interpress, 1981

Madeyski Jerzy, Rago Danuta and Siemaszko Zbyv 1988

Malecki, Jan.M, *A History of Krakow For Everyone,* Krakow: Literackie, 2008

Marsden, Philip, *The Bronski House,* London: HarperCollins, 1995

Michener, James, *Poland ,* London: Corgi, 1984.

Milosz, Czeslaw, *The Captive Mind,* London: Penguin Books, 1980

Morawinska, Dr Agnieszka, *Polish Painting 15th- 20th Century,* Warsaw: Auriga, 1984

Morawinska, Dr Agnieszka, *The National Museum in Warsaw, Director's Choice,* London: Scala Arts & Heritage Publishers Ltd, 2016

Nowak, Jan, *Courier from Warsaw,* London: Collins/Harvill, 1982

Oseka, Andrzej and Skrodzki, Wojciech, (Transl: Keplicz, Krystyna), *Contemporary Polish Sculpture,* Warsaw, Arkady, 1977

Ostrowski, Jan K. *Cracow,* Warsaw: Wydawnictwa Artystyczne I Filmowe, 1992

Paczynska, Maria, *The Historical Atlas of Poland,* Wroclaw: Dept of the State Cartographical Publishers, 1981

Piwocka, Magdalena, *The Tapestries of Sigismund Augustus,* Krakow: Wawel Royal Castle State Art Collections, 2007

Ruhemann, Helmut, *The Cleaning of Paintings,* London: Faber and Faber Ltd, 1968

Siewkiewicz, Henryk, *The Teutonic Knights,* (transl. Alicia Tyszkiewicz), New York: Hippocrene Books, 1966

Stepien, Halina, *Malarstwo Maksymiliana Gierymskiego,* Wroclaw: Ossolinskich, 1979

Swiechowski, Zygmunt, (translated by Baldyga, Jerzy and Kozinska-Baldyga, Alina) *Romanesque Art in Poland, Warsaw,* Warsaw: Arkady, *1983*

Szablowski, Jerzy, *Collections of the Royal Castle of Wawel,* Warsaw: Arkady, 1975

Walek, Janusz, *A Panorama of Polish History,* Warsaw, Interpress, 1982

Walek, Janusz, *A History of Poland in Painting,* Warsaw, Interpress Publishers, 1988

Walek, Janusz, *Female Portraits by Leonardo da Vinci,* Krakow: Anna, 1994

Zamoyski, Adam, *The Polish Way,* London: John Murray, 1987

Zamoyski, Adam, *The Last King of Poland,* London: Jonathan Cape, 1992

Zamoyski, Adam, *The Princes Czartoryski Museum,* Krakow: DEKA, 2001

Zamoyski, Adam, *Warsaw 1920,* London: HarperCollins, 2008

Zygulski, Zdzislaw, Jr, *An Outline History of Polish Applied Art,* (transl.by Stanislaus Tarnowski), Warsaw: Interpress, 1987

www.ingramcontent.com/pod-product-compliance
Lightning Source LLC
Chambersburg PA
CBHW051307220526
45468CB00004B/1240